THE INTERNATIONAL SCIENTIFIC SERIES
VOLUME LXXVI

THE INTERNATIONAL SCIENTIFIC SERIES

THE EVOLUTION OF THE ART OF MUSIC

BY

C. HUBERT H. PARRY

D. C. L. DURHAM, M. A. OXON.

MUS. DOC. OXON., CANTAB., AND DUBLIN; HON. FELLOW
OF EXETER COLLEGE, OXFORD

NEW YORK AND LONDON

D. APPLETON AND COMPANY

1918

PREFACE

THE following outline of the Evolution of Musical Art was undertaken, at the invitation of Mr. Kegan Paul, somewhere about the year 1884. Its appearance was delayed by the constantly increasing mass of data and evidence about the music of savages, folk music, and mediæval music; and by the necessity of exploring some of the obscure and neglected corners of the wide-spread story of the Art. And though the subject was almost constantly under consideration, with a few inevitable interruptions, the book was not completed till 1893.

Obligations in many directions should be acknowledged—especially to Mr. Edward Dannreuther, for copious advice, suggestions, and criticisms during the whole time the work was in hand; to Miss Emily Daymond, of Holloway College, for reading the proofs; to Mr. W. Barclay Squire, for untiring readiness to make the resources of the Musical Library of the British Museum available; to Mr. A. J. Hipkins, for advising about the chapter on Scales; and to Mr. Herbert Spencer, Mr. H. H. Johnston, and many others for communications about the dancing and music of savage races.

The title, under which the book was first published in 1893, was evidently misleading, and has therefore been slightly amplified, with the view of suggesting the intention of the work

more effectually.   It is hoped that the drawback under which
it labours, through the impossibility of introducing many
musical illustrations in such a narrow space, may before long
be remedied by the publication of a parallel volume, consisting
almost entirely of musical excerpts and works which are not
easily accessible to the general public, so arranged as to show
the continuous process of the development of the Musical Art
in actuality.

CONTENTS

CHAPTER I

PRELIMINARIES

PAGE

The artistic disposition—Susceptibility and impulse towards expression—Music in the rough, in animals, in savages—Design essential—Expressive cries and expressive gestures leading to song and dancing—Melody and rhythm—The art based upon contrasts—Nervous exhaustion and its influence on the art—Tension and relaxation—Organisation **1**

CHAPTER II

SCALES

Definite relations of pitch indispensable—Slow development of scales —Slender beginnings—Practicable intervals—Scales variable in accordance with the purposes for which they are wanted—Melodic scales—Heptatonic and pentatonic—Ancient Greek system—Modes—Persian system—Subtle organisation—Indian system—Modes and ragas—Chinese system—Japanese—Javese —Siamese—Bagpipe scale—Beginnings of modern European system—Classification of notes of scale—Temperament . . **15**

CHAPTER III

FOLK-MUSIC

Music of savages—First efforts in the direction of design—Elementary types—Reiteration of phrases—Sequences—Tonality—Ornament—Pattern tunes—Universality of certain types of design—Racial characteristics—Expression and design—Highest forms—Decline of genuine folk-music **47**

vii

CHAPTER IV

INCIPIENT HARMONY

PAGE

Music and religion—Music of early Christian Church—Doubling
melodies—Organum or diaphony—Counterpoint or descant—
Singing several tunes at once—Motets—Influence of diaphony
—Canons—Cadences—Indefiniteness of early artistic music—
Influence of the Church   82

CHAPTER V

THE ERA OF PURE CHORAL MUSIC

Universality of choral music—Aiming at beauty of choral effect—
Contrapuntal effect—Harmonic effect—Secular forms of choral
music—Madrigals—Influence of modes—Accidentals—Early
experiments in instrumental music—Imitations of choral forms
—Viols—Lutes — Harpsichords — Organ — Methods — Homogeneity   103

CHAPTER VI

THE RISE OF SECULAR MUSIC

Reforming idealists—First experiments in opera, oratorio, and cantata — Recitative — Beginnings indefinite—Expression — Tendency towards definition—Melody—Arias—Realism—Tendency
of instrumental music towards independence   125

CHAPTER VII

*COMBINATION OF OLD METHODS AND NEW
PRINCIPLES*

Renewed cultivation of contrapuntal methods—Influence of Italian
taste and style upon Handel—His operas—His oratorios—J. S.
Bach—Influences which formed his musical character—Differ-

PAGE

ence of Italian and Teutonic attitudes towards music—Instrumentation—Choral effect—Italian oratorio—Passion music—
Public career of Handel—Bach's isolation—Ultimate influence
of their work   157

CHAPTER VIII

CLIMAX OF EARLY INSTRUMENTAL MUSIC

Early instrumental music contrapuntal—Fugue—Organ music—
Orchestral music—Harpsichord and clavichord—Suites and
partitas—"Das wohltemperirte Clavier"—Unique position of
J. S. Bach in instrumental music   175

CHAPTER IX

BEGINNINGS OF MODERN INSTRUMENTAL MUSIC

Systematisation of harmony—The early Italian violinists—Distribution of contrasted types of movements in groups—Violin
sonatas—Harpsichord sonatas—Operatic influence—Overture
and sinfonia   193

CHAPTER X

THE MIDDLE STAGE OF MODERN OPERA

Formality of the opera seria—Intermezzos—Comic features—Style
—Gluck and expression—Piccini—Mozart—Italian influence—
Idomeneo—Instrumentation—Teutonic aspiration—Artistic
achievement   213

CHAPTER XI

THE MIDDLE STAGE OF "SONATA" FORM

Self-dependent music and design—Successive stages of development
—Subject and form—Influences which formed the musical
characters of Haydn and Mozart—Symphonies—Orchestration
—Quartetts—Increase of variety of types—High organisation
in a formal sense   233

CHAPTER XII

BALANCE OF EXPRESSION AND DESIGN

PAGE

Development of resources—Importance of Mozart's work at the
particular moment—Beethoven's impulse towards expression—
His keen feeling for design—Preponderance of sonatas in his
works—His three periods—Richness of sound—The pianoforte
—The orchestra—Use of characteristic qualities of tone—
Expansion of design—Expression—The scherzo—Close texture
of Beethoven's work—His devices—Programme . . . 249

CHAPTER XIII

MODERN TENDENCIES

Characterisation—Increase of impulse towards the embodiment of
definite ideas external to music—Spohr—Weber—Mendelssohn
Berlioz—Instrumentation—Resuscitation of oratorio—Its peculiarities—Change in the aspect of choral writing—Secular choral
works—Declamation—Solo song—Treatment of words—Expression and design—Pianoforte music—Obviousness and obscurity
—Realism—Great variety of traits and forms .   . . 273

CHAPTER XIV

MODERN PHASES OF OPERA

Italian disposition and its fruits—French opera—German ideals—
Wagner—Early influences—Instinct and theory—Exile and
reflection—Maturity—Methods and principles—Leit motive—
Tonality—Instrumental effect—Design and expression again—
Declamation and singing—Profusion of resources . .   306

SUMMARY AND CONCLUSION 333

INDEX 339

THE ART OF MUSIC

CHAPTER I

PRELIMINARIES

THERE are probably but few people in the world so morose as to find no pleasure either in the exercise or the receipt of sympathy, and it is to be hoped there are very few so blind or perverse as to regard it as an undesirable and useless factor in the human psychological outfit. Whether it is the higher development of an original instinct which enabled mankind to rise above the rest of the animal world by co-operation and mutual helpfulness, or whether it is the outcome of the state of mutual dependence which is the lot of human beings it is obviously a quality without which society could hardly continue to exist in the complicated state of organisation at which it has arrived. The jarring interests of hurrying, striving millions require something more than mere cold-blooded utilitarian motives to keep them properly balanced; and in matters of everyday life the impulses which tend to mutual helpfulness and forbearance are fed by the ordinary phases of this omnipresent instinct. But there are many kinds and infinitely variable degrees of sympathy, and some people love best to bestow it, and some there are who much prefer to receive it. And apart from the ordinary sympathetic consideration of every-day life on the one hand, and of the devoted sympathetic heroism which often rises to the pitch of entire sacrifice of self on the other, most people have some special lines and subjects which excite their sympathetic instincts, and make

them specially conscious of the delight of fellowship in tastes
and interests, whether it be politics, science, literature, art, or
sport; and in such circumstances the instinct, without passing
the bounds of normal healthiness of tone, may rise to a degree
of refined responsive sensitiveness, which is productive of a very
high quality of happiness.

But of all types of humanity, those who are possessed with
artistic dispositions are notoriously most liable to an absorbing thirst for sympathy, which is sometimes interpreted by
those who are not artistic as a love of approbation or noto-
riety; and though a morbid development of the instinct may
sometimes degenerate into that unhappy weakness, the almost
universal prevalence of the characteristic cannot be summarily
accounted for on such superficial grounds, but deserves more
discriminating consideration. The reason that artistic and
poetic human beings are generally characterised by such a conspicuous development of their sympathetic instincts appears
to lie in the fact that they are peculiarly susceptible to beauty
of some kind, whether it be the obvious external kind of
beauty, or the beauty of thought and human circumstance;
and that the keenness of their pleasure makes them long to
enhance their own enjoyments by bringing their fellow-men
sympathetically into touch with them. From this point of
view the various arts of painting, sculpture, music, literature,
and the rest, are the outcome of the instinctive desire to
convey impressions and enjoyments to others, and to represent in the most attractive and permanent forms the
ideas, thoughts, circumstances, scenes, or emotions which
have powerfully stirred the artists' own natures. It is the
intensity of the pleasure or interest the artist feels in what
is actually seen or present to his imagination that drives him
to utterance. The instinct of utterance makes it a necessity
to find terms which will be understood by other beings in
whom his appeal can strike a sympathetic chord; and the
stronger the delight in the thought or feeling, the greater is
the desire to make the form in which it is conveyed unmistakably clear and intelligible. But intelligibility depends
to a great extent in all things upon principles of structure,

and structure implies design; hence the instinctive desire to make a thought or artistic conception unmistakably intelligible is a great incentive to the development of design.

Design has different aspects in different arts; but in all it is the equivalent of organisation in the ordinary affairs of life. It is the putting of the various factors of effect in the right places to make them tell. In some arts design seems the very essence and first necessity of existence, and though in music it is less easily understood by the uninitiated than in other arts, it is in reality of vital importance. Music indeed cannot exist till the definiteness of some kind of design is present in the succession of the sounds. The impression produced by vague sounds is vague, and soon passes away altogether. They take no permanent hold on the mind till they are made definite in relation to one another, and are disposed in some sort of order by the distribution of their up and down motion or by the regularity of their rhythmic recurrence. Then the impression becomes distinct, and its definiteness makes it permanent. In most arts it is the permanence of the enjoyment rather than that of the artistic object itself which is dependent on design. In sculpture, for instance, the very materials seem to ensure permanence; but undoubtedly a piece of sculpture which is seriously imperfect in design soon becomes intolerable, and is willingly abandoned by its possessor to the disintegrating powers of rain and frost, or to some corner where it can be conveniently forgotten. Painting does not seem, at first sight, to require so much skill in designing, because the subjects which move the artist to express himself are so obvious to all men; but nevertheless the most permanent works of the painting art are not those which are mere skilful imitations of nature, but those into which some fine scheme of design is introduced to enhance the beauty or inherent interest of the artist's thought.

In music, form and design are most obviously necessary, not only because without them the impression conveyed is indefinite and fugitive, but also because the very source and origin of its influence on human beings is so obscure. To some people beauty of form in melody or structure seems the chief excuse for the

2

art's existence; and even to more patient observers it seems to be on a different footing from all the other arts in respect of its meaning and intention. Even the most unsophisticated dullard can see what inspired the painter or the sculptor to express himself, but he cannot understand what music means, nor what it is intended to express; and many practical people look upon it as altogether inferior to other arts, because it seems to have no obviously useful application. Painting naturally appears to the average mind to be an imitative art; and, drawing a conclusion from two premises which are both equally false, some people have gone on to suppose that the only possible basis of all arts, including music, is imitation, and to invent the childish theory that the latter began by imitating birds' songs. There is no objection to such a theory if considered as a pretty poetical myth, and instances of people imitating birds in music can of course be substantiated; but as a serious explanation of the origin of music it is both too trivial and too incompatible with fact to be worth discussing. In reality, both arts are much on the same footing, for painting is no more a purely imitative art than music. People deliberately copy nature chiefly to develop the technique which is necessary to enable them in higher flights to idealise it, and to present their imaginings in the terms of design which are their highest sanction. It is just when a painter deliberately sets himself to imitate what he sees that he least deserves the name of an artist. The devices for imitating nature and throwing the unsophisticated into ecstasies, because the results are so like what they themselves have seen, are the tricks of the trade, and, till they are put to their proper uses, are on no other footing than the work of a good joiner or a good ploughman. It is only when they are used to convey the concentrated ideals of the mind of the artist in terms of beautiful or characteristic design that they become worthy of the name of art. Music is really much on the same footing, for the history of both arts is equally that of the development of mastery of design and of the technique of expression. The only real difference is that the artist formulates impressions received through the eyes, and the musician formulates the direct expression of man's innermost feelings and sensibilities. In fact, the arts of painting and sculpture and their kindred are the expression of the outer surroundings of man, and music of what is within him; and consequently the former began with imitation, and the latter with direct expression.

The story of music has been that of a slow building up and extension of artistic means of formulating in terms of design utterances and counterparts of utterances which in their raw state are direct expressions of feeling and sensibility. Utterances and actions which illustrate the raw material of music are common to all sentient beings, even to those which the complacency of man describes as dumb. A dog reiterating short barks of joy on a single note at the sight of a beloved friend or master is as near making music as the small human baby vigorously banging a rattle or drum and crowing with exuberant happiness. The impulse to make a noise as an expression of feeling is universally admitted, and it may also be noticed that it has a tendency to arouse sympathy in an auditor of any kind, and an excitement analogous to that felt by the maker of the noise. A hound that has picked up the scent soon starts the responsive sympathy of the chorus of the pack; a cow wailing the loss of her calf often attracts the attention and response of her sisters in neighbouring fields; and the uproarious meetings of cats at night afford familiar instances of the effect such incipient music is capable of exerting upon the feline disposition.

Human beings are quite equally sensitive to all forms of expression. Even tricks of manner, and nervous gestures, and facial distortions are infectious; and very sensitive and sympathetic people are particularly liable to imitate unintentional grimaces and fidgets. But sounds which are uttered with genuine feeling are particularly exciting to human creatures. The excitement of a mob grows under the influence of the shouts its members utter; and takes up with equal readiness the tone of joy, rage, and defiance. Boys in the street drive one another to extravagances by like means; and, as Cicero long ago observed, the power of a great speaker often depends not so much on what he says, as upon the skill with which he uses the expressive tones of his voice. All such utterances are music in the rough, and out of such elements the art of music has grown, just as the elaborate arts of human speech must have grown out of the grunts and whinings of primeval savages. But neither art nor speech begins till something definite appears in the texture of its material. Some intellectual process must be brought to bear upon both to make them capable of being retained in the mind; and the early steps of both are very similar. Just as among the early ancestors of our species, speech would begin when the indefinite noises which they first used to communicate with one another, like animals, passed into some definite sound which conveyed to the savage ear some definite and constant meaning; so the indefinite cries and shouts which expressed their feelings began to pass into music when a few definite notes were made to take the place of vague, irregular shouting. And as speech grows more copious in resources when the delicate muscles of the mouth and throat are trained to obedience in the utterance of more and more varied inflections, and the ear is trained to distinguish niceties which have distinct varieties of meaning; so the resources of music increased as the relations of more and more definite notes were established, in obedience to the development of musical instinct and as the ear learnt to appreciate the intervals and the mind to retain the simple fragments of tune which resulted.

The examination of the music of savages shows that they hardly ever succeed in making orderly and well-balanced tunes, but either express themselves in a kind of vague wail or howl, which is on the borderland between music and informal expression of feeling, or else contrive little fragmentary figures of two or three notes which they reiterate incessantly over and over again. Sometimes a single figure suffices. When they are clever enough to devise two, they alternate them, but without much sense of orderliness; and it takes a long period of human development before the irregular haphazard alternation of a few figures becomes systematic enough to have the aspect of any sort of artistic unity. Through such crude attempts at music, scales began to grow; but they developed extremely slowly, and it was not till special races had arrived at an advanced state of intellectuality that men began to pay any attention to the relations of notes to one another, or to notice that such abstractions could exist apart from the music. And it has even sometimes happened that races who have developed up to an advanced standard of intellectuality have not succeeded in systematising more than a very limited range of sounds.

But complete musical art has to be made definite in other respects besides mere melodic up and down motion. The successive moments had to be regulated as well as mere changes of pitch, and this was first made possible by the element of rhythm.

All musical expression may be broadly distributed into two great orders. On the one hand, there is the rhythmic part, which represents action of the nature of dance motions; and on the other, all that melodic part which represents some kind of singing or vocal utterance. Rhythm and vocal expression are by nature distinct, and in very primitive states of music are often found independent of one another. The rhythmic music is then defined only by the pulses, and has no change of pitch; while purely melodic music has change of pitch, but no definition or regularity of impulse. The latter is frequently met with among savage races, and even as near the homes of highest art as the out-of-the-way corners of the British Isles. Pure, unalloyed rhythmic music is found in most parts of the uncivilised globe; and the degree of excitement to which it can give rise, when the mere beating of a drum or tom-tom is accompanied by dancing, is well known to all the world. It is also a familiar fact that dancing originates under almost the same conditions as song or any other kind of vocal utterance; and therefore the rhythmic elements and the melodic elements are only different forms in which the same class of feelings and emotions are expressed.

All dancing is ultimately derived from expressive gestures which have become rhythmic through the balanced arrangement of the human body, which makes it difficult for similar actions to be frequently repeated irregularly. The evidence

2

of careful observers from all parts of the globe agrees in describing barbarous dances as being obvious in their intention in proportion to the low standard of intelligence of the dancers. Savages of the lowest class almost always express clearly in their dance gestures the states of mind or the circumstances of their lives which rouse them to excitement. The exact gestures of fighting and love-making are reproduced, not only so as to make clear to the spectator what is meant by the rhythmic pantomime, but even in certain cases so as to produce a frenzy in the mind of both spectators and performers, which drives them to deeds of wildness and ferocity fully on a par with what they would do in the real circumstances of which the dancing is merely an expressive reminiscence.

In these respects, dancing, in its earlier stages, is an exact counterpart of song. Both express emotions in their respective ways, and both convey the excitement of the performers to sympathetic listeners; and both lose the obvious traces of their origin in the development of artistic devices. As the ruder kinds of rhythmic dancing advance and take more of the forms of an art, the significance of the gestures ceases to be so obvious, and the excitement accompanying the performance tones down. An acute observer still can trace the gestures and actions to their sources when the conventions that have grown up have obscured their expressive meaning, and when the performers have often lost sight of them ; and the tendency of more refined dancing is obviously to disguise the original meaning of the performance more and more, and merely to indulge in the pleasure of various forms of rhythmic motion and graceful gesture. But even in modern times occasional reversions to animalism in depraved states of society revive the grosser forms of dancing, and forcibly recall the primitive source of the art.

In melodic or vocal music the process has been exactly analogous. The expressive cries soon began to lose their direct significance when they were formalised into distinct musical intervals. It is still possible to find among lowly organised savages examples of a kind of music which is so little defined in detail that the impulsive cry or howl of expression is hardly disguised at all by anything which could be described as a definite interval. But the establishment of a definite interval of any sort puts the performer under restrictions, and every step that is made in advance hides the original meaning of the utterance more and more away under the necessities of artistic convention. And when little fragments of melody become stereotyped, as they do in every savage community sufficiently advanced to perceive and remember, attempts are made to alternate and contrast them in some way; and the excitement of sympathy with an expressive cry is merged in a crudely artistic pleasure derived from the contemplation of something of the nature of a pattern.

It is obvious that the rhythmic principle and the melodic principle begin very early to react upon one another. Savages all over the world combine their singing and their dancing; and they not only sing rhythmically when regular set dances are going on, but when they are walking, reaping, sowing, rowing, or doing any other of their daily labours and exercises which admit of such accompaniment. By such means the rhythmic and the melodic were combined, and it is no reckless inference that from some such form of combination sprung the original rhythmic organisation of poetry.

But the tendency to revert to primitive conditions is frequently to be met with even in the most advanced stages of art; and an antagonism, which it is one of the problems of the art to overcome, is persistent throughout its history. In very quick music the rhythmic principle has an inevitable tendency to predominate, and in very slow music the melodic principle most frequently becomes prominent. But it must be remembered that the principle which represents vocal expression applies equally to instrumental and to vocal music, and that rhythmic dance music can be sung. The difference of principle between melodic quality and rhythmic quality runs through the whole art from polka to symphony; and, paradoxical as it may seem, the fascination which some modern sensuous dance-tunes exercise is derived from a distinctly canta-

bile treatment of the tune, which appeals to the dance instinct
through the languorous, sensuous, and self-indulgent side of
people's natures.

The antagonism shows itself as much in men as in the art
itself. Dreamers and sentimentalists tend to lose their hold
upon rhythmic energy; while men of energetic and vigorous
habits of mind set little store by expressive cantabile. Composers of a reflective and romantic turn of mind like Schumann
excel most in music which demands cantabile expression; and
men like Scarlatti, in rhythmic effect. This rule applies even
to nations. Certain branches of the Latin race have had a
very exceptional ability for singing, and have often shown
themselves very negligent of rhythmic definiteness; while the
Hungarians manifest a truly marvellous instinct for what is
rhythmic; and the French, being a nation particularly given
to expressing themselves by gesticulation, have shown a most
singular predilection for dance rhythm in all branches of art.
In the very highest natures the mastery of both forms of
expression is equally combined; and it is under such conditions,
with musicians who have both methods of expression well
under command, that music rises to its highest perfection; as
the use of the two principles supplies the basis of the widest
contrast of which the art is capable.

In this respect the two contrasting principles of expression
are types of a system of contrasts which is the basis of all
mature musical design; and when the ultimate origin of all
music, as direct expression of feeling and an appeal to sympathetic feeling in others, is considered, it is easy to see that
the nature of the human creature makes contrast universally
inevitable. Fatigue and lassitude are just as certain to follow
from the exercise of mental and emotional faculties as from
the exercise of the muscles; and fatigue puts an end to the
full enjoyment of the thing which causes it. It is absolutely
indispensable in art to provide against it, and it is the instinct
of the artist who gauges human sensibilities most justly in
such respects that enables him to reach the highest artistic perfection in subtlety as well as scope of design. The mind first
wearies and then suffers pain from over-much reiteration of a

single chord, or of an identical rhythm, or of a special colour, or of a special fragment of melody; and even of a thing so abstract as a principle. In some of these respects the reason is easily found in some obvious physiological fact, such as exhaustion of nervous force or waste of tissue; but it appears certain that the only reason why a similar explanation cannot be enunciated in connection with the more intangible departments of human phenomena is that the more refined and subtle properties of organised matter are not yet perfectly understood But it holds good, as a mere matter of observation, that the laws which apply in cases where the physiological reasons are clear apply also in less obviously physical cases. It is perfectly obvious that when any part of the organism is exhausted, its energy can only be renewed by rest. But rest does not necessarily imply complete lassitude of all the faculties. It is a very familiar experience of hard-worked men that the best way to recover from the exhaustion of a prolonged strain is to change entirely the character of their work. Many of the phenomena of art are explicable on this principle. Up to a certain point the human creature is capable of being more and more excited by a particular sound or a particular colour; but the excitement must be succeeded by exhaustion, and exhaustion by pain, if the exciting cause is continued. If the general excitement of the whole being is to be maintained, it must be by rousing the excitable faculties of other parts or centres of the organism; and it is while these other faculties or nerve-centres are being worked upon that the faculties which have been exhausted can recover their tone. From this point of view a perfectly balanced musical work of art may be described as one in which the faculties or sensibilities are brought up to a certain pitch of excitation by one method of procedure, and when exhaustion is in danger of supervening, the general excitation of the organism is maintained by adopting a different method, which gives opportunity to the faculties which were getting jaded to recover; and when that has been effected, the natural instinct is to revert to that which first gave pleasure; and the renewal of the first form of excitation is enhanced by the consciousness of memory, together with that sense of

renewal of a power to feel and enjoy which is of itself a peculiar and a very natural satisfaction to a sentient being.

In the earlier stages of the art the struggle to arrive at a
solution of the problem this proposes is dimly seen. As man
had only instinct to find his way with, it is not surprising
that he was long in finding out means of managing and distributing such contrasts. In the middle period of musical
history, when musical mankind had learnt its lesson, and
took a complacent view of its achievement, the method and
use of such contrasts became offensively obvious; but in the
modern period they are disguised by infinite variety of musical
and æsthetical devices, and are necessarily made to recur with
extraordinary frequency in proportion to the exhausting kinds
of excitation employed by modern composers. In mature art
the systematisation of such contrasts is vital, and in immature
art it is incipient; and this fact is the most essential difference between the two.

Of such types of contrast that of principle between the
rhythmic and the melodic on one hand, and of emotional and
intellectual on the other, are the widest. The manner in
which they are applied in the highest works of absolute
music, such as symphonies and sonatas, will hereafter come
under consideration.

In the earliest stage of musical evolution these respective
principles show themselves especially in the manner in which
definition is obtained, since, as has been pointed out, definiteness is the first necessity of art. From melodic utterance
came the development of the scale, from dancing the distribution of pulses. The former is the result of man's instinct to
express by vocal sounds, the latter of his instinct to express
by gestures and actions; and in the gradual evolution of the
art the former supplies the element of sensibility, and the
latter that of energy; and when the nature of both is considered it will be felt that these characteristics are in accordance with the nature of their sources.

To sum up. The raw material of music is found in the
expressive noises and cries which human beings as well as
animals give vent to under excitement of any kind; and

their contagious power is shown, even in the incipient stage, by the sympathy which they evoke in other sentient beings. Such cries pass within the range of art when they take any definite form, just as speech begins when vague signals of sound give place to words; and scales begin to be formed when musical figures become definite enough to be remembered. In the necessary process of making the material intelligible by definition, the rhythmic gestures of dancing played an important part, for by their means the succession of impulses was regulated. Both vocal music and dancing actually originate in the same sources; as they are different ways of manifesting similar types of feeling. But they are in their nature contrasted, for in the one case it is the sound which forms the means of expression, and in the other it is a muscular action; and the music which springs from these two sources is marked by a contrast of character in conformity with their inherent differences. This contrast presents itself as the widest example of that law of contrasts which runs through the whole art, and forms, next to the definition of material, its most essential feature.

The law of contrasts forms the basis of all the important forms of the art, for a most obvious and natural reason. The principle of sympathetic excitement upon which the art rests necessarily induces exhaustion; and if there was no means of sustaining the interest in some way which allowed repose to the faculties that had been brought into exhausting activity, the work of art could go no further than the point at which exhaustion began. It is therefore a part of the business of the art to maintain interest when one group of faculties is in danger of becoming wearied, by calling into play fresh powers of sensibility or thought, and giving the first centres time to recover tone. And as there would be no point in such a device if the first group of faculties were not called into exercise again when they had revived, the balance and rationale of the process is shown in mature periods of art by a return to the first principle of excitation or source of interest after the establishment of the first distinct departure from it, which embodied this inevitable principle of contrast.

Taking the most comprehensive view of the story of musical evolution, it may be said that in the earlier stages, while the actual resources were being developed and principles of design were being organised, the art passed more and more away from the direct expression of human feeling. But after a very important crisis in modern art, when abstract beauty was specially emphasised and cultivated to the highest degree of perfection, the balance swung over in the direction of expression again; and in recent times music has aimed at characteristic illustration of things which are interesting and attractive on other grounds than mere beauty of design or of texture.

CHAPTER II

SCALES

THE first indispensable requirement of music is a series of notes which stand in some recognisable relation to one another in respect of pitch; for there is nothing which the mind can lay hold of and retain in a succession of sounds if the relations in which they stand to one another are not appreciably definite. People who live in countries where an established scale is perpetually being instilled into every one's ears from the cradle till the grave, can hardly bring themselves to realise the state of things which prevailed before any scales were invented at all. And the familiar habit of average humanity of thinking that what they are accustomed to is the only thing that can be right, has commonly led people to think that what is called the modern European scale is the only proper and natural one. But it is quite certain that human creatures did exist for a very long time without the advantage of a scale of any sort; and that they did have to begin building up the first indispensable necessity of musical art, by deciding on a couple of notes or so which seemed satisfactory or attractive when heard one after the other; and that they did have to be satisfied with a scale of the most limited description for a very long period.

What interval the primitive savage chose at the outset was probably very much a matter of accident; and inasmuch as scales used for melody are much less exact and stable than those which are used for harmony, it is quite certain that the reiteration of any interval whatever which men first took a fancy for was only approximate, and that only in course of ages did instinctive consensus of opinion, possibly with the help of some primitive instrument, fasten definitely upon a succession of sounds which to modern musicians would be clearly recognisable as a fourth or a fifth, or any other acoustically explicable pair of notes.

It is advisable to guard at the outset against the familiar misconception that scales are made first and music afterwards. Scales are made in the process of endeavouring to make music, and continue to be altered and modified, generation after generation, even till the art has arrived at a high degree of maturity. The scale of modern harmonic music, which European peoples use, only arrived at its present condition in the last century, after having been under a gradual process of modification from an accepted nucleus for nearly a thousand years. Primeval savages were even worse off than mediæval Europeans. They did not know that they wanted a scale; and if they had known it they would have had neither acoustical theory nor practical experience to guide them, nor even examples to show them how things ought not to be done. But it is very probable that in the end they selected an interval which would approve itself to the acoustical theorist as well as to the unsophisticated ear of a modern lover of art. What that interval would be it is difficult to guess, and pure theoretic speculation is almost certain to be at fault in any decision it comes to on the subject; but examination of the numerous varieties of scales existent in the world, and of such as are recorded approximately by ancient wind instruments, with the help of theory, may ultimately come very near to solving the problem.

With reference to this point, it may be as well to recognise that in the great number of scales which have developed up to a fair state of maturity, there are no two notes whatever that invariably stand in exactly the same relation to one another throughout all systems. It might well be thought that the octave could be excluded from consideration, as if it were not part of a scale, but only the beginning of a new series. But even the octave is said to be a little out of tune in accordance with the authorised theory of Chinese music. However, this is clearly only a characteristic instance of the relation between theory and art, for no Chinese singer would be able consistently to hit an exact interval which was just not a true octave, even if he was perverse enough to try. Of other familiar intervals the varieties are infinite. In our own system the fifth is less in tune than in many other systems, and in the Siamese scale there is nothing like a perfect fifth at all. The fourth is an interval which is curiously universal in its appearance; but that, again, does not appear in the true Siamese scale, or in one of the Javese systems. An agreement in such intervals as thirds and sixths is not to be expected. They are known to be difficult intervals to learn, and difficult to place exactly in theoretic schemes; and the result is that they are infinitely variable in different scales Some systems have major thirds, and some minor; and some have thirds that are between the two. Sixths are proportionately variable, and are often curiously dependent upon the fifth for any status at all; and of such intervals as the second and seventh, and more extreme ones, it must be confessed that they are so obviously artificial, that even in everyday practice in countries habituated to one scale they are inclined to vary in accordance with individual taste, and the lack of it.

Of all these intervals there are two which to a musician seem obviously certain to have been the alternatives in the choice of a nucleus. As has been pointed out, sixths, thirds, sevenths, and seconds are all almost inconceivable. They are all difficult to make sure of without education, and are unstable and variable in their qualities. There remain only the intervals of the fourth and the fifth; and evidence as well as theory proves almost conclusively that one of these two formed the nucleus upon which almost all scales were based; and one of the two was probably the interval which primitive savages endeavoured to hit in their first attempts at music.

But at the outset there comes in a very curious consideration which must of necessity be discussed before going further. If a modern musician, saturated in the habits of harmonic music, was asked for an opinion, he would say instantly that it was impossible that any beings could have chosen the fourth as their first interval; for that seems as hard to hit as thirds and sixths, and is even more inconclusive and unsatisfying to our ears. But nevertheless the fact remains that it is more often met with than the fifth in barbarous scales, and if modern habits of musical thought can be put aside the reason becomes obvious. Our modern harmonic system is an elaborately artificial product which has so far inverted the aspect of things, that in order to get back to the understanding of ancient and barbarous systems we have almost to set our usual preconceptions upside down. The modern European system is the only one in which harmony distinctly plays a vital part in the scheme of artistic design. Our scale has had to be transformed entirely from the ancient modes in order to make the harmonic scheme of musical art possible; and in this process the attitude of the cultivators of other systems towards their scales has been lost sight of, and their perception of them has become almost a lost sense. All other systems in the world are purely melodic. They present a single part as the whole material of music, and their scheme of æsthetics is totally alien from such a highly artificial and intellectual development as that of modern European music. In melodic systems the influence of vocal music is infinitely paramount; in modern European art the instrumental element is strongest. The sum of these considerations is, that whereas in modern music people count their intervals from the bass, and habitually think of scales as if they were built upwards, in melodic systems it is in most cases the reverse. The most intelligent observers of Oriental systems notice that those who use them think of these scales as tending downwards; and in certain particulars it is undoubtedly provable that the practice of the ancients was in like manner exactly contrary to ours. To take one consideration out of many as an illustration. The leading note of modern music always tends upwards; in other words, the note which lies nearest to the most essential note of the scale, which is always heard in the final cadence, and is its most characteristic melodic feature, is below the final and rises to it. But this is exactly the reverse of the natural instinct in vocal matters, and contrary to the meaning of the word cadence.

Most of the natural cadences of the voice in speaking tend downwards. When a man raises his voice at the end of a sentence he is either asking a question or expressing astonishment, and these are expressions of feeling which are in a minority. Pure vocal art follows the rule of the inflections in speaking; and in melodic systems, which are so much influenced by the voice, cadences which rise to the final sound are almost inconceivable. They might be possible as expressing great exaltation of feeling and power; but in most cases a cadence means, artistically, a point of repose, and it is only in very exceptional cases that a point of repose can be imagined on a high note; for the sustainment of a high note implies tension of vocal chords and effort, and such sustained effort can scarcely be regarded as a point of repose. In modern music the cadence is a harmonic process, and not a melodic one; and the upward motion from the leading note to the tonic in cadences becomes intelligible as successive positions of upper portions of the essential harmonies which happen to coincide with æsthetic requirements of melody when supported by the chords which supply the other requisites of a cadence simultaneously.

In melodic systems the majority of cadences are, as the word implies, made downwards; and undoubtedly in a majority of cases the scale was developed downwards. In such circumstances the difficulty of accounting for the more frequent appearance of the fourth than the fifth in scales used only for melodic purposes disappears, for, going downwards, it is perfectly natural and easy to hit the interval of the fourth. Moreover, a notable peculiarity in the construction of many and various scales increases the likelihood of the fourth having been first chosen downwards, while it also explains the early appearance of the interval of a third. It is an indubitable fact that scales are developed by adding ornamental notes to the more essential notes which have been first established; that is, notes which lie close to the essential notes, and to which the voice can waver indefinitely to and fro. A note of this kind would not at first be very exact in its relative position. Mere uncertainty of voice would both suggest it and make it variable; but undoubtedly it became a conspicuous feature of the cadences very early. If the fourth below was chosen by a musical people in developing the melodic scale downwards, it is likely to be verified by the frequent appearance of a note a semitone above it, as this would be the first addition made to the scale, and would serve as the downward-tending leading note of the system.

There are many facts which justify this theory of the development of the scale, notably the construction of ancient Greek scale, and of the modern Japanese and the aboriginal Australian scale, such as it is, and even of the scale indicated by the phonographed tunes of some of the Red Indians of North America. The first scale which history records as having been used by the Greeks is indeed absolutely nothing more than a group of three notes, of which those which are furthest apart make the interval of the fourth, and the remaining note is a semitone above the lower note. This is precisely the group of notes which analogy and argument alike lead us to expect in the second stage of scale-making under melodic influences, and it affords an almost decisive proof that the first interval chosen was the downward fourth. The Japanese system had no possible direct connection with the Greek system, but the same group of notes is prominently characteristic, and is undoubtedly used with persistent reiteration in their music. A modern European can get the effect for himself by playing C, and the A♭ and G below it one after another, and reiterating them in any order he pleases, so long as he makes A♭ the last note but one, and G the final. The result is a curious reversal of our theories of musical æsthetics, for G seems to become the tonic, and C the note of secondary importance—a state of things which is only conceivable if we think of the scale as tending downwards instead of upwards.

But it is not to be denied that some races seem to have chosen a rising fifth as the nucleus of the scale, though it is much less common. The voice has to rise in singing as well as to fall, and it is conceivable that some races should have thought more of the rise, which comes early in the musical phrase, than of the fall, which naturally comes at the end. One of the most astute and ingenious analysts of musical scales, Mr. Ellis, thought that early experimenters in music found out the fifth as the corresponding note to the fourth on the other side of the note from which the fourth was first calculated. The proof of the fifth's being recognised early— beyond its inherent likelihood—lies in the fact that some bar· barous scales comprise the interval of an augmented fourth, such as C to F♯, which is only intelligible in a melodic system on the ground of the F♯ being an ornamental note appended to the G next above it. The original choice of a fifth or a fourth as the basis or starting-point may have had something to do with the fact that nearly all known scales which have arrived at any degree of completeness can be grouped under two well-contrasted heads. The scales of China, Japan, Java, and the Pacific Islands are all pentatonic in their recognised structure. That is, they theoretically comprise only five notes within the limits of the octave, which are at various distances from one another. But in this group the fifth above the lowest note is a prominent and almost invariable item. The rest of the most notable scales of the world are structurally heptatonic, and comprise seven essential notes in the octave. Such are the scales of India, Persia, Arabia, probably Egypt, certainly ancient Greece and modern Europe. And in these the fourth was the interval which seems to have been first recognised. To avoid misconception, it is necessary to point out that all these scales have been subjected to modifications in practice, and their true nature has thereby been obscured. But the situation becomes intelligible by the analogy of our own use of the modern scales. Ours are undoubtedly seven-note scales, as even children who practise them are painfully aware; but in actual use a number of other notes, called accidentals, are admitted, both as modifications and as orna- ments. The key of C is clearly represented to every one by the white keys of a pianoforte, but there is not a single black note which every composer cannot use either as an ornament or as a modification without leaving the key of C. Similarly, nearly all the pentatonic scales have been filled in, and the

natives who use them are familiar with other notes besides
the curious and characteristic formula of five; but in the background of their musical feelings the original foundation of
their system remains distinct, just as the scheme of the key
of C remains distinct in the mind of an intelligent musical
person even when a player sounds all the black notes in a
couple of bars which are nominally in that key.

It undoubtedly made a great difference whether the fifth or
fourth was chosen, for it is noticeable that small intervals like
semitones are rare in five-note systems and common in seven-
note systems; and this peculiarity has a very marked effect
in the music, for those which lend themselves readily to the
addition of semitones have proved the most capable of higher
development. It is unnecessary to speculate on the way in
which savages gradually built their scales by adding note to
note, as the historical records of Greek music go so far back
into primitive conditions that the actual process of enlargement can be followed up to the state which for ancient days
must be considered mature. It is tolerably clear that the
artistic standard of the music of the Greeks was very far
behind their standard of observation and general intelligence
in other matters. They spent much ingenious thought upon
the analysis of their scales, and theorised a good deal upon
the nature of combinations which they did not use; but their
account of their music itself is so vague that it is difficult to
get any clear idea of what it was really like. And it still
seems possible that a large portion of what has passed
into the domain of "well-authenticated fact" is complete
misapprehension, as Greek scholars have not time for a
thorough study of music up to the standard required to judge
securely of the matters in question, and musicians as a rule
are not very intimate with Greek. But certain things may
fairly be accepted as trustworthy. Among them is, of course,
the enthusiasm with which the Greeks speak of music, and
their belief in the marvellous power of its effects. The stories
of Orpheus and Amphion and others testify to this belief
strongly, and mislead modern people into supposing that
their music was a great art lost, when the very details and

style of their evidence tend to prove the con(rary. It is not in times when art is mature that people are likely to tell stories of overturning town walls or taming savage animals with it; but rather when it is in the elementary stages, in which the personal character of the performer adds so much to the effect. It is a sufficiently familiar fact that in our own times a performer of genius can move people more and make more genuine effect upon them with an extremely simple piece than a brilliant *virtuoso* of the highest technical powers can produce with the utmost elaboration of modern ingenuity. A crowd of people of moderate intelligence go almost out of their minds with delight when a famous singer flatters them with songs which to musicians appear the baldest, emptiest, and most inartistic triviality. The moderns who are under such a spell cannot tell what it is that moves them, and neither could the Greeks. They would both confess to the power of music, and the manner of their confession would seem to imply that they were very impressionable, but had not arrived at any high degree of artistic intelligence or perception. The Greeks, moreover, were much nearer the beginning of musical things, and may be naturally expected to have been more under the spell of the individual sympathetic magnetism of the performer than even uneducated modern people; and the accounts we have of their system tend to confirm these views. Its limitations are such as do not encourage a belief in high artistic development, for at no time did the scheme extend much beyond what could be reproduced upon the white keys of the pianoforte and an occasional B♭ and C♯; and all the notes used were comprised within the limits of the low A in the bass stave and the E at the top of the treble stave. The first records indicate the time when the relations of three notes only were understood, which stood in much the same relation to one another that A F E do in our modern system. This clearly does not represent the interval of a third with a semitone below it, but the interval of a fourth looking downwards with F as a downward leading note to E. This was called the tetrachord of Olympos. In time the note between A and F was added, which gave a natural flow down

from A to E. This was well recognised as the first nucleus of the Greek system, and was called the Doric tetrachord. It was enlarged by the simple process of adding another group of notes which corresponded exactly to the first, such as E, D, C, B, below or above, thereby making a balance to the other tetrachord. It is possible that their musical sense developed sufficiently to make use of the artistic effects which such a balance suggests; and it is even likely that the desire for such effects was the immediate cause of the enlargement of the scale. In course of time similar groups of notes, called tetrachords, were added one after another, till the whole range of sounds which the Greeks considered suitable for use by the human voice was mapped out. The whole extent of this scale being only from A in the lower part of the bass stave to A in the treble, indicates that the Greeks preferred only to hear the middle portion of the voice, and disliked both the high and low extremes, which could only be produced with effort; and it proves also that their music could not have been of a passionate or excitable cast, because the use of notes which imply any degree of agitation are excluded. The last note which is said to have been added in the matter of range was the A below the lowest B, which was attributed to a lyre-player of the name of Phrynis in 456 B.C. But this note was considered to stand outside the set of tetrachords, and was not used in singing, but only to enable the harp-player to execute certain modulations.

The Greek musical system being a purely melodic one, it was natural that in course of time a characteristic feature of higher melodic systems should make its appearance. For the purposes of harmony but few arrangements of notes are necessary; but for the development of effect in melodic systems it is very important to have scales in which the order of arrangement of differing intervals varies. In the earliest Greek nucleus of a scale, the Doric, there was a semitone between the bottom note and the next above it in each tetrachord—as between B and C, or E and F. In course of time the positions of the semitones were altered to make different scales, and then the tetrachord stood as B, C♯, D, E, or, as in our modern minor scale, D, E, F, G. This was called the Phrygian, and was considered the second oldest. Another arrangement with the semitone again shifted, as B, C♯, D♯, E, resembles the lower part of our modern major scale, and was known as the "Lydian." When the tetrachords were linked together at first they overlapped; as in the Doric form, if the lower tetrachord was B, C, D, E, the one added above it would be E, F, G, A, the E being common to both tetrachords. This was ultimately found unsatisfactory, and a scheme of tetrachords which did not overlap was adopted about the time of

Pythagoras. Thus the Doric mode stood as E F G A B C D E, the semitones coming between first and second and fifth and sixth; the Phrygian mode became like a scale played on the white notes of the pianoforte beginning on D; and the Lydian like our ordinary major scale; and more were added, such as the Æolic, which is like a scale of white notes beginning on A; the Hypolydian, like one beginning on F, and so forth.

The restrictions of melodies to these modes secured a well-marked variety of character, to which the Greeks were keenly alive; and they expressed their views of these diversities both in writing and in practice. The Spartan boys were exclusively taught the Doric mode, because it was considered to breathe dignity, manliness, and self-dependence; the Phrygian mode was considered to have been nobly inspiring also, but in different ways; and the Lydian, which corresponded to our modern major mode, to be voluptuous and orgiastic, probably from the fact that the semitones lay in the upper part of the tetrachords, which in melodic music with a downward tendency would have a very different aspect from that of our familiar major mode under the influence of harmony. But this mode was not in great favour either in ancient times or in mediæval times, when attempts were made to revive the Greek system.

In this manner a series of the notes which were supposed to be fit for human beings to sing were mapped out into dis-

tinct and well-defined positions. But one of the most important developments of the scale still remained to be made. In
modern times the scale has become so highly organised that
the function of each note and the particular office each fulfils
in the design of compositions is fairly well understood even
by people of moderate musical intelligence. What is called
the tonic, which is the note by which any key is named, is
the most essential note in the scale, and the one on which
every one instinctively expects a melody or a piece of music
in that key to conclude; for if it stops elsewhere every one
feels that the work is incomplete. To the tonic all other
notes are related in different degrees—the semitone below, as
leading to it; the dominant, as the note most strongly contrasted with it, and so forth. But to judge from the absence
of comment upon such functions of various notes of the scale
by Greek writers, and the obscurity of Aristotle's remarks on
the subject, it must be assumed that the ideas of the Greeks
on such a head were not clearly developed. In the beginning,
when there were only three notes to work with, it seems as
if their musical reason for existence necessarily defined their
functions. But it is probable, as frequently happens in similar
cases outside the range of music, that composers speculated
in arrangements of the notes which ignored the purposes
which brought them into existence; and that, as the scale
grew larger and larger, people ceased to recognise that any
particular note was more important than another. It is true
they had distinct names for every note in a mode, and two
are specially singled out as important, namely, the "middle"
note and the "highest," which all modern writers agree was
what we should call the lowest. If anything can be gathered
from the ancient writings on the subject at all, it would seem
to be that the middle note, the " mese," was something like our
dominant, and the "hypate," which we should call the lowest,
was the note to close upon. If this was so, the original functions described on page 20 were still recognised in theory;
but the wisest writers on the subject in modern times think
that matters got so confused that a Greek musician would end
upon any note that suited his humour. This vagueness coin-

cides with the state of the scales of all other melodic systems; and though the Greeks were more intelligent than any other people that have used a melodic system, it is very likely that without the help of harmony it was almost impossible for them to organise their scale completely.

The Greeks subjected their scales to various modifications in the course of history. It was very natural that such intellectualists as they were should try experiments to enhance the opportunities of the composer for effect. One experiment was made very early, which was to add a note like C♯, but less than a semitone above the C, which stood next above the lowest note of the old Doric tetrachord; and this was called the chromatic genus. Other experiments were tried in sub-dividing into yet smaller intervals; but the various writers who describe these systems indicate that they were not altogether successful, as the chromatic genus was regarded as mawkish and insipid, and the enharmonic genus as too artificial.

The Greek system may therefore be considered to have arrived at its complete maturity in the state in which a range of sounds extending only for two octaves was mapped out into a series of seven modes, which can be fairly imitated on a modern pianoforte by playing the several scales which begin respectively on E, F, G, A, B, C, D, without using any of the black keys. The difference between one and another obviously lies in the way in which the tones and semitones are grouped, and the device affords a considerable opportunity for melodic variety. But it appears improbable that the Greeks arrived at any clear perception of the functions of the notes of the scale after the manner in which we regard our tonic and dominant: the full development of this phase of scale-making had to wait till after the attempt to systematise ecclesiastical music on what was supposed to be the ancient Greek basis in the early middle ages; when the new awakening of the sense of harmony soon caused scales to take entirely new aspects. But this being the highest artificial development of the scale element of music in connection with harmony must be considered later, as there are many other melodic systems like that of the ancient Greeks in principle but different in their order of arrangement.

In the many and various melodic systems of the world, scales are found of various structure, but the building of all of them has evidently been achieved by similar processes. Races show their average characteristics in their scales as much as they do in other departments of human energy and contrivance. Such as are gifted with any degree of intellectual activity have always expended a singular amount of it on their scales; and the result has been pedantically minute, or theoretic, or extravagantly fanciful in proportion to their inclinations in these respects. The Chinese, as might be expected, have been at once minutely exact in theory and bombastically complacent in fancy. The races of the great Indian peninsula have been wildly fanciful in their imagery, and equally extravagant in ingenious grouping of notes into modes; while the Persians and Arabs have been remarkable for their high development of instinct in threading the difficult and thorny ways of acoustical theory in such a manner as to obtain a very perfect system of intonation. The Persian system is probably the most elaborate scale system in the world. Nothing appears to be known of early Persian music, though the earliest records give examples of scales which are already very complete, implying a very long period of antecedent cultivation of the art. In the tenth century they had already developed a scale which has the appearance of being singularly complete, as it comprised all the intervals which are characteristic of both our major and minor modes, except the major seventh, which is our upward-tending leading note. That is, it appears as the scale of C with both E flat and E natural, and both A flat and A natural, but B flat only instead of our familiar leading note B. This shows that they certainly did not at that time attempt cadences of the kind so familiar in modern harmonic music, but kept to the forms which were suitable to a melodic system. They did not, however, long rest satisfied with a scale of such simplicity. By the time of Tamerlane and Bajazet the series of notes had been enlarged by the addition of several more semitones, and had been

systematised into twelve modes, on the same principle and for
the same purposes of melodic variety as had been the case with
the Greeks. In fact, the first three agree exactly with the
ancient Ionic, Phrygian, and Mixolydian modes of the Greeks,
but go by the very different names of Octrag, Nawa, and
Bousilik. But even this did not go far enough for the subtle
minds of the Persians and Arabians. A famous lute-player
adopted a system of tuning which gave intervals that are
quite unknown to our ears; as, for instance, one note which
would lie between E♭ and E, and another between A♭ and A,
in the scale of C. The former is described as a neutral
third, neither distinctly major nor minor, which probably
had a pleasant effect in melodic music; and the latter, as a
neutral sixth.

Going still further, they applied mathematical treatment of
a high theoretical kind to the further development of the
scale. They evidently discovered the curiously paradoxical
facts of acoustics which make an ideally perfect scale impossible, and, to obviate the difficulties which every acoustical
theory of tuning presents, they subdivided the octave into no
less than seventeen notes. Their object was not to have such
a large number of notes to make melodies with, or to employ
quarter tones, but to have a copious variety to select from as
alternatives. The arrangement of these notes was quite
systematic, and gave two notes instead of the one familiar
semitone between each degree of the scale and the one next
to it. That is to say, between D and C there would be two
notes, one a shade less than a semitone (making the interval
known as the Pythagorean limma 243 : 256), and another
a little less than a quarter tone from D (making the interval
known as the comma of Pythagoras (524288 : 531441). And
similar intervals came between D and E, and so on through
the scale. By this ingenious arrangement they secured
absolutely true fifths and fourths, a major third and a major
sixth that were only about a fiftieth of a semitone (that is,
a skisma) short of true third and sixth, and a true minor
seventh. Theoretically this is the most perfect scale ever
devised. Whether it really was used exactly in practice is

another matter. Even under harmonic conditions, when notes are sounded together, it is impossible for the most expert tuners to make absolutely sure of intervals within such narrow limits as the fiftieth of a semitone; while it is well known that in melodic systems the successions of notes used by the performers are only approximately true; for the finest ear in the world can hardly make sure of a true third or a true sixth when the notes are only sounded one after the other. In modern times this remarkable system of the Persians has been changed still further, by the adoption of twenty-four equal quarter tones in the octave. But this plan really lessens the delicate perfection of the adaptability of the system; for though it looks a larger choice of notes, it will not give such absolutely true intervals as the earlier scheme. With all this wonderful ingenuity in dividing off the range of sounds for use and defining the units exactly, it appears that the Persians and Arabians had but an uncertain sense of what we call a tonic, and, as far as can be gathered, stopped short of classifying the notes in accordance with their artistic functions, just as the Greeks seem to have done.

In strong contrast to the Persians the inhabitants of the great Indian peninsula appear to have sedulously avoided applying mathematics to their scales; and though the Indian scales are even more complicated and numerous than the Persian, they have been handed down from generation to generation for ages, purely by aural tradition. Unfortunately this avoidance of mathematics has caused the subject of Indian scales to be extremely obscure, and the extraordinarily high-flown imagery which is used in Indian treatises on music renders the unravelling of their system the more difficult. The method used for arriving at the actual scales used by musicians is to ascertain the exact length of the subdivisions of the strings which are indicated by the positions of the frets upon the lute-like instrument called the vina, which has been in universal use for many hundreds of years, and to test and compare the notes which are produced by sounding the strings when "stopped" at such points. The frets are supposed to mark the points at which the string should be stopped with

the finger to get the different notes of the scale; but in
practice a native player can always modify the pitch by
making his finger overlap the fret more or less, and thereby
regulate the fret to get the interval which tradition taught him
to be the right one. In fact the frets on different instruments
vary to a considerable degree—even the octave is sometimes
too low and sometimes too high; but through examining a
number of specimens a rude average has been obtained, which
seems to indicate a system curiously like the modern European
system of twelve semitones. But it is clear that this can be
only a rough approximate scheme upon which more delicate
variations of relative pitch are to be grafted, for the actual
system of Indian scales is far too complicated to be provided
for by a mere arrangement of twelve equal semitones.

As in the case of the Persian and Arabic system, the
Indian scale does not come within the range of intelligible
record till it is tolerably mature and complete from octave
to octave. In order to get a variety of major and minor
tones and semitones, the scale was in ancient times divided
into twenty-two small intervals called s'rutis, which were a
little larger than quarter tones. A whole tone contained
four s'rutis, a three-quarter tone three, and a semitone two.
By this system a very fair scale was obtained, in which the
fourth and fifth were very nearly true, and the sixth high
(Pythagorean). In what order the tones and semitones were
arranged seems to be doubtful; and in modern music the
system of twenty-two s'rutis has disappeared, and a system
of the most extraordinary complexity has taken its place.
The actual series of notes approximates as nearly as possible
to the European arrangement of twelve semitones; and the
peculiarity of the system lies in the way in which it has been
developed into modes. The virtue of the system of modes
has already been pointed out, as has the adoption of a few
diverse ones by the Greeks. The Indians went so far as
to devise seventy-two, by grouping the various degrees of the
scale differently in respect of their flats and sharps. The
system can be made intelligible by a few examples out of
this enormous number. Our familiar major mode forms

one of them, and goes by the name of Dèhraśan-kârabhárna. Our harmonic minor scale also appears under the name of Kyravâni, the Greek modes also make their appearance, and every other combination which it is possible to get out of the semitones, but always so that each degree is represented in some way or another. The extremes to which the process leads may be illustrated by the following. Tânarupi corresponds to the following succession—

C, D♭, E♭♭, F, G, A♯, B, C.

Gavambódi to

C, D♭, E♭, F♯, G, A♭, B♭♭, C.

This obviously carries the modal system as far as it can go in the way of variety.

But besides these modes the Indians have developed a further principle of restriction in the "ragas," which are a number of formulas regulating the order in which the notes are to succeed each other. The rule appears to be that when a performer sings or plays a particular raga he must conform to a particular melodic outline both in ascending and descending. He may play fast or slow, or stop on any note and repeat it, or vary the rhythm at his pleasure; it even appears from the illustrations given that he may put in ornamental notes and little scale passages, and interpolate here and there notes that do not belong to the system, so long as the essential notes of the tune conform to the rule of progression —Just as in modern harmonic music certain discords must be resolved in a particular way, but several subordinate notes may be interpolated between the discord and the resolution.— An example may make the system clearer. The formula given for the raga called Nâda-nâmakrya is C, D♭, F, G, A♭, C in ascending, and C, B, A♭, G, F, E, D♭, C in descending. In practice it is evident that the performers are not restricted to the whole plan at once. G may go either to F descending or to A♭ ascending, and A♭ may either go to C or back to G and so on; but the movement from any given note must be in accordance with the laws of the raga, up or down. The

example of this raga given in Captain Day's Music of Southern
India helps to make the system clear.

In the mode of Máya-málavagaula, and the raga Náda-námakrya.

et cet.

By such means the freedom of the performer is restricted,
but curious special effects are obtained. For instance, the
ascending scheme of Mohànna is C, D, E, G, A, C, which
produces precisely the effect of Chinese or any other pentatonic music, though the Indian music belongs to the heptatonic
group of systems; and close as the restrictions seem to be,
it may be confessed that, judging from the examples given, a
great deal of variety can be obtained without transgressing
them. A similar device to that of the ragas is very commonly
met with even in modern European music, when a composer
restricts a melody to a particular group of notes in order to
give it more definite character.

Pursuing their love of categorising still further, the Indians
restrict particular ragas to particular hours of the day, and
they used also to be restricted to particular seasons of the
year. As was the case with the Greeks and their modes,
the different ragas have different attributes, and are believed
respectively to inspire fear, wonder, anger, kindness, and so
forth. And moreover they are all personified as divine beings,
and have wives and histories, and are the subjects of elaborate
pictures, and apparently also of fanciful poems. This all
points to a very long period of development, and to a considerable antiquity in the established system; for even people

who **luxuriate in imagery** and fancifulness like the Indians, do
not attribute divine qualities to a scheme which they themselves have only devised in comparatively recent times.   The
whole story points to a considerable gift for the organisation
of artistic material; but it is nevertheless recorded that the
Indians have little feeling for anything like a tonic, or for
relative degrees of importance in the notes that compose the
scale; and there seems little restriction as to which note in
the scale may be used for the final close.

The ancient Greek, and the Persian and Indian systems,
are the most important of the heptatonic order, all of which
appear to have been developed from the basis of the fourth;
and these have served for the highest developments of pure
melodic music.   Some of the pentatonic systems (with modes
of five notes) have also admitted of very elaborate and
artistic music; but the standard is generally lower, both in
the development of the scale and of the art for which it
serves.

The system which is usually taken as the type of the pentatonic group is the Chinese, which stands in strongly marked
contrast to the Persian and Indian systems in every way.
The passion for making ordinances about everything, and
the obstinate adherence to schemes which have received the
approval of authority, which characterise the Chinese, make
themselves felt in their scale system as everywhere else.
According to authorised Chinese history, their music is of
marvellous antiquity, and copious details are given about
the surpassing wonders of the ancient music, and of the great
emperors from nearly 3000 B.C. onwards, who composed music,
and ordinances for its regulation; but the account is so over-
whelmed by grandiose and absurd myths and extravagances that
it is impossible to trace the development of the scale.   It has
been altered several times, but the alterations are by no means of
the nature of developments. About 1300 B.C. the scale is said to

have corresponded to C, D, E, G, A,

which may be taken to be the old pentatonic formula.

About 1100 B.C. it was amplified to C, D, E, F♯, G, A, B, C

Later still, when a great
Mongol invasion occurred, the Mongols changed the F♯ to F,
and made the scale like our major mode. But then some of
the musicians wanted to use F and some F♯, and Kubla Khan,
founder of the Mogul dynasty, ordained that there should
be both F and F♯ in the scale, which accordingly became
C, D, E, F, F♯, G, A, B, C. About a couple of hundreds
of years later the F♯ was abolished again, and soon after
that the late form of the pentatonic scale was adopted,

which stands as C, D, F, G, A.

But meanwhile the Chinese had from early ages a complete set
of twelve semitones just as we have, but arrived at, as their
history tells, in a singular semi-scientific manner. According
to the very careful and conscientious treatise of Van Aalst, the
Chinese say that there is perfect harmony between heaven
and earth; and that as the number 3 is the symbol of heaven
and 2 of earth, any sounds that are in the relation of 3 to 2
must be in perfect harmony. They accordingly cut two tubes,
one of which is two-thirds the length of the other, and took
the sounds which they produced as the basis of their musical
system. Fanciful as the story is, it points to the germ of
truth, that the interval of the fifth, which is produced by
such a pair of tubes, was really the nucleus of the pentatonic
system. And according to their story they went on to find
out other notes by cutting a series of twelve such tubes, each
of which was either two-thirds of the next longer, or gave
the octave below the note obtained by that measurement. To
all appearance this gave them a complete series of semitones.
The tubes so cut were the sacred regulators of the national
scale, and were called the "lus." They were also held to be
the twelve moons, and also the twelve hours of the day, and
other strange things; and the fact that they were all these
wonderful things at once made it indubitable that the scale

was perfect and not to be meddled with. But in fact nearly all the intervals were out of tune. The fifth tube would ostensibly give a note a third above the lowest tube—as, if the lowest was C, the second would give G, the third D, the fourth A, and the fifth E. But that note would really be too high, and the intervals would go on getting more and more out of tune till they arrived at the octave, which would be the worst of all. But the matter was ordained so. The "lus" were made in accordance with the sacred principles of nature; and therefore though the scale does not sound agreeable it is right, and so it must remain. In order to keep the scale in accordance with these sacred principles the "lus" were made of such durable materials as copper and jade; and though it appears that the "lus" are no longer in use, the system on which they were constructed still regulates the Chinese scale.

But this must not be taken to imply that all these twelve semitones were to be used in the same piece of music. Their only service was to enable the characteristic pentatonic series to be made to start from different pitches. Practically the Chinese only use one mode at a time. In early times they only used a series corresponding to the notes produced by the first five "lu" pipes; that is, C, D, E, G, A, which is their old pentatonic form. The modern series is theoretically that which corresponds to C, D, F, G, A. The use of the semitones is to enable the series to be transposed bodily, which does not alter the mode, except by varying the degree in which the notes are out of tune. On great ceremonial occasions the hymns have to be sung in the "lu," which is called after the moon in which it is celebrated. So if in a ceremony which took place in the first moon the pentatonic series began on C, the hymn would be sung a semitone higher each successive moon, till at a ceremony in the twelfth moon it would begin on B, a seventh higher than the first; and then at the next performance the hymn would drop a whole major seventh, and be sung in notes belonging to the scale of C again. To be hedged in with such conditions as these cannot be expected to be encouraging to art, and it is not to be wondered at that

he Chinese system is the most crudely backward and in-
apable of development of any of the great melodic systems.
But at the same time it must not be ignored that notwithstanding such obstacles, and the fact that musicians are looked
down upon as an inferior caste in China, the Chinese do
manage to produce good and effective tunes; and it cannot
be denied that the pure pentatonic system lends itself peculiarly to characteristic effects, and to the production of impressions which are more or less permanent. Its very restrictions
give it an appearance of strangeness and definiteness which
attract notice, and with some people liking.

Nations which have not been so tied and bound by ordinances and dogmatic regulations have managed to develop
pentatonic systems to a much higher degree of artistic elasticity, and the result has naturally been in some cases to
minimise the characteristic pentatonic effect. The Japanese
were among the foremost to expand their system in every
practicable way. They have nominally as complete a series
of twelve semitones as European musicians, but, like all other
cultivators of melodic music, they only use them to select from.
Authorities may be confessed to differ, but their scale-system
seems to be pentatonic in origin, like that of the Chinese;
though, unlike them, they distribute their intervals so as to
obtain twelve different modes of five notes each. For instance,
one mode of five notes, called Hiradioschi, corresponds to C,
D, E♭, G, A♭; another, Kumoi, to C, D♭, F,* G, A♭; another,
Iwato, to C, D♭, F, G♭, B†; from which it is to be observed
that they fully appreciate the artistic value of semitones; which
again distinguishes them from the Chinese, who rarely use such
intervals. They are said to make use of the octave, the fifth,
and the fourth in tuning, and to tune their thirds and sixths
by guesswork, and not by any means scientifically. The
thirds are said to be often more like the "neutral thirds"
described in connection with Persian music, which are neither
major nor minor, but between the two. A Japanese musician,

---

* Mr. Pigott gives a note equivalent to E.
† Mr. Pigott gives a note equivalent to B♭.

who seems fully competent to form an opinion, has expressed
doubts as to whether their scale was true pentatonic or not.
In face of the distinct grouping of five notes which is almost
invariable, this view seems rather paradoxical; but the frequent
occurrence of a fourth with a semitone above the lower note
is so like the early tetrachord of the Greeks, with a sensitive
downward-tending leading note (see p. 23), that the doubt
cannot be said to be without some appearance of justification.
The mode Kumoi, quoted above, would in that sense represent
two tetrachords, C, D♭, F—G, A♭ C, like those of Olympos,
put one above another; and the effect of them may be gauged
by the process suggested on p. 20.

There are two other important systems of melodic music
which are most probably true pentatonic, but quite different
from either Chinese or Japanese. The oldest of them is the
Javese. In this case there is no possibility of unravelling
the process of development of the scales; we can only take
the results as examined by Mr. Ellis and Mr. Hipkins, whose
methods seem thoroughly trustworthy, and gather what we
can from the facts. The Javese have two plans of tuning,
one called Gamelan Salendro, and the other Gamelan Pelog,
which differ so much that they cannot be played together.
In the Gamelan Salendro scale there are five notes, which
are fairly equidistant from one another, and each of the
intervals exceeds a whole major tone, such as C and D, by
a considerable interval. To our European ideas such a scale
seems almost inconceivable. To compare it with our major
scale of C, the first degree would be from C to a note half-
way between D and E♭, the next degree would be between
E and F but nearer to F, the next would be a quarter of a
tone higher than G, and the next about half-way between A
and B♭, and the next move would be to the octave C above
the starting-point. How such a scale could be tuned by ear
almost passes comprehension, and implies a very remarkable
artificial development of scale-sense in the musicians who use
it. The Gamelan Pelog is a very different mode, and almost
as singular. The first step would be from C to a note a
little higher than E, the second to a note a little below F,

the third note would be just below G, the next a little below B, and the remaining step would reach the octave C. This is evidently a very elaborate artificial development of some simpler pentatonic formula that has long passed out of record. The Siamese system is almost as extraordinary. It is not now pentatonic, though supposed to be derived originally from the Javese system. The scale consists of seven notes, which should by rights be exactly equidistant from one another; that is, each step is a little less than a semitone and three-quarters. So that they have neither a perfect fourth nor a true fifth in their system, and both their thirds and sixths are between major and minor; and not a single note between a starting note and its octave agrees with any of the notes of the European scale. The difficulty of ascertaining the scale used in practice lay in the fact that when the wooden har-monicon, which seemed the most trustworthy basis of analysis, was made out of tune, the Siamese set it right by putting pieces of wax on the bars, which easily dropped off. Their sense of the right relations of the notes of the scale is so highly developed that their musicians can tell by ear directly a note is not true to their singular theory. Moreover, with this scale they have developed a kind of musical art in the highest degree complicated and extensive.

This survey would not be complete without reference to the scale of the Scotch bagpipe. This, again, is a highly artificial product, and no historical materials seem available to help the unravelling of its development. Though often described as pentatonic, the scale comprises a whole diatonic series of notes, from which modes may be selected. These notes do not agree with our ordinary system, and their relations are merely traditional, as they are tuned empirically by ear. Taking A as a starting-point, the next note is a little below B; the next is not C, but almost a neutral third (p. 29) from A; the next very nearly a true fourth above A, that is, a little below our D; the next almost exactly a true fifth from A, that is, very near E; the next a neutral sixth from A (p. 29), between E and F; and the remaining note a shade below G. The type is more like the ancient Arabic than any

4

other, and not really the least like the Chinese, though the impression conveyed by the absence of the leading note sometimes misleads people into supposing they are akin. Whether it is really a pentatonic scale, as some have thought, is therefore extremely doubtful. Even if the modes were really of five notes, that is not a proof that its constitution is of the pentatonic order, as has been indicated in connection with the Indian and Japanese system; both the fifth and the fourth are very nearly true, and as it seems based on the old Arabic system, which was not pentatonic, the argument would tend to class it with the Indo-European and Persian seven-note systems.

The above summary is sufficient to show the marvellous variety of the scales developed by different nations for purely melodic purposes. The simple diatonic system of the Greeks, the subtly ingenious mathematical subdivisions of the Persians and Arabs, the excessive modal elaborations of the Hindus, the narrow and constricted stiffness of the Chinese, the ambiguous elasticity of the Japanese, and the truly marvellous artificiality of the Javese and Siamese systems, are all the products of human artistic ingenuity working instinctively for artistic ends. Similarity of racial type seems to have caused men to produce scales which are akin. They are all devised as means to ends, and when the mental characteristics and artistic feeling of the races who devised the scales have been similar the result has been so too. The seven-note systems are mostly characteristic of Caucasian races, and the five-note scales of the somewhat mixed but probably kindred races of Eastern Asia. And this does not so much indicate that they borrowed from each other as that the same types of mind working under artistic impulse produced similar results. One important defect they have in common. Though in most of them the relations of the notes are actually defined with the utmost clearness, in none have they arrived at the artistic completeness of maturity which is implied by classification. This remained to be done under the influence of harmony.

It is quite clear that the early Christians adopted the principles and some of the formulas of melody of the ancient

Greek system—in the state to which it had arrived at about
the beginning of our era—for as much music as their simp.e
ritual required. But none of it was written down, and in
those centuries of general disorganisation in which the collapse
of the Roman Empire was going on, the traditions became
obscure and probably conflicting in different centres. To
remedy this state of things efforts were made, especially by
Ambrose, Bishop of Milan, and one of the many Popes named
Gregory, to establish uniformity by restoring the system of
the Greek modes and making the music they used conform to
it. Knowledge of every kind was at that time at a very low
ebb, and the authorities who moved in the matter had very
limited and indefinite ideas of what Greek music had been.
But between them they contrived to organise an intelligible
arrangement of various modes, and it was of no great consequence that they got most of the names wrong. Ambrose
authorised four modes, the (1) Dorian, (2) Phrygian, (3)
Lydian, and (4) Mixolydian—corresponding more or less to
the ancient Greek (1) Phrygian, (2) Doric, (3) Syntono-Lydian,
and (4) Ionic. These were called the authentic modes. Gregory
nominally added four more, which were not really new modes,
but a shifting of the component notes of the modes of Ambrose;
for as by Ambrose's regulations musicians were only allowed
to use the scale of D between D and its octave, by Gregory's
arrangement they might use the notes *a*, *b*, *c* below the lower
D instead of in the higher part of the scale. And similarly
with the other three. Gregory's group were called plagal
modes. In later days four more modes were added: the mode
beginning on C, and that beginning on A and their plagals;
and two hypothetical modes which were not supposed to be
used, namely, that beginning on B and its plagal. The total
amounted therefore to fourteen modes, of which two were not
actually used. It was very soon after this organisation of
modes that attempts at harmony began to be made, either by
doubling an ecclesiastical tune at another pitch, such as the
fourth or the fifth, or by really trying to get two tunes to go
together. The idea of harmony in the modern sense did not
develop into clearness for centuries; but musicians got more

and more expert in contriving to make various melodies go together without ugly combinations, and by degrees the meaning of chords and their possible functions in a scheme of art began to dawn upon men's intelligence. Meanwhile artistic instinct led composers to modify the ecclesiastical modes. Even when they were only used melodically, certain imperfections had made themselves felt. The mediæval musicians had quite an intense detestation of the interval of the augmented fourth, such as appears between F and B; and singers were allowed to take the note a semitone lower than B, that is, B♭, wherever the notes forming the objectionable interval occurred close together in a passage of melody. This was not at first dictated by a feeling for the ugliness of the harmonic effect of the notes, but for that of their melodic effect; it was not till men's sense for harmony began to grow and expand that the ugliness of the interval in harmony became equally apparent. Then one modification led to another. The adoption of B♭ got rid of the ugly interval between F and B, but it created a new one between B♭ and E; and to obviate this, a new flat had to be introduced for E. Then, as men's harmonic experiences increased, a still further alteration began to suggest itself strongly. At first the principal melody of the plain song had been generally in the bass, and had been doubled in the higher parts; then it was transferred to the middle parts, and other melodies called counterpoints were written round it; and then, finally, a totally new aspect of things for art was reached when men began to feel that the tune was at the top. The change of attitude is illustrated by the change in the details of the cadences. As long as their feeling for the pure melodic side of music predominated, musicians regarded the passage of the last note but one of the principal melody one step downwards to the tonic as the principal feature of the cadence. When they began to accompany this passage by harmony, their attention was soon drawn away from this part in the combination to the notes that accompanied it in other parts. At first it was customary to accompany the last note but one with the third below or the sixth above, and pass to the unison or the octave for the conclusion. And

as long as nothing else was added this did very well, though in
the favourite modes the accompanying part moved up a whole
tone instead of a semitone. The aspect of things was changed
when men found out that it sounded well to accompany the
penultimate step of the plain song by the fifth below as well
as the third or sixth, as E and C by A, or A and F by D ;

then the effect of the minor

third created by the system of most of the modes began to
appear objectionable; because the artistic sense of musicians
made them long for definite finality at the conclusion of a
piece of music, and this was not produced by such a process
as the progression of the chord of A minor to the chord
of D minor, or of D minor to G. To obviate this a sharp
was added by musicians to the third of the penultimate chord,
as to C in example (a) above, and to F in example (b), thus
creating the upward-tending leading note, and giving a better
effect of finality to the progression. The move was opposed
by ecclesiastical authority, but in vain; the artistic instinct
of musicians was too strong, and the major penultimate chord
with its sensitive leading note became an established fact
in music.

It is not possible here to trace the gradual transformation
of the modes through every detail. Step by step, in analogous
ways to those described above, the modes were subjected to
further modifications by the addition of more sharps and flats.
Men's sense of the need for particular chords in particular
relations to one another drove them on in spite of themselves;
and the most humorous part of the story is, that after centuries of gradual and cautious progress they ultimately completed a scale which they had known all along, but had
rather looked down upon as an inferior specimen of its kind.
This simply proves what is now quite obvious, that for melodic
purposes such modes as the Doric (beginning on D) and the
Phrygian (beginning on E) were infinitely preferable to the
Ionic (beginning on C), and that when they began to add

harmonies they had not the least notion whither their course was going to lead them. They first attempted harmony in connection with the melodic modes which they thought most estimable, under the familiar misconception that what was best in one system would be best in all, and only found out that they were wrong by the gradual development of their artistic sense for harmony in the course of many centuries. At last, in the seventeenth century, men began to have a distinct sense of an artistic classification of the notes of the scale. The name note or tonic of a scale arrived finally at its decisive position as the starting-point and the resting-place of an artistic work. The establishment of the major chord on the dominant note—the fifth above the tonic—gave that note the position of being the centre of contrast to the tonic ; and upon the principle of progress to contrast, and back to the initial starting-point, the whole fabric of modern harmonic music is built. The other notes fell into their places by degrees. The mediant (as E in C) chiefly as the defining note for major or minor mode; the subdominant (as F in C) as a subordinate centre of contrast in the harmonical system of design, and as the sensitive downward-tending leading note to the third in the final chord in the cadence. The leading note (as B in the key of C) had a melodic function in strengthening the cadence, and served as the major third of the dominant chord; the supertonic (as D in the key of C) served as fifth of the dominant chord, and as the basis of the harmony which stands in the same relation to the dominant of the key as that stands to its tonic. And the remaining diatonic note (the submediant, as A in C) appears chiefly as the tonic of the relative minor mode, and otherwise as the most indefinite note in the system. This does not of course exhaust the functions of the various notes. To give them all would require a treatise on modern composition. They are always being expanded and identified with fresh manipulations of the principles of design by able composers. The fact is worth noting that the complete classification of the functions of the various items of the scale puts the European harmonic system of music—as a principle suited for the

highest artistic development—at least eight centuries ahead
of all melodic systems. For it took musicians fully that
time to arrive at it from the basis of the old melodic system
of the Church.

The last stage of refinement in the development of our scale
system was the assimilation of all the keys—as they are
called—to one another; that is, the tuning of the twelve
semitones so that exactly the same modes can be started from
any note as tonic. But it took men long to face this, and the
actual adoption of the principle necessitated a further modification of the scale.

As long as people could remain content with approximately
diatonic music, and a range of few keys, they did not become
painfully aware of the difficulties which acoustical facts throw
in the way of perfect tuning. Till the end of the sixteenth
century musicians did not want more accidentals than B♭, E♭,
F♯, C♯, and G♯. But as their sense for possibilities of harmony and modulation expanded they began to make A♭ stand
for G♯, and D♭ for C♯, and D♯ for E♭, and endeavoured to
get new chords and new artistic effects thereby. When they
began to find out the artistic value of modulation as a means
of contrast and variety, by degrees they came to want to use
all the keys. But under the old system of tuning B♭ was by
no means the same thing as A♯, and any one who played the
old G♯, C, and E♭ under the impression that it was the same
chord as C, E, and G transposed, was rudely undeceived by
an unpleasant discordance. The men whose instincts were
genuinely and energetically artistic insisted that our system
must accept a little imperfection in all the intervals for the
sake of being able to use all keys on equal terms. The
struggle was long, and various alternatives were proposed
by those who clung to the ideal of perfectly tuned chords—
such as splitting up the semitones as the Persians had done.
But in the end the partisans of the thoroughly practical and
serviceable system of equal temperament won the day. The
first important expression of faith was J. S. Bach's best-
known work, the two books of Preludes and Fugues in all
the keys, called by him the "well-tempered clavier." An

ideally tuned scale is as much of a dream as the philosopher's stone, and no one who clearly understands the meaning of art wants it. The scale as we now have it is as perfect as our system requires. It is completely organised for an infinite variety of contrast, both in the matter of direct expression—by discord and concord—and for the purposes of formal design. The instincts of human creatures for thousands of years have, as it were, sifted it and tested it till they have got a thing which is most subtly adapted to the purposes of artistic expression. It has afforded Bach, Beethoven, Schubert, Wagner, and Brahms ample opportunities to produce works which in their respective lines are as wonderful as it is conceivable for any artistic works to be. A scale system may fairly be tested by what can be done with it. It will probably be a good many centuries before any new system is justified by such a mass of great artistic works as the one which the instincts and efforts of our ancestors have gradually evolved for our advantage.

CHAPTER III

FOLK-MUSIC

THE basis of all music and the very first steps in the long story of musical development are to be found in the musical utterances of the most undeveloped and unconscious types of humanity; such as unadulterated savages and inhabitants of lonely isolated districts well removed from any of the influences of education and culture. Such savages are in the same position in relation to music as the remote ancestors of the race before the story of the artistic development of music began; and through study of the ways in which they contrive their primitive fragments of tune and rhythm, and of the principles upon which they string these together, the first steps of musical development may be traced. True folk-music begins a step higher, when these fragments of tune, as nuclei, are strung together upon any principles which give an appearance of orderliness and completeness; but the power to organise materials in such a manner does not come to human creatures till a long way above the savage stage. In such things a savage lacks the power to think consecutively, or to hold the relations of different factors in his mind at once. His phrases are necessarily very short, and the order in which they are given is unsystematic. It would be quite a feat for the aboriginal brain to keep enough factors under control at once to get even two phrases to balance in an orderly manner. The standard of completeness in design depends upon the standard of intelligence of the makers of the product; and it cannot therefore be expected to be definite or systematic when it represents the intellectual standard of savages. Nevertheless the crudest efforts of savages throw light upon the true nature of musical design, and upon the manner in which human beings endeavoured to grapple with it. The very futility of the arrangement of the musical figures in the tunes of savages is most instructive, and the gradual development of power to arrange them in an intelligible order is clearly seen to proceed parallel to the general development of capacities of all kinds in the human race.

At the very bottom of the process of development are those savage howls which have hardly any distinct notes in them at all. Many travellers record such things, and try to represent them in the European musical stave. For instance, the natives of Australia are described by a French traveller as beginning a howl on a high note and descending a full octave in semitones; and the Caribs are described by an English traveller as doing the same thing. Every one who knows

anything about music is aware that the stave notation cannot in this case represent the reality, as a downward scale of correct semitones is beyond the powers of any but very highly trained singers even in advanced stages of musical development. Another traveller quotes some Polynesian cannibals as gloating over their living victims, shortly to be devoured, and singing gruesomely suggestive passages of rising quarter tones. In all such cases the process must have been a gliding of the voice up or down, without notes that were strictly defined either in relation to one another or to any general principle. This process of gliding is familiar in every stage of art, even the most advanced, and always implies direct

* Compare the following Hungarian tune for the same type of expression made into music :—

human expression in the action, for it is obviously out of the range of any scale. But in advanced stages of art it is a mere accessory which the performers use for expressive purposes at their own discretion, and it is not often indicated in the actual writing of the musical material of compositions. With the savage it is pure human expression no further advanced than the verge of formulation into musical terms.

The first step beyond this is the achievement of a single musical figure which is reiterated over and over again. Of this form the aborigines of Australia are recorded to afford the following example :—

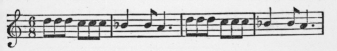

This simple figure they are said to have gone on singing over and over again for hours. It seems to represent a melancholy gliding of the voice downwards—the first artistic articulation of the typical whine above described—and as far as it represents any scale, it indicates the use of the downward fourth as the essential characteristic interval, with a downward-tending leading note (see page 23). A similar example of the reiteration of a single figure is quoted by a traveller from Tongataboo, which is also described as being repeated endlessly over and over again :—

et cet.

It is extremely difficult to make sure what intervals savages intend to utter, as they are very uncertain about hitting anything like exact notes * till they have advanced enough to have instruments with regular relations of notes more or less indicated upon them. But if the latter illustration can be trusted, it represents the nucleus of the pentatonic system

* See note at the end of the volume.

(page 21), with a sort of ornamental glide round one of the
essential notes.

Reiteration similar to that shown in the above examples is
also described by Mr. A. H. Savage Landor in his account of
his travels among the "hairy Ainu," the peculiar and isolated
race that now inhabit the Kurile Islands, north of Japan.
He says, "The same phrase recurs again and again in their
songs." And again, "Ainu music . . . is monotonous and
continually repeats itself."

From a very different and distant group of natives, the
Macusi Indians of Guiana in South America, comes a formula
of repetition which is one step further advanced, as there is a
contrast of two melodic formulas, A and B.

The design is obviously unsymmetrical, and the real impulse
of the singers seems to have been to derive pleasure from the
mere sense of contrast between the two little musical figures,
and, like children, to reiterate the first phrase till they were
tired of it, and then to sing the second a little for a change,
and then to go back to A for a little, and then sometimes to
reiterate B till they were tired of that, and then to go back
to A again, and so on. They are said to have gone on doing
this for hours.

As we rise in the human scale the phrases get longer and
more varied; and the relation of phrase to phrase becomes
more intelligible, and the order in which they occur becomes
more symmetrical. The relative lack of mental power shows
itself in weakness and indefiniteness of design. A sort of
music will go on for a long time, but be totally devoid of
systematic coherence; indeed, resembling nothing so much as

attempts at stories made by excitable children or people of weak intellect, who forget their point before they are half-way through, and string incidents together which have in reality nothing to do with one another.* There is a most remarkable example of this kind of helplessness in a long Trouvère song in an English manuscript of the thirteenth century. It tells the story of Samson, and begins by reiterating a very genial little fragment of tune,

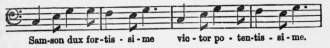

Sam-son dux for-tis - si - me   vic - tor po - ten-tis - si - me.

which rambles on pleasantly for some time, and then—as if there had been enough of it—is replaced by another phrase of similar type, which in turn gives place to another, without any attempt at system or balance or co-ordination of the musical material. It is as if the singer went on with a little phrase till he was tired of it, and then tried another till he was tired of that, and so on as long as the words required.

A type of this sort, with a little more sense of system, is quoted from Mozambique :—

It must be confessed that this must either have been improved

* See note at the end of the volume.

upon in the recording, or else it is not pure native music. But by reading between the lines it is easy to see that the music had organisation enough to start from a high point and end on the low point of repose, and that three different types of fairly well-defined figures were successively alternated without further attempt at balance than the repetition of the first phrase

Reiteration interspersed among vague meandering indefinite passages of song of a characteristic phrase which has taken the fancy and laid hold of the mind seems to belong to the same order of design as the familiar rondo. A remarkably clear example is quoted from the music of the natives of British Columbia :—

As the standard of human organisation improves, the capacity to balance things more regularly becomes evident; and the power to alternate simple figures more systematically immediately produces a primitive type of more definite character than the specimen of the rondo above quoted.

The following example of Feejee music illustrates the type with very fair regularity :—

This type of design persists through the whole story of musical art with different degrees of extension in the phrases which are alternated. The familiar aria form of the middle period of opera is merely an alternation of characteristic material and contrasting keys, and the more highly organised rondo of symphonic art is a constant alternation of one special musical passage with others which contrast with it. In the Feejee tune there are only two figures which are alternated.

As an extraordinarily compact example of reiteration with different phrases alternating with the recurrences of the principal figure, the following Russian tune is worth examination, and it certainly puts the type in almost the closest limits conceivable :—

The tune is specially interesting because it reverses the familiar order of the rondos, and puts the essential characteristic figure second to the contrasting figures each time; and this rather emphasises the universality of the general principle of knitting a whole movement together by the reiteration of a characteristic feature. In this case the tonal form is obscure, for the tune begins on D and ends on C, so the curious little figure indicated by the asterisk is apparently the only thing that holds the tune together; but the management of the alternations shows a skill and subtlety which enhances the effect of the whole. For the little figure is approached first from D, next from C, next from A, and last from E; and in the last case the figure itself is neatly varied by raising the pitch of its initial note.

The principle of constant reiteration of a figure or a rhythm to unify a movement is of familiar occurrence. It is illustrated in the reiteration of a figure of accompaniment to long passages of free melody, as in the slow movement of Bach's Italian concerto, and in the organ fantasia in C; it is also illustrated in the familiar form of the ground bass so often used by Lulli, Purcell, Stradella, Bach, and others; which consists of the incessant repetition of a short formula in the bass with the utmost variety of melody, figure, harmony, and rhythm that the composer can contrive in the upper parts. The device of reiteration is also happily used to give a characteristic expression to the whole of a movement, as in the first chorus of Dvorak's "Spectre's Bride," and in the Nibelung music in Wagner's "Ring;" and carrying implication to the utmost, the same principle is the basis of the "variations" form, which is simply the reiteration of a recognisable formula of melody or harmony in various disguises.

Of the ways in which such reiteration may be managed there are many examples in folk-music. One that indicates a certain advance in artistic perception is the reiteration of the same phrase at different levels, which corresponds to the type known in more advanced music as a sequence; which indeed is one of the most important devices known to composers for giving unity and intelligibility to progressions, and is used constantly by every composer of any mark from Lasso and Palestrina to Wagner.

The two following tunes from different parts of the globe will serve to illustrate the primitive type.

The first is a Russian peasant tune quoted in a book of the last century :—

The second is English of the Elizabethan era :—

This last represents a much higher standard of musical perception, as unity is maintained without strict uniformity of one principle of procedure. Indeed, there are a considerable number of devices which imply design in this tune which should not be overlooked. The closeness of the first half to the central note C, and the wide range of the second half, give an excellent principle of contrast; and the consistency of the principle of contrast is maintained by making the levels of the sequence close in the first half and wide in the second; further, the ends of each half are ingenious extensions of the principal figure, and as each of them breaks the regularity of the repetitions it throws the essential points of the structure into relief; and as the first half ends on C, and the second on the tonic F, the principle of contrast is carried out with comprehensive variety; and, what is of highest importance in such a case, the tune is knit into complete unity by the definiteness of the tonality.

The principle of defining design by tonality marks a considerable advance in musical intelligence, as it implies a capacity to recognise special notes as of central importance in the scheme, and others as subordinate. In the above example the C at the end of the first half has the feeling of being a point of rest, though not a final point; but the F at the end is an absolute point of repose, and is felt to round off the design completely. If the last note had been G or E instead of F, the whole thing would have sounded hazy and incomplete. This impression of finality is produced solely by the feeling for the key, which is an outcome of long human experience of certain types of progression and melody. In this individual instance the key is understood through the harmonic implications of the melody; for the end implies what is called a regular dominant-tonic cadence, and would probably not give the effect of finality at all to musicians only accustomed to melodic music. Indeed, the melodic systems are not well adapted to such forms, since they have none of them any such strong definition of a tonic as is characteristic of harmonic music. The modern European scheme of art rests upon a systematisation of the scale which recognises certain notes as being final, and all the other notes as having relative degrees of importance, while all have their special functions in determining design; and this principle is perfectly invaluable for establishing the unity of a piece of music. But it is purely the result of harmonic development, for in all melodic systems the notes are more on an equality. Their functions are not decisively fixed, and a tune can begin or end with any note of the scale. This makes it much more difficult to establish the unity of a piece of music, and the possibilities of variety in intelligible designs are thereby limited. Indeed, long consistent development of a single movement is impossible in pure melodic music; the resources of art are not various enough to admit of it; and even in short tunes, if the music is to be fully intelligible in design, it has to be so without the resource of a well-defined pair of contrasting points like tonic and dominant. But, on the other hand, melodic systems admit of an arbitrary choice of any particular note, which can be emphasised so persistently that it takes rank as a sort of tonic. The pentatonic systems are happy in this respect, because the definiteness of difference in the relation between one pair of notes and another helps the mind to fasten on special notes with ease, and to accept them as of vital importance to the design.

The following Chinese tune will serve to illustrate this device, as it is all threaded upon the single note D :—

It will also serve to illustrate again the same principles as those illustrated by the Russian tune quoted on p. 53, as it is practically little more than a series of variations on the figure of the first two bars.

A similar use of a note like a tonic is to be observed in the following Indian tune, which will also be useful as illustrating at once a capacity for contriving a longer sweep of melody, a higher sense for clear and decisive balancing of contrasting phrases, and also the Oriental love of ornamentation :—

The Indians of the Orient contrive to make long passages of melody; but the order of the recurrence of the characteristic figures is very frequently incoherent. The rondo type is, however, fairly common. But it must be acknowledged that many of the tunes are not true examples of folkmusic, but rather of a conventional art-music, which represents the skill of more or less cultivated musicians. The ornamental qualities are characteristic features of nearly all Oriental music, and demand more than passing consideration.

With genuine Orientals the love of unmeaning decorative ornamentation is excessive in every department of mental activity, whether literature, art, or music. This is generally a sign that the technical or manipulatory skill is far in excess of the power of intellectual concentration. When mental development and powers of intellect and perception are too backward to grasp a design of any intricacy or a conception that is not obvious and commonplace, the human creature who is blessed with facility of execution expends his powers in profusion of superfluous flourishes. In European countries the type is most commonly met with among popular operatic singers; but it is also plentiful among showy pianists, violinists, and other virtuosi, who rejoice the hearts of those members of the general public who are as unintelligent as themselves. Indeed, the truth is of wide application, and need not be confined merely to music; for it is noticeable that people who delight in excess

of ornament and decoration are almost always of inferior intellectual power and organisation. Ornament is the part of anything which makes for superficial effect. It may co-exist with
a great deal of force and fire, as in what is called Hungarian
music, which is really a gipsy development of Hungarian substance; and it may be used as an additional means of expression,
as it is in some Scotch and Irish tunes; but when it is purely a
matter of display, it generally implies either undeveloped mental
powers or great excess of dexterity. The Siamese are among
the most musical nations, and most skilful in performance;
but their mental development has only begun in comparatively
recent times, and the masses of the people are still child-like
in intellectual matters. A thoroughly competent observer
says that their vocal performances seem to be made of nothing
but trills and runs and shakes, and it is certainly much the
same with their instrumental music. The florid character of
Egyptian music is also notorious; but the most curious example
of the kind is what is familiarly known as Hungarian music.
The original Hungarian music is extraordinarily characteristic
in rhythm and vigorous in melody, but devoid of ornament.
The recognised musicians of Hungary are gipsies, who are of
Oriental descent, and are well known for their taste for finery
and ornamentation all the world over; and in their hands
Hungarian music has become the most ornamental thing of
its kind that Europeans are acquainted with. The ornaments
are perfectly meaningless, except as implying singular dexterity of manipulation and an extraordinary aptitude for
purely superficial invention in the decorative direction. The
following is an example of parts of a Hungarian tune, and
of the version with the ornamentation added by the gipsy
performers. The beginning stands as follows :—

And the close:—

Nearly all the music of South-Eastern Europe exhibits th
same traits. The Roumanian folk-music and dance-music
very vivid in neatness of phraseology; full of little trills an
jerks, and characterised also by quaint and rather plaintiv
intervals, such as are very familiar in many Eastern quarter
The following fragment is unusually simple in part, but ve
characteristic as a whole:—

Similar peculiarities, both of intervals and of ornament
are shown in the tunes of Smyrna and the islands of th
Hellespont. And even in Spain, in the southern district
and in the Balearic Islands, where traces of Oriental influenc
are still to be met with in other lines besides music, th
characteristic features of the tunes of Eastern Europe are m
with in combination with higher qualities of design.

Racial differences, which imply different degrees of em

tionalism and imaginativeness, and different degrees of the power of self-control in relation to exciting influences, are shown very strongly in the folk-music of different countries. No people attempt folk-tunes mechanically without musical impulse. The very fact of musical utterance implies a genuine expression of the nature of the human being, and is, in varying degrees, a trustworthy revelation of the particular likings and tastes and sensibilities of the being or group of beings which gives vent to it. The natural music of a demonstrative people is rhythmic and lively; of a saturnine people, gloomy; of a melancholy and poetical people, pathetic; of a matter-of-fact people, simple, direct, and unelaborated; of a savage people, wild and fierce; of a lively people, merry and light; of an earnest people, dignified and noble. It remains so through all the history of art; and though the interchange of national products has more or less assimilated the arts of certain countries, the nature of man still governs his predilections, as is easily seen by the average differences of tastes in art in such countries as Italy, France, and Germany.

Before discussing folk-music in general, certain circumstances have to be taken into consideration. A large proportion of the tunes came into existence in connection with poems and ballads which told some story or tragic event of local interest, and each tune was made to fit all the verses, whether they were cheerful or tragical. Such a tune is likely to be little more than a mere design, which might be very pleasant and complete as melodic design in itself, but would leave it to the singer to put the necessary expression corresponding to the varying sentiment of the words, by giving to a rise in the melody the character of exultant happiness or poignant anguish, and to a fall either reposeful satisfaction or hopeless despair. Any attempt to infuse strong expression into music makes the systematic management of design more difficult, because it is liable to break through the limitations which make design possible, and to force the composer into climaxes and crises at moments which are difficult to adapt to the general conventional rules of orderliness. The greater part of the history of music turns upon this very point; for composers have been constantly attempting to enlarge their resources so as to be able to bring more and more expression into use without spoiling the consistency of the design. For, as has been indicated in connection with the Englisb sequence tune (page 55), different principles of design can be set off against one another; and when the terms of one principle of order are broken for any purpose, such as expression or variety, they can, in advanced states of art, be supplemented by some other principle of form or expression.

The difficulty of introducing expression without spoiling the design was felt as much by the makers of folk-tunes as by composers of more advanced music; and the way in which nations looked at expression and design is the source of the most deep-seated differences between the different national products. Indeed, the whole of the folk-music of the world may be broadly classified into two comprehensive divisions. On the one hand, there are all those tunes whose ostensible basis of intelligibility is the arrangement of characteristic figures in patterns; and on the other, all those which by very prominent treatment of climaxes imply a certain excitement and an emotional origin. The various national groups of folk-music may be classified by the extent to which they incline to one or other of these types. No nation is restricted entirely to one or the other, but the preponderance with some nations is decisively in favour of emotional tunes, and with others of formal tunes. The formal tunes are the most primitive types, and also undoubtedly the least interesting and beautiful.

Before proceeding, therefore, to the highest type of folk-tune, it will be well to consider the universality of certain simple principles of design in all branches of folk-music. The simplest arrangement is the alternation of two characteristic figures in various patterns. The crude attempt of savages to make some sort of pattern out of two figures has been illustrated from the Macusis and Feejees. A primitive but more successful pattern is the following Russian peasant's tune :—

Here are only two figures, as in the Macusi tune, but the
treatment implies an immense difference of artistic sense;
for four principles of design are combined to give the tune
variety and unity—rhythmic contrast, melodic contrast, and
contrast of pitch, all held together by unity of tonality. The
tune centres on A, starting from it and returning to it. The
first half emphasises the part of the scale which lies above
A, and the second half the part that lies below it. The
rhythmic system is consistent, but inverted in the two halves;
so that the characteristic anapæst comes at the beginning of
the phrases in the first half, and at the end in the second.
It is also noteworthy as a very neat little subtlety that the
high note which completes the balance of the range of the
two contrasting halves of the scale is obtained by a slight
variation of the first principal figure.

To shorten the discussion of the principles upon which
such patterns are contrived, it will be of service to take the
letter A to represent the figure or complete phrase with
which the tune begins, and B to represent the second, and
if there is a third to call it C, and so on. The greater
portion of the folk-tunes of the world are simple patterns,
based upon all possible interchanges of strongly characteristic
figures similar to the possible combinations of A, B, or A, B,
C, in symmetrical order. It is truly extraordinary what an
amount of variety proves to be possible. The simplest type
of all is A, B, A, without disguise. And of this there are
literally thousands of examples, ranging from very short
phrases to long passages like the arias of the old Italian
operas. As types of the most compact kind with slight
variations the following will serve:—

Hungarian.

Poitevin.

Welsh.

From the mountains of Galicia in N.W. of Spain.

Every possible order that can give the impression of balance is adopted; and special types of character are often emphasised by the way in which particular figures are insisted upon. The plaintiveness of the following old Servian tune is intensified by harping on the phrase that contains the curious augmented interval, and by the ingenuity with which the accent is shifted in different repetitions :—

As the sense for design grows stronger, and skill in putting things to effective issues improves, the repetitions are varied to enhance the interest. The following for its size is very comprehensive. It comes from Bas Quercy :—

Each clause ends on a different note except the first and last, and this gives a very strong impression of variety in unity.

The device of repeating two different phrases successively (as A, A, B, B) is very familiar, and so is the alternation ending with the second phrase (A, B, A, B). Both of these necessitate a feeling for tonality, as without it the unity would not be complete. In other words, the tonality supplies the impression of unity, and the successive alternations the contrast. When the tonality is not decisive the effect is quaintly incoherent, as in the following Russian tune :—

Of the same A, A, B, B, with a little coda at the close to strengthen the impression of unity, the old form of the tune "In dulci jubilo" is a good instance :—

MS. of A.D. 1305.

An illustration of A, B, A, B, with a variation of B to strengthen the close, is the following Slavonic tune :—

In the more highly organised types the simplicity of such methods of procedure is very much disguised. Very often

the figures are not repeated in their entirety, but only characteristic portions of them, especially those portions which
occupy the most prominent positions, such as the first part
of the phrase or the figures of the cadence.

In the most highly organised examples also the phrases
become much longer, and are subject to variations which
strengthen the design to a remarkable degree. A fine instance is the following Scotch tune :—

In this the effect of contrast between A and B is mainly
achieved by difference of position in the scale, as B is almost
entirely composed of fragments and variations of fragments
of A; so that the whole tune is knit together with the
utmost closeness. Tonality, relation of pitch, rhythm, and
characteristic figures of melody are all used with remarkable

skill to attain the end of variety of contrast within unity. A
tune of this sort indicates a great power of mental concentration in the nation which produces it; but the elaborate
ingenuity with which it is knit together is by no means
rare. Nearly all strong and responsible races possess tunes
of this kind, which will bear a very careful analysis in every
detail.

But by way of contrast it will be well to take a passing
glance at the tunes of advanced but less concentrated races.
In southern countries the impulse is neither towards concentration of design nor often towards any degree of expression.
Very simple forms are met with, such as the Galician tune
on page 64. But in the more highly organised tunes there
is often but little consistency. The song is a sort of wild
utterance of impulse by the types of creatures who do not
criticise but only enjoy. The Basques have extraordinarily
long rambling tunes, which in a sort of vague way suggest disposition of materials like those above described (A, B, A, &c.).
But there is no closeness of texture as in the Scotch tune, nor
is any concentration of mind shown by any feature of form
or idea. In some Spanish tunes there is a sort of luxury of
irregularity which may be illustrated in a small space in the
following example from the neighbourhood of Barcelona :—

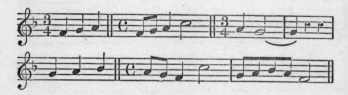

When analysed at close quarters there are some interesting
and subtle principles of cohesion even in this tune, but the
general effect produced is a sort of careless abandonment to
impulse. A characteristic feature of Spanish folk-tunes is a
curious jerk which commonly occurs at the end of phrases;
and this not only appears in tunes from various districts of
Spain, but has crossed the seas, and continues to appear in

places where the Spaniards were once masters, as in Sicily and
in South America. A very characteristic example of this very
feature comes from Vera Cruz in Mexico :—

There is very little of close-knit orderliness about this tune,
but it is a good illustration of an impulsive type, and the
sequence in the second half illustrates the same principle
of cohesion as the Russian and English tunes on page 55.
As an illustration of the Spanish jerk from Sicily a small
fragment will suffice :—

The Italians also possess this jerk; possibly it remains as a
relic of former Spanish occupation. The indolent insouciance
of their tunes is familiar. They are sometimes cast on very
simple lines, and are melodically attractive, but are not often
highly organised or closely knit.

Passing on to more reserved and self-contained but highly
reflective races, folk-music is found to become more and more
simple and plain. There is an enormous quantity of genuine
early German folk-music; but it is quite singularly deficient
in vividness of any kind, and is devoid of marked characteris

tics in the way of eccentric intervals and striking rhythms. Expression is sometimes aimed at, but always in a self-contained manner; that is, in such a manner that both the outline of the melody and the general distribution of its phrases adapt themselves to closely coherent and intelligible principles of design; and the designs themselves are on an average of a higher order and represent stronger instincts for organisation than the tunes of other nations which in actual details of material are more attractive. There are certain obvious features in early German folk-tunes which show an inclination for coherence and completeness of design. In a very large majority of tunes the first couple of phrases—making, as it were, the first complete musical sentence—is repeated, thereby giving a strong sense of structural stability. The middle portion of the tune often provides contrast to the stability of the first portion by being broken up into shorter lengths, or by being poised upon different centres and notes of the scale; and the final portion is very frequently marked by a singular melisma or dignified flourish in the final cadence, which serves to give additional weight and firmness to the return to the tonic of the song, which clinches the design into completeness. This melismatic device is one of the most characteristic features of old German songs, and is, of course, an ornamental process; but it is generally applied with great sense of expressive effect, and never gives the impression of being introduced for the sake of display. A tune, which was printed at least as early as 1535, will serve to illustrate most of these points:—

Besides the points above mentioned, the tune indicates a
fine sense for knitting things together, by presenting a formula
of melody and rhythm successively in different phases. The
portion of the second phrase marked C is derived from B (by
imitating its diatonic upward motion); and in its turn it serves
as the basis for the whole of the middle part E and F, by appearing in successive repetitions in a rising sequence. Again,
the passage marked H, and the whole of the final cadence K,
are successive variations of the last bar but four, G, which is
in itself a kind of mixture of A and D. And it is most noteworthy that in the course of the repetition the figure G grows
more like D, till at K it gives the impression of being a
perfect counterpart to the cadence of the first half of the
tune; and the impression is enhanced by the introduction
of the little parenthesis I, which at the same time neatly
defers the last recurrence of the highest note of the song,
so that it shall not come three times running in the same
rhythmic position.

Other points which are characteristic of German folk-music
are the irregularity of the metre, in mixing up threes and
fours, the diatonic and serious nature of the tunes, and the
absence of any obvious sense of vivid rhythm. The impression produced by a large range of these tunes is far more intellectual and responsible than is the case with southern tunes,
and they admit of closer analysis. This implies a race that
takes things more seriously, and instinctively makes for something that will stand the test of close and frequent scrutiny
and endure. The light-heartedness and excitability of southern

6

races makes them care less for the element of permanence, which is one of the essential objects of art (see p. 3), and they place themselves in an attitude of receptivity to the pleasures which appeal to them most quickly, and rather resent the attitude of instinctive reserve which makes men hesitate to abandon themselves to an impression before they have to a certain extent tested its soundness.

Permanence in a work of art depends to a great extent on its being able to stand the test of frequent scrutiny without betraying serious flaws; and this is only achieved by considerable concentration of faculty and self-restraint. Folk-music is often most successful in abandonment to impulse, but the type of human being which takes even its folk-songs seriously is likely to succeed best in higher ranges of pure art work; and it may be confessed that the relative standards of later art in various countries are the natural result of qualities which betray themselves in genuine folk-music. With regard to principles of design in general, it may be said that Germans rarely adopt the plan of consecutively reiterating short phrases, either simply or with variations, in the manner shown in the Russian and Oriental examples quoted. When they repeat phrases it is either to re-establish a balance after contrast, as in the rondo form, or to make essential parts of the structure correspond, as in the tune above quoted. The close of the whole often corresponds to the close of the first half, and sometimes the first half is repeated in its entirety at the conclusion of the tune; and again at times the tune appears to have very high qualities of design which defy anything but a very close analysis. As an example of this type the following especially beautiful tune is worth quoting :—

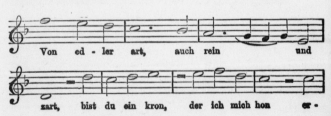

Von ed - ler art, auch rein und

zart, bist du ein kron, der ich mich hon er -

ge-ben gar, glaub' mir   für war   das hertz in mir

krenkt sich nach dir   dar-umb ich gern auff all   dein er hilff

mir, ich hab' nit tros • • • • tes mer.

This is obviously a strong emotional utterance, and the
chief basis of form is the alternation of implied tonics—
alternately F and D—as if the keys were major and
relative minor; which is an alternation very often met
with in folk-music, specially amongst northern peoples, such
as the Scandinavians. Then there is the contrast of long
sweeping phrases and short broken ones; the variety of the
closing notes of each phrase; the long sweep of the opening and closing phrases, which are thereby made to match;
and the subtle balance of the curves which constitute the
melody.

Characteristic formulas are rather rare in German folk-
music. The most noticeable in old folk-tunes is a curious
pathetic rise up to the minor seventh of the scale through
the fifth. Many tunes begin in this way, as—

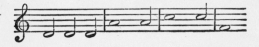

And again :—

The same interval occurs in Scandinavian tunes, as in the following from Upland :—

In more modern German folk-music the influence of harmony becomes strongly apparent. Harmony represents the higher standard of intellectuality in mankind, and the Germans have always had more feeling for it than southern races. In folk-music the harmonic basis is, of course, very simple and obvious; but it is sometimes very apparent, and shows itself even in a strong inclination to construct melodies on the basis of arpeggios. The Tyrolese adopt arpeggios for their singular jodels, which are the most ornamental forms of vocal music in Teutonic countries. In their case, however, the excess of decoration does not so much imply low organisation or superficial character, but rather the very exuberance and joy of life in the echoing mountains; and the physical effect which mountain life has upon them is shown by the extraordinarily wide compass of their songs. The arpeggio form of melody was found out very early in pastoral districts of Germany through the help of the horn. The following is part of a "cow-horn" tune of the fourteenth century, from Salzburg:—

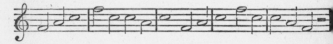

The folk-tunes of England present much the same features as the German tunes. There is next to no superfluous ornamentation about them, but a simple directness, such as characterises most northern folk-tunes. As in the German tunes, there is an absence both of eccentric intervals and of striking and energetic rhythms. There are plenty of dance tunes, but, like the German and Dutch and Scandinavian tunes, they rather imply an equal flow of contented and joyous spirits, **than the** vehement gestures, the stamping, and the concentration of muscular energy which are represented by the dance tunes of many southern races and of savages. In a very large proportion of the tunes there are clear evidences of a liking for simple and definite design, which is shown in the orderly arrangement of characteristic phrases. The most familiar form is singularly like a form prevalent in German tunes, which consists of the repetition of the first phrase for balance and stability, then a contrasting phrase, and finally a return to the first phrase, or a part of it, to conclude with ; and this principle of design underlies many tunes in which it is just shaded off so as to conceal its obviousness. The following is a concise example to the point :—

It is worth noting that the final repetition of A is effectively varied by the interruption of the parenthesis C, just in the same manner and in the same place that the recurrence of the high note is deferred at I in the German tune on page 71. There are far more instances of reiteration of short figures in English than in German tunes, and a single figure varied or given at different positions in the scale sometimes does duty for the whole tune. An extremely characteristic example, in which there is a large quantity of such reiteration, is the well-known "Carman's Whistle :"—

Features of these kinds make the tunes rather more human than a large proportion of German tunes; but, as might be expected, there is very little of strong emotional expression in English folk-music, except in such rare examples as "The Poor Soul sat sighing," and "Willow willow." There is, however, a good deal of expression of a less powerful kind—gaiety, humour, tenderness, and playfulness; but pathos is rare, and morbid or feverish passion is entirely absent. The more genuinely English the folk-music, the more it breathes the genuine love of country, of freedom, of action and heartiness. From the wonderful early tune "Sumer is icumen in" to the few uncontaminated examples of the present day the same qualities of style are apparent—a style which gay nations would call too plain and matter-of-fact, but infused with much more character, and showing more genuine taste, freshness, and variety, than almost any folk-tunes but those of the very highest standard.

So far the process of development is very easily followed. The savage stage indicates a taste for design, but an incapacity for making the designs consistent and logical; in the lowest intelligent stage the capacity for disposing short contrasting figures in an orderly and intelligent way is shown; in the highest phase of the pattern-type of folk-tune the instinct for

knitting things closely together is shown to be very remarkable; and the organisation of the tunes becomes completely
consistent from every point of view. A still higher phase is
that in which the skill in distributing the figures in symmetrical
patterns is applied to the ends of emotional expression.

The tunes which imply an emotional impulse indicate it
by the manner in which the rise to a high note is made the
conspicuous feature of the tune. The difference between high
and low organisation is shown in much the same way as in
pattern-tunes. In the low standards of pattern-tunes there
are but few principles of cohesion; in the highly organised
ones (such as the Scotch tune on page 67) there are many
interlaced. Similarly in emotional tunes of the lowest grade
there is only one climax, in the most highly organised tunes
there are many, and in the best there is a steady gradation
of climaxes; so that the higher points succeed one another
in such a way as to make the emotional expression of the
tune stronger at successive moments.

It is very common, even in tunes which have the general
character belonging to the pattern order, to make a special
rise to the highest point in the middle, or early in the latter
part of the tune (*e.g.*, "Weel may the keel row"). Hungarian
tunes illustrate both types very happily; and the finest
tunes in the world combine the emotional aspect with the
finest adjustment of design. With the Hungarians both
the dance tunes and vocal tunes are so full of energetic
intervals and rhythms that even when there are no crises the
impression produced is often emotional. Many Scotch tunes
are in the same category. The latter branch of folk-music
affords many examples of fine emotional tunes. Indeed, for
the simple type of tune combining emotional crises with very
distinct and simple form, it would be difficult to find anything
better than the following:—

The successive sweeps up to the high note in the first half lead beautifully to the pathetic F natural in the second half, and the expression is finely intensified by the rise to the highest crisis on G immediately after.

As a very characteristic example from a different part of the world, the following from Murcia, in the south of Spain, is worth examining :—

The rises and falls are singularly systematic, and the relations of the different points are admirably diversified, and always well calculated both for relative contrast and human expression.

Irish folk-music—probably the most human, most varied, most poetical, and most imaginative in the world—is particularly rich in tunes which imply considerable sympathetic sensitiveness; and the Anglo-Scotch border folk-music is not far behind. In many tunes of these districts the very design itself seems to be the outcome of the sensibility of the human creature. The cumulation of crises rising higher and higher is essentially an emotional method of design. The rise and fall and rise again is the process of uttering an expressive cry, and the relaxation of tension during which the human creature is gathering itself together for a still more expressive cry. The Murcian tune is good in this respect, but as a simple emotional type the following Irish tune is one of the most perfect in existence :—

The extreme crisis is held in reserve till the last. In the first half of the tune the voice moves in low ranges of expression, rising successively to the very moderate crises A and B. The portion in bracket is merely a repetition of the phrases A and B, with slight additions of ornament and a different close, the artistic point of which it is not necessary to discuss here. At the beginning of the second half the voice begins to mount to a higher crisis at C, and intensifies that point by repetition at D, and finally leaps to its uttermost passion at E, and then falls with a wide sweep (comprising one more moderate crisis) to the final cadence. Within the limits of a folk-tune it is hardly possible to deal with the successive crises more effectively.

As art-music grows and pervades the world, pure folk-music tends to go out of use among the people. Reflections of respectable taste invade the homes of the masses more and more, and familiar fragments which are adopted from various sources by purveyors of tunes for light popular operas and such gay entertainments take the place of the spontaneous utterances of the musical impulse of the people. Civilisation reduces everything to a common level, and "the people" cease to make their own tunes, and accept vulgarised and weakened portions of the music of the leisured classes, and of those who wish to be like them. The rapid extinction of the tunes which successively catch the people's ears as compared with the long life of those that went to their hearts in old days, is an excellent vindication of the fact that what is to be permanent in music needs a genuine impulse in feeling as well as the design which makes it intelligible. True folk-music is an outcome of the whole man, as is the case with all that is really valuable as art. The features which give it its chief artistic and historical importance (apart from its genuine delightfulness) are those which manifest the working of the perfectly unconscious instinct for design, and those in which the emotional and intellectual basis of the art is illustrated by the qualities of the tunes which correspond with the known characters of the nations and peoples who invent them. Folk-tunes are the first essays made by man in distributing his notes so as to express his feelings in terms of design. Highly sensitive races express themselves with high degrees of emotional force and variety of form; placid races show perfect content in simple design with little meaning; races of moderate intelligence who have considerable skill in manipulation and love of effect, introduce much ornamentation; serious and strong races, and those with much reserve of disposition, produce very simple and dignified tunes; and so on in varying degrees. Modes of life and climatic conditions all tell upon the product, and ultimately colour in no little degree the larger artistic developments which are the counterparts of these slender beginnings. Folk-music supplies an epitome of the principles upon which musical art is founded; and though a long period had to elapse from the point where conscious artistic music began, during which musicians were busy with other problems than those of design; when the art had progressed far enough for them to concentrate attention on design again, the same principles which appear in folk-music were instinctively adopted in all the forms of mature art.

CHAPTER IV

INCIPIENT HARMONY

IT can hardly be doubted that music was called into existence by religious feelings as soon as by any of which human creatures are capable. Even the most primitive rites are accompanied by something of the nature of music, and the religious states of awe and wonder and of ecstasy and devotion are all familiarly liable to engender musical utterance. The relation of religion to various arts varies with its principles and objects, and with the dispositions of the people who profess it. The religion of the ancient Greeks comprised everything which expressed the emotional inner being of man—such as dances, theatrical performances, orgies, and an infinite variety of curious ceremonies which expressed every phase of what a man in modern times would consider essentially secular feelings. Similarly, many religions, of all times and types, comprise dancing of a frenzied description, and functions which call forth the most savage instincts of the human creature. In such cases the music is not limited to things which a modern Christian would regard as suitable for church purposes; for the Christian religion is distinguished from all others by its inwardness and quietude, and the absence of any outward energetic signs of excitement; and it is only on rare occasions that eccentric outbursts of ecstatic fervour in any of its professors find utterance in lively gesticulations or rhythmic dance. From the very first the spirit of the religion was most perfectly and completely reproduced in its music, and even the various phases it passed through in many succeeding centuries are exactly pictured in the art which most closely presents the spiritual side of man.

In the early middle ages the warlike priest was not an

unfamiliar object; but nevertheless the spirit of the religion and religious life was essentially devotional and contemplative; and it followed that all the music employed in church ceremonies was vocal or choral, and almost totally devoid of any rhythmic quality and of everything which represented gesticulatory expression. This state of things was eminently favourable to the development of certain artistic features which were a necessary preliminary to the ultimate building up of the modern musical art. Dance music demands very little in the way of harmony. The world could go on dancing to the end of time without it; and whatever harmony is added to pure dance tunes, even in days of advanced art, is generally of the simplest and most obvious description. But vague melodic music, and vocal music which is sung by voices of different pitch, seem to call imperatively for the help of harmony; and unless the instinctive craving for choral harmony had led men to overcome its initial difficulties, the art could never have developed that particular kind of regularity in time which is independent of dance rhythm. It was the necessity of regulating the amount of time which should be allowed to particular notes when singers sang together, which brought about the invention of the standards of relative duration of notes, and the whole system of breves, semibreves, minims, and crotchets; and also the invention of the time signatures, which do not necessarily imply rhythm, but supply the only means by which various performers can be kept together, and irregular distribution of long and short notes made orderly and coherent. It is perfectly easy to keep instruments or voices together when the music is regulated by a dance rhythm; but in pure choral music, such as was cultivated from the tenth century till the sixteenth, it is quite another matter; for the parts were so far from moving upon any principle of accent, that one of the most beautiful effects, which composers sought after most keenly, was the gliding from harmony to harmony by steps which were so hidden that the mind was willingly deceived into thinking that they melted into one another. The mystery was effected by making some of the voices which sang the harmony move and make a new harmony, while the others held the notes that belonged to the previous harmony; so that the continuity of the sound was maintained though the chords changed. This would have been impossible without some means of indicating the duration of the notes, and no style could so soon have brought men to face the necessity of solving the problem involved as the growing elaboration of choral music, of that unrhythmic kind which was the natural outcome of religious feeling of the Christian devotional type.

It is very remarkable how soon after the first definite appearance of Christian Church music as a historical fact men began to move in the direction of harmony. The harmonic phase of music has been exactly coeval with the development of that particular kind of intellectual disposition which continued to manifest itself more and more as modern Europe slowly emerged from the chaos which followed the collapse of the Roman Empire. It is as if harmony—the higher intellectual factor in music—began with the first glimmerings of modern mental development, and grew more and more elaborate and comprehensive, and more adapted to high degrees of expression and design, simultaneously with the growth of men's intellectual powers. As long as the Church reigned supreme, harmony remained more or less in the background, and made its appearance mainly as the result of the combination of the separate melodies which various voices sung at once. But towards the end of the sixteenth century it began to assert itself as the basis of certain new principles of design, and in the succeeding century, as secular life grew more and more independent of ecclesiastical influences, it became more and more the centre and basis upon which the whole system of artistic musical design was founded; and it ultimately became not only the essence of the structure, but a higher and richer means of immediate expression than was possible by the subtlest and most perfect treatment of any other kind of musical device.

But the first steps in this important development were slowly and laboriously achieved under the influence of the

ncient Church. There seems no reason to doubt that the
music used in the early Christian ritual was of Greek origin,
nd that certain traditional formulas for different parts of
he service had been handed down from generation to genera-
ion by ear. These were certainly quite unrhythmic and also
rather melodically indefinite; but the circumstances under
which they were used were so favourable to their preserva-
ion that they possibly obviated the difficulty which such
vagueness puts in the way of accuracy of transmission. For
anything which is part of a ritual has a tendency to be very
carefully guarded, and in course of time to be strictly stereotyped; because whatever people hear and see when they are
in the act of worship seems to share the sacredness of the
unction, and ultimately becomes itself a sacred thing which
it is profanation to meddle with. But it was nevertheless
inevitable that after the lapse of a few centuries the practice
of different churches should have ceased to be quite uniform,
and the authorities of the Church endeavoured in the fourth
and sixth centuries to give special sanction to the traditions
which appeared to have the best credentials. It was then
that the connection of the music of the Church with the
ancient Greek system was definitely acknowledged (as described on page 41); and though the regulations for systematising the art did not quite agree with the Greek system,
owing to lack of opportunity to discover exactly what that
was, the slight discrepancies did not affect the artistic consequences that followed. The Ambrosian and Gregorian
schemes included a number of vocal formulas, consisting of
traditional melodies, which became the basis of an extraordinarily prolonged and comprehensive development. They
were the few established facts of musical art then existing,
and upon them the fabric of modern music soon began to be
built.

The immediate source of a most important new departure
seems to have been the simple fact that men's voices were of
different calibres; for as some were deep basses and some
high tenors, and some between the two, it was manifestly
inconvenient that they should all sing their plain song at

the same pitch. Some could not sing it high, and some could
not sing it low. In extreme cases low basses and high tenors
could sing an octave apart, but as a rule that was too wide
for convenience; so men had to find some other relation of
pitch at which it would be convenient to sing the plain
song or chants simultaneously. In such a case it is of
first importance to find a relation of pitch which shall sound
agreeable in itself, and also one which would not cause
certain notes of one part in the reduplicated melody to jar
with certain notes in the other part. It must be clearly
understood that such a process of doubling was not what is
called singing in thirds or sixths in modern times. When
people sing in that manner now, they do not each sing the
same melody. The upper voice takes the melody, and the
lower adds major or minor thirds, and sings tones or semitones, according to the nature of the scale or key in which
the music is written. Thus if two voices sing the following

simple succession of notes together,

it is not a reduplication of melodies, but a process of harmonisation. The upper voice sings a semitone in the first step
A, where the lower sings a whole tone; and in the last step
B, the upper voice sings a whole tone where the lower sings
a semitone. If the melodies were justly reduplicated at the

third, the result would be as follows,

Such a progression would have the tones and semitones in
the same places in both melodies, but the effect would be
hideous to modern ears, and would have been impossible to
early mediæval musicians, because they had not developed their
scale sufficiently to supply such conflicting accidentals. And
the same difficulties present themselves with all the intervals

that they could have chosen, except two, which are the fifth and the fourth. It also happens that the human mind is so slow to develop any understanding of the effects of harmony, that men only learned to endure even infinitesimally dissonant chords by slow degrees. The combination in which there is the least element of discordance after the octave is the fifth,

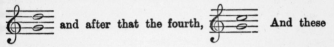 and after that the fourth, And these

two were the first which men learned to endure with equanimity. It took them centuries to settle down to the comfortable acceptance of such familiar combinations as thirds and sixths, and it took fully a thousand years after their sense of harmony had begun to dawn before they could accept the simplest discords without some preliminary devices to save the ear from being too roughly assailed by the sudden jar. It is a pregnant fact that the process has gone on till the present day, and that the combinations which human ears accept without preliminary and without protest have been largely added to in the present century. In later times the progress has been more and more rapid, but in early times it was most astonishingly slow. Men allowed some of our most familiar combinations as notes of passage—purely subordinate details—and by their use in that manner they became accustomed to the sound of them; but they were very long in coming to the state of musical intelligence which recognises even a third as a stable and final combination. The test of complete satisfactoriness for any interval is the possibility of leaving off upon it without giving a sense of artistic incompleteness and a desire in the mind for something further. In modern times no chord is complete at the end of a composition which does not contain a third; but the mediæval musicians could not even put up with it in the final chord till the art had undergone some five centuries of development. Its relative roughness had much the same effect that a discord has to modern ears; and so whereas in modern times a man feels that he wants something more when he is without it, in mediæval

7

times he would have wanted something more because he had got it.

These complicated circumstances produced the result that when men first tried singing anything but pure melody in one line at a time, they doubled the melody at the fifth above or the fourth below. This result seems hideous to modern ears, since fifths have acquired a new significance in the development of harmonic music. But to people whose minds are chiefly concerned with melodic effects it still seems a natural procedure. Not only is it sometimes adopted in modern Europe by singers in the streets and by other people of low musical intelligence, but a most trustworthy observer states that the same phase of reduplication is beginning to be adopted in Japan, and is the only thing approaching to harmony which is used in genuine Japanese music. If Japanese music is spared the contamination of modern European popular music, it will probably go through the same phases as early mediæval music, and the Japanese sense of harmony will develop in the same manner as that of Europeans did long ago.

It is well to keep clearly in mind that this new departure did not really amount to harmonisation, nor did it imply a sense for harmony. In the beginning it was merely the doubling of a melody, just like the familiar doubling at the octave in modern times, but at intervals which were less wide apart. Harmonisation implies the understanding of the relations of different chords or combinations to one another. Human creatures had to go through a long probationary period, and to get accustomed to the sounds of chords in themselves, before they could begin instinctively to classify them in the manner in which they ultimately came to serve as the basis of modern harmonic art.

Men began to move in the direction of real effects of harmony when, instead of making their voices go in strict parallels at some definite interval apart, they began to mix up different intervals together. The way in which this was at first effected was chiefly by interchanging fifths, fourths, and octaves or unisons, and by the use of stationary notes (such as are commonly described in modern times as pedals)

as an accompaniment to plain-song. The following will illustrate their skill, about the tenth century, in varying the
monotony of consecutive fifths or fourths :—

Te hu-mi-les fa-mu-li   mo-du-lis ven-er-an-do pi-is.

5   4   4   4   4   4   1   1

This passage as far as the asterisk is merely the plain chant
accompanied by a pedal (the same device as the drone which
has been familiar for ages), which does not constitute or
imply harmony. From that point there are only three intervals which do not accord with the ancient and crude principle
of the "organum"—the one fifth, and the two unisons with
which the whole concludes. This, it may be confessed, is not
a very great advance in the direction of harmonisation, but it
shows how the feeling for intermingling a variety of harmonies
began to develop.

In the course of the eleventh, twelfth, and thirteenth
centuries, musicians found out how to introduce ornamental
notes, and learned to like the sound of the interval of the
third, especially at the last step before the final note of all
when the movement ended in unison. But their difficulties
were enhanced by their attitude towards harmonisation. The
basis of operations was always some given melody, such as a
passage of an old Church hymn or chant; and to this they
endeavoured to add another independent voice part by calcu-
lating what interval they would have to move at each step in
the part added to obtain satisfactory consonances in relation
to each step of the original melody. The theorists of those
days, who were surprisingly numerous, endeavoured to give
rules by which a musician should be able to fit a new part to
any given melody. A treatise of the thirteenth century says :
—" If the chant (that is, the lower part) ascends the interval

of a second, and the organum (the part added) moves down

the interval of a third, they will make a fifth :

If the chant ascends a third, and the organum descends a

tone, they will be at the fifth :   If the chant

mounts a fifth, and the organum descends a fourth, they will

be together :   If the chant descends a second,

and the organum beginning at the fifth ascends a third, they

will make an octave :   And similar directions

were given for a great variety of contingencies in various
treatises, both earlier and later. The kind of result obtained
may be judged from a fragment of a thirteenth-century
hymn :—

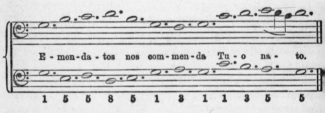

E - men - da - tos   nos   com - men - da   Tu - o   na -   to.

1   5   5   8   5   1   3   1   1   3   5   5

This is what was originally meant by counterpoint. It was
point set against point, or note against note; and nearly
all the early music in which voices of different calibres were
combined was of this description. Composers found it quite
sufficiently difficult to carry out a simple scheme of this kind
without trying any further to enhance its effect, except by an
occasional ornament, such as the D and C in crotchets just
before the end in the example. They hardly seem to have

thought of varying the monotony of the simultaneous progressions of the parts until they began to attempt something more than mere two-part counterpoint; and, moreover, composers or singers who first endeavoured to improve upon such homogeneity of the simultaneous motion of parts were hampered by the fact that they had not the means to indicate it. In the primitive melodic music of the Church there was neither rhythm nor any need to regulate the values of the notes in respect of their length. No doubt they had long notes and short ones, but it was left to the taste and discretion of the performer to decide how long and how short they should be; and the early forms of musical notation (which were merely marks put over the syllables at varying heights to help the memory of the singer) gave no indication of the length of time that the notes were to last. Even when "organising" in fifths and fourths and the simple kinds of note against note counterpoint came into practice, it was still possible to do without rules of measurement so long as the singers moved from note to note and from syllable to syllable simultaneously. But it is to be inferred that after a time singers began to extemporise improvements and ornaments to the descant, which made the keeping of the voices together somewhat difficult; and by degrees the necessity of infusing order into the proceedings drove musicians to invent signs which indicated the relative lengths of time that the singers should hold the various notes. The rules which were first devised were curiously complicated and puzzling. There were no bars, and even the relative value of notes varied in accordance with certain symbols which were placed at the beginning of the music, and also with the forms of certain obscure scrawls and contorted signs called ligatures, which were allowed to stand for several successive notes at a time. The rules given for some of these signs are so obscure that even at the present day they can hardly be considered as decisively understood and settled, and the task of the singers who had to read them seems almost superhuman. It can only be supposed that they did things very much by ear, as they had done for many previous centuries. But the devices of notation enabled composers to treat their respective voices with more independence, and to proceed to new kinds of musical achievement.

But every new step they took brought them face to face with new difficulties. The addition of two parts instead of one to a "canto fermo" made the calculations necessary to bring about agreeable consonances much more arduous; and to add three, so as to make an ordinary piece of four-part writing, was considered to be a feat of almost superhuman concentration. The excessive difficulty which such things presented in early days is sufficiently indicated by the nature of the productions of the most celebrated composers, which have the same sort of aspect as the artistic efforts of a baby just out of its cradle, when it tries to represent mankind or its favourite animals. It may have been the severity of these difficulties which caused composers to adopt a less laborious but more hazardous way of arriving at the effect of harmonisation; which was none other than to take two or more tunes and force them to go together by easing off the corners and adapting the points where the cacophony was too intolerable to be endured. This may seem a very surprising and even laughable way of obtaining an artistic effect, but in reality the actual practice of combining several tunes together is by no means uncommon. Several savage and semi-civilised races adopt the practice, as, for instance, the Bushmen at the lower end of the human scale, and the Javese, Siamese, Burmese, and Moors, about the middle. In these cases the process usually consists of simultaneously singing or playing short and simple musical figures, such as savages habitually reiterate, with the addition in some cases of a long sort of indefinite wailing tune which goes on independently of all the rest of the performance. The Javese carry such devices to extremes, producing a kind of reckless, incoherent instrumental counterpoint, very much like a number of people playing various tunes at once, with just sufficient feeling for some definite central principle to accommodate the jarring elements. The following is a portion of a phonographed record of some Javese music performed by several instrumental performers. The directions of the stems up and down indicate the several instruments, and their respective tunes or musical figures can be unravelled by strictly following the notes which have the stems turned the same way.

Of the same type is the combination of dancing and story singing, which is illustrated in a practice met with among the Portuguese lower classes, of playing a couple of simple figures on the mandolin and repeating them ceaselessly without any change, while a singer wails out a long poem in extremely long notes which have very little to do with the accompaniment.

This curious practice is more easily intelligible when the element of rhythm comes in and makes it possible to base the combination upon short figures, and to present the whole in an instrumental form. Vocal melodies, which are necessarily more wide in their range, require much more manipulation; for the constantly changing forms of melody present fresh difficulties of assimilation at every step. But the practice of combining tunes seems to have become universal quite suddenly, and it led very quickly to fresh developments. And it is worth noting that one of these developments was precisely the same in principle as that adopted by the Bushmen and the Javese and other semi-savage experimenters in such things; which was to accompany the main combination of two melodies by a short musical figure which could be incessantly reiterated as an accompaniment. In mediæval music this was a sort of nonsense part, and was sung to nonsense syllables, such as "Balaam," or "Portare," or "Verbum," or "Angelus," or any other single word which could easily be adapted to a sort of pseudo-rhythmic group of notes, which would fit in while

the other two or three voices got through their respective
tunes. When the word "Alleluia" was chosen for reiteration
it presents a rather more sensible appearance; but this was
clearly an accident, as it happens to be used on one occasion
as an accompaniment to two tunes, one of which is concerning
love, and the other about the pleasures of good fellowship.
The practice was so well understood that the composer merely
wrote the word once at the beginning of the piece, and the
singers (generally those who took the lower part) fitted it
in as seemed to them good. A short fragment of such a
motet, combining Latin and French words with a nonsense
part, will be sufficient to show what a singular art-product
resulted :—

Povre se-cors ai en - core re-co-vré,   A ma dame que je avoie servi

Gaude   chorus   om - ni-um fi - del-i - um.

An - ge - lus,   An - ge-lus,   An - ge - lus.

In such pieces as this it was generally rather a matter of
chance what combinations were produced. The composer
was for the most part at the mercy of the tunes he attempted
to combine, and he was necessarily absolved from the rules
which theorists laid down for the adding of counterpoint to
a canto fermo. The main object seems to have been to get
the chief points, on which stress could be laid, to form consonances, and to let passing notes clash as they would. And
it is very remarkable that the instinct of the composers even
in adapting tunes together worked in the direction of successions of fifths and fourths, like those which made up the early
form of the organum. The example quoted above is rather
an extreme case of independence, if not of recklessness; but

even in this case the old type of the organum is discernible in the relations between the lower and the upper parts, which move in fifths and octaves.

In other compositions by the mediæval musicians it is common to meet with a structure which consists almost entirely of successions of fifths disguised by the ornamental notes which are interspersed. The nature of such compositions may be best judged from an example of the thirteenth century by the Trouvère poet and musician, Adam de la Hale :—

The framework of this fragment consists of a succession of octaves and fifths, which is almost as regular and unchanged as the old diaphony of the ninth and tenth centuries ; but the succession is disguised and made expressive by ornamental or subsidiary notes introduced between the main blocks of octaves and fifths. The rest of the little song (which would take too much room to quote) is of exactly the same construction, and so are many pieces of sacred and secular music of these early centuries. As composers developed their skill in adapting voice parts to one another, in course of time they even managed to write in four parts with some facility, and this necessarily made them more accustomed to the effect of the less purely harmonious consonances; for though they tried hard to restrict themselves in the main to what they called the perfect concords, such as octaves, fifths, and fourths, it was impossible to write in more than two parts without frequently introducing a complete triad with third and fifth, and scarcely less frequently the intervals of the sixth, major and minor.

It is not necessary to follow out the progress of these early centuries in detail. It pursued its slow course on the same lines. Composers found out artistic devices which facilitated their labours, and enabled them to approximate to more pleasing and artistic results. But the average quality of their works of every kind is marvellously crude, harsh, and incoherent. Almost every elementary rule of art which a modern musician holds inviolable is broken incessantly, and there are hardly any pieces of music, by the most learned or the most intelligent musicians up to the fourteenth century, which are not too rough and uncouth to be listened to by even the most liberal-minded and intelligent musician without such bewilderment as often ends in irrepressible laughter. The little rondeau of Adam de la Hale, part of which is quoted above, stands almost alone for genuine expressiveness, and even a certain attractiveness, amongst a great mass of experiments which are simply chaotically clumsy and homogeneous.

A still more rare and wonderful exception, which is important on other grounds besides its musical effectiveness, is the famous English canon, "Sumer is icumen in," which is probably of little earlier date. This is clearly a folk-tune (and a very beautiful one) which lent itself easily to being sung as a round by several voices in succession, with a sort of drone bass. It is an almost unique example of its kind for the time when it was written; and it proves, in a manner which cannot be ignored, that composers had already at this early date a very definite idea of the canonic form, which was one of the earliest and simplest devices of contrapuntal music, and almost the only one which was cultivated with any success before the sixteenth century. The significant point about this canonic form, in relation to the evolution of musical art, is its singular homogeneousness. It affords hardly any effect of artistic variety or contrast, and of itself no special means of expression. In fact it is really no more than a technical device—a sort of exercise of skill, like any game which men play just for the amusement of overcoming a difficulty. But in these early stages of development the distinction between art and artifice had hardly arisen. Considering the state of the art at the time of its first appearance, this form becomes a very important event in the story. It was a very natural outcome of the improvement of pure choral music that the different voices should sometimes be made to sing the same words and phrases after one another instead of simultaneously; and in later times, when men had developed higher artistic sense, one of the most elastic and comprehensive of musical forms was developed on that principle. But in those early days, when musical intelligence was so undeveloped, it was natural that composers should endeavour to follow out a simple contrivance of the sort to the bitter end, and should imagine that they had really achieved an artistic result when they had manipulated the flow of a voice part in such a way that another voice beginning a little later should be able to sing the same melody always a little way behind the leader. The device undoubtedly took the fancy of early composers very strongly, as was natural when so few devices of any kind were possible; and they expended so much energy upon it that in the fifteenth century they developed quite an abnormal skill in futile note-spinning and puzzle-making. It is not to be denied that canons can be made not only very effective but beautiful; the mistake which most of the early composers and many modern ones have made is to take the means for

an end, and assume that the device is worth doing for its
own sake. The canonic form is a further illustration of the
state of the art from another point of view, as it is purely
a combination of voice parts, and not a device of harmony
at all. The result is harmony of a sort, but in no sense a
phase of harmony which implies any feeling for system or
harmonic order. The harmonies are the accident and not
the essence of the device; and the product was in the early
examples both rhythmically and structurally incoherent, and
so far homogeneous.

Another defect in the form which is characteristic of undeveloped artistic sense is that the voices go on all through
without material breaks. There is no relief or change in the
amount of sound which the ear receives, and therefore there
is a lack of variety. This feature is equally characteristic of
a large amount of the early choral music of other kinds.
Composers seem to have thought that it was an advantage
to keep the parts going; and when they gave any voice a
rest of long duration, it was generally less for the sake of
artistic effect than because they found it so difficult (in a
triplum or quadruplum) to keep all the parts in continual
activity. One part indeed was necessarily kept going. For
it was the almost universal practice that each movement was
developed upon some ready-made melody, such as a plain
chant, or even a secular tune put into long notes. This was
generally put in the tenor, and the other parts were added by
calculations such as those quoted on page 90. And if this
canto fermo stopped, there was nothing left to build upon.
Here again the product was homogeneous. The principle of
adding fresh voice parts to a given melody on contrapuntal
principles suggested of itself no contrasts except those of
pitch, nor any natural divisions or articulations of the artistic
organism, such as balanced phrases and periods. The music
flowed from end to end indefinitely, and the only indications
of completeness supplied were the definite point in the scale
from which the start was made, and the conventional close at
the end, sometimes, but by no means always, on the same tone
as that from which the movement set out.

A strong trace of the melodic system to which the old form of art belonged is recognisable in the cadences. These were not processes like a modern cadence, in which two blocks of contrasted harmony succeed one another; but progressions in which the most important features were the descent of the modal part—or canto fermo upon which the contrapuntal structure was built—one step downwards upon the tonic of the mode; and its accompaniment in another part by a third below or a sixth above in the penultimate step, passing finally into the octave or the unison.

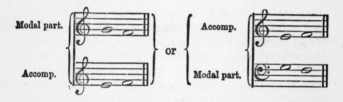

The whole aspect and texture of this old music is so different from the modern style, that it seems almost inconceivable to most people, when they first come into contact with it, that it could have had any musical effect at all, much less that it could be the direct source of the elaborate modern fabric. The most familiar rule that the tyro in the study of harmony learns to his cost is to avoid consecutive fifths and octaves; but the rule of the mediæval musicians was distinctly and unquestionably to write more of them than of anything else. As has been pointed out before, the basis and substructure of many compositions was a series of such fifths and octaves disguised by ornamental notes and passing notes. In other particulars also the difference from modern views is very marked; such as, for instance, in the use of discords. These early musicians used many discords, and very harsh ones too, but hardly ever in any way like modern composers. They were always purely accidental discords, and were in no sense either used as means of contrast, nor to propel the music on from point to point, as is their frequent function in modern times. The melodic outline of one part jostled against that of another voice part, and, as it were, disregarded what its neighbour was doing for a short while, till it landed upon some note which brought it again into consonance with its surroundings. The very idea of using chords of varying degrees of harshness as a means of effect does not seem to have dawned upon composers until after some centuries of experience. The early phase of the progress of harmony from homogeneity to heterogeneity is distinctly traceable in this respect. In the first stage there is no variety at all; all are fifths or fourths consecutively. A slight variety appears when fourths and fifths are mixed up with one another and with octaves; but it is very slight, as the difference between one and the other in degree of consonance is scarcely marked enough to afford a sense of contrast. When the force of circumstances drove composers to use the less perfectly consonant combinations of thirds and sixths, they enlarged the scope of their resources, and their materials became more systematically heterogeneous; but it took them a long time to realise the effects which could be made by using thirds as contrasts to more perfect consonances. Ultimately the composers with the higher instincts learnt to use the qualities of the different consonances for relatively similar effects of contrast to such as are produced by the relations of concord and discord in modern music; and then going a step still further, composers at last found out how to use real discords, such as were not the result of jostling passing notes only, but systematically introduced and under artistic control. They of course only used one kind of discord, which was obtained by one voice holding on a note which had been consonant in one chord while the other voices went on to other positions which made the combination into a discord. The appearance of this device immensely enhanced the vitality of the music; and though the moderation of composers in the use of it was extreme, it brought a tone into the art which soon began to dispel the ancient traditions of successions of fifths and fourths interspersed with discords which only came by chance and fulfilled no artistic function. The curious makeshifts of motets made up of several tunes twisted and hammered into a dubious conformity by degrees ceased to make their appearance. Composers still had to make their counterpoint upon the basis of a canto fermo, or a canon, or some equally primitive device, because without some kind of regulating principle they wandered and were lost like children without guides. But a more musical spirit pervaded their attempts, and they found out how to dispose the progressions of their parts so as to obtain contrasts of tone, and to make the voices flow at once with more real independence and interdependence. The influence of the old homogeneous organum ceased in time; and a real, though limited, heterogeneity took its place. And before the end of the fifteenth century composers really understood something of the delicate art of varying the amount and distribution of sound by sometimes having all the voices singing full together, and sometimes letting some of them stop here and there. And they even got so far as to understand how to make the utterances of different voices coherent by making them take up short fragments of melody or musical figures imitatively; and how to make the general texture of a movement uniform by the pervading style and mood of the musical ideas.

But the musical ideas themselves were singularly vague and indefinite. Even the tunes which composers borrowed were put into such enormously long notes that whatever individuality there was in them inevitably disappeared. It is quite impossible to recognise a tune when single notes are prolonged to an extent equivalent to half-a-dozen bars in slow time. And this extension was mercilessly practised by the best mediæval musicians in order to lengthen their movements, and give more time for the spinning out of their strange kinds of counterpoint. Spontaneity was of course out of the question. The store of known technical resources was too limited, and every musical work was the product of arduous and laborious concentration, or of peculiar ingenuity. Even expression of any kind was rare, for, strange as it seems, in such immature products the chief pleasure lay in arriving at a new experience through the overcoming of some technical difficulty. Their minds were so fully occupied with the difficulties they had to overcome that they could think of

little else. And even up to the end of the fourteenth century
the effect produced by getting a certain number of voices to
go together at all seems to have been so new and attractive
that it was hardly necessary to go any further afield to strike
men with wonder at the achievement.

All this development naturally proceeded under the wing
of the Church. The system of the modes prescribed by
ecclesiastical authority, and such rules of counterpoint as
ecclesiastical theorists discovered, pervaded such secular music
as there was quite as much as the genuine Church music.
There were plenty of attempts made to compose secular motets,
and lively secular tunes with a sense of rhythm in them made
their appearance therein, but the contrapuntal procedure was
the same in all; and the same phases of progress are noticeable
in one as in the other. Even folk-tunes were influenced by
the modes which were taught by the Church ; and the more
highly organised songs of the Troubadours, little as their
authors wished it, had to submit to the universal influence.
The ecclesiastics were the only people who had devised any
system for recording music accurately, and therefore even if a
man wished to strike out an independent line, his musical
utterances were sure to be recorded in terms which only the
musicians trained in the school of the Church knew how to use.

The Troubadours indeed stand outside the line of the direct
development of modern music, as their efforts seem to have
been purely melodic ; and though there are some beautiful
tunes still remaining which are attributed to them, they
represent a development of lyrical music which appears to
have had no immediate consequences. It was the fruit of
an isolated outburst of refined poetic feeling, and when its
natural home in the South of France was harried and ruined
by the Church the impulse dwindled and ceased.

But the crude efforts of the early contrapuntists, whether
secular or ecclesiastical, served as the immediate foundation
of one of the greatest eras in the history of musical art, and,
through that era, as the ultimate source of the characteristic
system of harmony which forms the distinguishing feature of
modern music.

CHAPTER V

THE ERA OF PURE CHORAL MUSIC

THE early period from the ninth till the end of the fifteenth century was, as it were, the babyhood of modern music, when ideas and modes of musical thought were indefinite, unsystematised, and unpractical. The Church, like a careful mother, watched over and regulated all that was done, and the infantile efforts scarcely emerged at any time into definiteness either of form or expression.

The two centuries which followed, up to the beginning of the seventeenth century, were the period of the youth of modern music—a period most pure, serene, and innocent—when mankind was yet too immature in things musical to express itself in terms of passion or of force, but used forms and moods of art which are like tranquil dreams and communings of man with his inner self, before the sterner experiences of life have quite awakened him to its multiform realities and vicissitudes. The manner in which the inevitable homogeneity of an early stage of art presents itself is still discernible from every point of view. The most comprehensive fact is that almost all the music of these two centuries is purely choral—that is, either written for several voices in combination without independent accompaniment, or devised upon methods which were invented solely for that kind of performance. It followed from this general fact that the methods of art were also homogeneous; for the processes which are fit to be used by voices alone are more limited in range and variety than those which can be employed by instruments, owing to the greater difficulty of taking awkward intervals and of sustaining the pitch, and to the necessity of adapting the notes to words; and also to the fact that the words often lessen the need of absolute principles

8

of design, by supplying a meaning to the music in general, when without them it would be incoherent.

The principal reason of this absorption of composers in the cultivation of choral music is obvious. It is a well-ascertained law of human nature, that men will not go out and labour in the desert at haphazard when they are fully occupied in extracting unlimited gold from a rich mine. Neither will they (in a healthy state of existence) abandon an occupation which is full of absorbing interest, and constantly presents fresh problems most tempting to solve, for the mere chance of amusement in some other direction. At the time when the great era of pure choral music was beginning, musical human beings, earnestly disposed, were just awakening to the singular possibilities of beauty which the combinations of many singing voices afforded. They were awakening to the actual beauty of the sound of chords sung by voices—to the beauty of delicate variety between one chord and another, and between chords in different positions (partly owing to the various qualities of the different registers of the voices)— to the beauty of the actual human expression of the individual voices, and to the beauty of the relations of the melodic forms of the different parts to one another. To win the delight of realising the various phases of these effects was enough to keep them fully occupied on even severer labour than the development of artistic technique; but the incitement quickened their musical instinct marvellously, and in a short time developed in them a delicacy of perception of artistic means and a sense of style which is almost unique in the history of the art. In later times composers are distracted by the varieties of style and taste which have been developed, in the necessary course of musical evolution, for different artistic purposes, such as the theatre and the concert-room; and they often introduce the formulas which belong to one kind of art into another to which they are quite unsuited; but in the early days there were no such distractions. Men's minds were occupied by the conditions of choral performance alone; and the better they understood what they were trying to do, the more refined and pure their artistic methods became

The turning-point from the helpless experimental crudity which marks the infancy of the art, to the comparative certainty of aim and execution which indicates its healthily maturing youth, was somewhere about the end of the fourteenth century. The state of transition is most strongly apparent in the works of the English composer Dunstable, who in some works still illustrates the bewildering amorphousness of the early stages of the art, and in others shows a fair mastery of both design and general effect; casting his vocal movements in thoroughly intelligible designs, and disposing his voice parts so as to obtain a really attractive quality of sound, not for the casual moment only, but in passages which are sufficiently long to be artistically effective. It marks no little advance in skill and in the mastery of technique, when composers were able to look beyond the mere overcoming of incidental difficulties and to make use of their devices for a purpose; and after Dunstable's time a definite purpose of some sort is more and more apparent in all they attempted.

It is probably common to all arts, that when the early stages of wrestling with technical difficulties have been passed, the aim of artists seems to be to produce effects which are more noteworthy for their beauty than for definiteness of expression and variety of characterisation. Distinctive definiteness of expression was certainly not the aim of the composers of the great choral period; and if it had been, they could not have succeeded without launching out beyond the limits of the art which they understood into that of experiment without precedent and without standards of test. Indeed, they were quite sufficiently occupied in applying the skill they had developed to the simple purpose of making groups of various voices produce effects of smooth and harmonious tone. In the main, the music was singularly indefinite in almost every respect. The style had grown up entirely under the influence of the Church, and composers had learnt how to solve their earliest artistic problems by using the old Church melodies as a basis whereon to add voice to voice and make a harmonious combination; and as the devotional sentiment of the Christian religion belonged to that inward class of spiritual emotions which expressed themselves vocally rather than by animated gestures, it followed that all this music was unrhythmic; and consequently it was also divested of all that kind of regular orderliness of structure which seems so indispensable in the maturer art of modern times.

It is true that composers had successfully elaborated methods for regulating the lengths of the notes, but the establishment of principles of relative duration tended rather to obscure the rhythmic or metrical order of the music than to define it at first, owing to the manner in which they applied them. The reason for this lay in the strong feeling musicians had for the independence of the voice parts. Their artistic instinct was specially attracted by the fascinating effect of diverse movement controlled into the unity of a perfect flow of harmony. To them it was still essential that each individual voice part should be pleasurable to sing, and the more subtly the independence of each singer or voice part was suggested, the more fascinating was the artistic effect. The result was that in one phase of this kind of art composers aimed chiefly at making the accents and climaxes of the various voice parts constantly alternate with one another. One voice part rose when another fell, one held a note when another moved, one came to its highest climax at one moment, and then descended, while another, as it were overlapping, moved up in its turn to another climax, and then in turn gave way. And as the skill of composers in managing such progressions improved, they found out how to distribute the climaxes of the various voice parts so as to make them gain in vital warmth by coming ever closer and closer; and the hearer could in a moderate degree be excited by the sound of successive crises in different qualities of tone, sometimes tenor, sometimes treble, sometimes bass; each of which seemed successively to rise into prominence within the smooth texture of the harmonious flow of sound, and then to be merged into it again as another voice took its place.

The tendency of all such devices was to obscure the rhythmic element of the music. But the necessity for orderliness in the relative lengths of notes brought about a clear recognition of underlying principles upon which the strong and weak accents were grouped. The mere fact that some particular long note had to be recognised as equal to two, three, four, six or more shorter ones, necessitated the development of a feeling for strong accents at the points where the longer and the shorter notes started together; and for a proportionate absence of accent at the points where the longer notes were holding, though the quicker notes were moving. But it was rather a point of art with the choral writers to avoid emphasising these mechanical accents, and to make the voices have independent cross accents with one another. In respect of pure contrapuntal skill, the beauty of effect of such devices depended upon the manner in which the composers managed to control them with the view to keeping the harmonies complete, full in sound, and ever subtly varying in quality. In early stages their control of relative qualities of chords and their power to group them effectively was very limited. Even their instinct for the actual effect of chords had to be developed by long experience. As has before been pointed out, in such devices as the old motets, in which various tunes were forced to go together, it was a matter of the purest chance what harmonies or cacophonies succeeded each other. But as composers gained experience they began to perceive the value of the effect of contrast and variety which could be obtained by distributing their chords with regard to their relative degrees of harshness. And it obviously became a most fascinating study to find out how to control the motions of the various voices so as to obtain at once constant variety of accent, alternation of crisis, and the particular effects of harmony of different degrees of fulness or slightness which were required for the attainment of satisfactory general effect.

The artistic problem was obviously by no means simple, and though there was little to distract composers or divert their energies into other lines of artistic speculation, very few arrived at complete mastery of resource and complete perception of the various shades of chord effect which are as necessary to the artistic result as the actual management of the strands of the counterpoint. But in one short period at the latter part of the sixteenth century a small group of composers achieved a type of art which for subtlety and refinement in the treatment of delicate shades of contrast has no parallel in the history of musical art. The very absence of strong emotional purpose or intention to characterise gave them a peculiar opportunity. Their whole attention was concentrated upon a limited field of effort, and the fruit of their labour was a unique phase of a pure, and as it were ethereal beauty, too delicate to satisfy mankind for long, and destined to be brought to an end by a period of reactionary experiment which produced things almost as crude, ugly, and barbarous as those of the twelfth and thirteenth centuries.

But meanwhile, though the central aim of composers was the development of skill in controlling the diverse voice parts so as to produce these varying effects of harmonious sound, yet there were many ways in which the tendency to branch out into diversity was shown. Among the most noteworthy of these was the adoption of a method of writing the voice parts which served as a contrast to the elaborate contrapuntal methods above described. In the most characteristic style of choral writing of the old contrapuntal kind a note was but rarely repeated for different syllables. The treatment of the singing voice parts resembled in this the inflections of human speech, in which mechanical reiteration of a note—which implies subordination to some external rule of form or rhythm —is rare. But the constant, ceaseless shifting of every voice is liable to become a strain on the attention when it goes on too long, and the mind begins to feel the need for some kind of repose.

It was probably as a means of relieving this strain that composers adopted a much simpler mode of procedure; in which the effect was not obtained by the relations of the melodic contours of the parts, but by successions of simple harmonies in which the voices often moved in blocks of chords, and also very often repeated the same notes to different syllables. This style is far more like the familiar modern processes of harmonisation; but there remains this marked difference, that whereas in modern harmony the chords always move in subordination to the principles of modern tonality—as illustrating the antitheses of tonic and dominant and other relatively contrasting centres—the old progressions of harmony moved under the regulations of the modes, with much less of definite system in their distribution, and also without the melody in the upper part which is commonly the outward and visible sign of the inward principle of design. The importance of the occasional adoption of this kind of procedure was very great, for it not only called men's attention more directly to the actual effect of chords as chords, but also led them inevitably to a more definitely rhythmic treatment of the music. It became, as it were, the door through which rhythm began to make its way into choral music of the purest kind; and though the finer artistic natures never submitted wholly to its spell except on rare and well-chosen occasions, the seduction it exercised was too great to be resisted, and even before the great period of choral music had arrived at its zenith its presence made itself subtly felt here and there in all departments of art.

The most important result of the adoption of a simpler method of harmonisation was that it awoke in men's minds a new perception of the aspects of harmony pure and simple, and a change of attitude towards design, which is betrayed by their very helplessness in sustaining the interest in a long passage which is harmonic rather than contrapuntal in its character. The increased facility which men gained in the management of their artistic resources led them to apply their skill to various forms of both sacred and secular music. The best secular forms were the madrigals, which were written under the same artistic conditions as the Church music, and aimed by similar treatment of independent voice parts at obtaining beautiful effects of melodic variety within the bounds of the controlling unity of the harmony. The moods naturally became a little lighter and more lively than in Church music, and the expression even a little more definite and more varied. And it happened also that the first collections of madrigals which won very marked success—which were brought out by Arcadelt in the middle decades of the sixteenth century—were singularly simple in their harmonic aspects, as the harmonies were allowed to move very much in blocks and to present the simple rhythms of the poems set, without the disguise of the familiar cross accents and the subtleties of choral counterpoint. It was under such circumstances that men began to feel the need of system in the distribution of the harmonies; and as the modes under whose restrictions they still worked hindered their finding any satisfactory system of contrast between one group of harmonies and another, they almost invariably lost themselves in mazes of pointless obscurity in the middle of a composition of any length. For though they could make a good beginning and a good end with simple chords, art required a long period of probation under quite new conditions before men found out how to deal with the development of a long movement successfully on any lines but the contrapuntal ones with which they were familiar. When Arcadelt and his contemporaries tried to sustain the interest without the contrapuntal methods, their skill soon failed them. But every effort in this direction told; and as men knew nothing better as yet in the way of harmonic design, it cannot be supposed that they noticed the defects of such early attempts as much as modern musicians do. Undoubtedly the hearing of such works made them more and more accustomed to the possibilities of harmony of the simpler kind, and in a great many smaller madrigals the composers soon hit upon very definite and tuneful effects which differ from modern works of a similar kind only in the quaint and attractive peculiarities inevitable to harmonisation in the old ecclesiastical modes. In the madrigals of the best time the finer contrapuntal methods were generally adopted; but men had so far progressed towards understanding the effect of harmonic design, that in many large examples, especially in those of the English school, tonality becomes sufficiently definite to admit occasionally of clear and effective treatment of modulation of the modern kind; which implies a conception of art quite alien to the purely contrapuntal and modal methods of the great choral composers.

A little consideration will show that the capacity to feel

the artistic effect of a change of key implies the adoption of
a new attitude in relation to art which is of the first importance. In melodic systems there is a wide range of possible
change of mode, but very little which amounts to change of
key. Differences of mode are differences in the relations of
various intervals to the most essential notes of the scale, such
as the initial or final of a tune, or any other notes on which
emphasis is especially laid. But differences of key are much
more subtle both in fact and effect. For they do not change
the order of the notes, but only the position of the centre
round which a uniform series is grouped; and the beauty of
the effect is partly derived from the identity of order in relation to a changed centre, and partly from the fact that this
identity causes certain notes to appear in one key which do
not exist in the other. Now, the original conception of the
art of the choral epoch was purely melodic: the central
thread of orderliness was the modal part, as it was called,
which moved, according to certain rules, within a range of
sounds of which either C, D, E, F, G, or A was the most
essential note; and whatever parts were added were regulated
by their relation to this part, which was most frequently the
tenor. Sharps and flats were in no case introduced to give
the effect of change of key, but merely to avoid intervals
which were considered offensive and inartistic, or to make
the close of the movement satisfactory to the ear. The idea
of introducing an F♯ into a passage in order to make a modulation from C to G, or a B♭ to pass from C to F, was alien to
the very heart of the modal system. When B♭ was introduced it was because the interval of the tritone or augmented
fourth between F and B was disagreeable; and when men
found that the introduction of a flat to B produced the very
interval they wanted to avoid between B♭ and E, they evaded
the obnoxious interval again by adding a flat also to E whenever it was required by the circumstances. But the object
was not to suggest a change of tonality, or to obtain variety
of harmony, but to soften the effect of a melodic passage.
The sharps were introduced on grounds which were less purely
melodic, as the dissatisfaction in a cadence consisting of the

succession of the chords of D minor and G, which drove musicians to sharpen the F, implies quite as much sense of the need for a penultimate major chord (which is a harmonic consideration) as for the rise of the semitone to the final, which is the melodic feeling. But, at any rate, it is quite clear that when once these supplementary notes had been added for one purpose, composers very soon made use of them for other purposes. They soon saw that it gave them an additional means of effect, and without thinking of anything so subtle or advanced as a change of key, they began to use them to obtain the effect of a difference of quality in harmony in the same position. They delighted in bringing passages close together which contained chords with F♯ and F♮, or C♯ and C♮ in them respectively. To people accustomed mainly to the diatonic series the effect must have been subtly enchanting; and composers, in their eagerness to avail themselves of all opportunities, occasionally overshot the mark, and made experiments to which modern ears, though as a rule tougher than ears of the sixteenth century, will not accord any appreciation. But the use of these accidentals gave men the opportunity to learn not only the important relations of tonic and dominant chords, but also further to develop a new conception of the nature of the musical scale. The truth is, that the frequent use of these accidentals ultimately assimilated the modes to such an extent, that little more than technical traditions, differences of style, and forms of cadences distinguished the music written in one mode from that written in another. This might be counted as a loss if it were not remembered that the old modal system was quite unfitted for the artistic purposes of harmony, and that the assimilation of modes into a system of keys was a necessary preliminary to the development of true harmonic music of the modern kind, and of those principles of harmonic design which are vital to its existence.

The masters of the great choral period never arrived at a definite acceptance of the contrast between tonic and dominant as a basis of design; but they understood the principle well enough to use progressions of such chords effectively in cadences of various kinds, and they arrived at a clear enough feeling for tonality in the latest years of the period to use passages which represent such contrasts of key as D minor and B♭ major, E minor and G, D minor and F. But the instinct of the higher class of composers for continuity in the flow of sound militated against any systematic use of such contrasts for purposes of design. Their movements started from some initial point, and wandered ceaselessly through unbroken mazes of counterpoint till the return to the starting-point in the close. There was nothing of the systematic modulation to a new key, and definite use of it as the principal element of contrast in the design which is familiar in modern music. But they soon found out the advantage of making subordinate recommencements start from chords which contrasted with one another; and the growth of their feeling for such contrasts grew with their freer use of accidentals, till the relation in which whole passages stood to one another was sufficiently clear and broad to give to a modern musician the impression of a very effective modulation.

It was in compositions of a lower order that composers were driven to experiment in rhythmical grouping of periods more like modern harmonic forms; for as in these they tried to set their poems directly and simply, they had no choice but to look for successions of chords which were effectively alternated and balanced. The general diffusion of skill in the management of voice parts brought into being a variety of popular forms which went by the names of Canzonas, Frottolas, and Villanellas, many of which were simple arrangements of popular street tunes, such as, but for the universal influence of the modes, would resemble modern part-songs; and besides these there was a very large amount of dance music for voices in parts, such as the Balletti, which were necessarily rhythmic and definite in the distribution of phrases and periods, and regularly grouped into bars. Many of these are remarkably bright, sparkling, and skilfully contrived with great feeling for vocal effect. The style of these works reacted upon the higher types of art, such as the madrigals; and in the latest phase of that form of art, which is represented at its best in

England during the latter part of Elizabeth's reign and in the time of James I., the actual subjects and figures of melody came to have a far more definite and distinct character, and the aspect of the works in general became far more animated, more pointed, and more rhythmic than it had been in earlier generations. The balance of style was admirably sustained by the great masters of the English school, Byrd, Wilbye, Weelkes Benet, Morley, Gibbons, and others, though they clearly aimed at more definite expression and more close attention to the words than would have been consistent with the artistic intentions of the early Netherland and Italian masters. But the expansion of the style in these directions bore with it the seeds of dissolution; and as soon as composers endeavoured to enlarge the scope of choral music yet further by imitating the methods of the early operas and cantatas, the mediæval type of choral art passed into mongrel forms, and very shortly ceased altogether.

In connection with the dissolution of the early form of art, it is impossible to overlook the fact that branches of art which were completely in the background and were held of but small consequence at the time when pure choral music was at its highest perfection, had great influence in bringing the era of its prosperity to an end. For even long before the days of such unique masters of choral art as Palestrina, and Lasso, and Gibbons, men had begun to divine that there were possibilities of new effects, and a wide extension of artistic resources to be got out of music for instruments. And even while these great masters were busy enriching the world with their masterly achievements, other men were busily making crude experiments in instrumental music, which were among the most potent influences in leading the world to prefer new kinds of music to the choral masterpieces of the latter part of the sixteenth century, and served to supply the substratum upon which the experimenting revolutionaries of the next generation began to build. While men had so much of their attention concentrated upon developing artistic methods which were most suitable for human voices in combination, instruments had naturally been considerably in the background, they had been very imperfect in construction, and had next to nothing to do with really high-class art in any independent form. But the early imperfect types of viols which had long been in use were by degrees improved under the influence of men's growing appreciation for beauty of tone and refinement of feeling for execution, and before the end of the sixteenth century, even when the great masters of choral music were in the heyday of their artistic prosperity, the earliest representatives of the unique and incomparable school of Italian violin-makers were already busy with their inimitable work. In kindred lines of workmanship men arrived at great perfection in the making of those troublesome but very fascinating domestic instruments, the lutes of all kinds ; and at the same time the early types of keyed instruments, such as harpsichords or virginals and clavichords and spinets, were rapidly approaching a condition sufficiently practicable to be worthy of the attention of genuine composers ; and organs were passing out of the cumbrous and unmanageable state in which there had to be almost as many bellows as notes, and the notes had to be put down with the whole fist, into a practicable condition which admitted of independent music being performed upon them. But the music for instruments was in a very backward state, because composers had no idea what to aim at in writing for them. When they wanted something of a superior artistic order for stringed instruments, they simply played madrigals, or wrote music in imitation of any of the varieties of choral music ; not realising that without the human tones and the varying degrees of effort and tension in the vocal chords, which gave expression to the rising and falling of the melodic material, the effect was pointless and flat. No doubt the skilful treatment of contrapuntal resources made these movements interesting to the performers to play; but apart from such personal considerations, all the early music of this kind, produced before the rhythmic treatment appropriate to instruments came into force, is altogether shadowy and colourless, and has no independent artistic status.

The case was different with dance tunes, for in such rhythmic ranges the instruments were in their proper sphere.

There is a very large quantity of such music for stringed instruments and harpsichords which represents the crude and primitive types of later sonatas and suites. These little works were written by composers of all countries, and an occasional example is met with which has real vivacity and effectiveness; but for the most part they are singularly clumsy and inartistic, and hardly ever present more than the slightest trace of refined artistic intention in the composer. They indicate a dim sense of abstract effect only in the alternations of quick and slow dances, and of dances in rhythm of three or four beats, and in attempts to regulate the structure of the individual dance tunes into equal and balancing groups of bars. The backward condition of the technique of performance on stringed instruments accounts for a good deal of the crudity and absence of expression in the music written for them; for mankind developed their skill in performance quite as slowly and laboriously as they developed the technique of composition; and the progress of both invention and execution has been at all times to a great extent interdependent.

The standard of lute music was slightly better than that of the music written for other stringed instruments. The instrument was very popular in refined sections of society; and the fact that it required less mechanical ingenuity to bring it to perfection, and that it was very portable and well adapted to the conditions of domestic performance and to the social arrangements of wealthy people, caused its technique to be brought to a high pitch before that of any other modern instrument. The sort of music written for it in the early days was much like that written for stringed instruments; and consisted mainly of dance tunes in sets, occasionally of imitations of choral canzonas and madrigals, and occasionally also of fanciful movements which would correspond to free preludes or fantasias in modern music. What gives these works a higher importance in relation to later instrumental music than the early viol music, is, that the element of personal skill and expression is much more apparent in them, and that the style is on the whole much more independent and more distinctively instrumental. The development of the ornamental department of music had to be achieved in the same fashion as that of all other features of the art; and there can be no doubt that the early stages of the invention of the rich and copious store of decorative material and of decorative principles, which are so characteristic of modern music, were achieved by the early composers for the lute. Even quite early in the sixteenth century, when the great choral style was by no means matured, lute music was already much cultivated; and though the forms of the movements, such as Ricercare, Passamessos, Preambules, and Pavanas, were at first crude and imperfect, and the ornaments childish and tame, yet such works and groups of movements formed the basis of a long and continuous improvement, ultimately finding highly artistic expression in the Ordres of Couperin and the Suites and Partitas of J. S. Bach.

The music for the harpsichord and its nearest relatives attained but slight independence in the days of the great choral composers. Arrangements were made of choral music, and imitations of the same were attempted; and a fair quantity of dance tunes similar to those written for the violins or viols was produced. Some lute music was adapted, and a certain number of independent fantasias and preludes were contrived; which were sometimes written in the choral style, and sometimes consisted of simple passages of runs and arpeggios. A certain amount of development of decorative material and of technique was achieved; but, on the whole, this branch of instrumental music was more backward than any other in those days.

On the other hand, organ music was relatively the most advanced, and the nearest to complete emancipation and independence. The requirements of ecclesiastical functions must have made considerable demands on the powers of organists from comparatively early times; and though the backward state of the mechanism of the instrument prevented them from achieving much distinction by brilliant display, they had ample occasion for experimenting in solo music, and the results they attained to were as fruitful as they are instructive. As in other branches of instrumental music, they frequently imitated the contrapuntal methods of choral music, and with more appropriate effect. But following the natural instincts of human kind, they endeavoured to adorn these movements with flourishes and turns and all the available resources of ornamental variation. They also developed a kind of performance which, without disrespect, may be compared to very bad and unintelligent modern extemporisation. The systematisation of chord progressions had yet to be achieved, and even the ablest composers were therefore, through lack of opportunity, in much the same position as any very inefficient modern organist is through lack of ability. They had little or no conception of genuine musical ideas of the kind which is adapted to instruments, and the need for purely ornamental performance was the more imperative. They therefore devised toccatas and fantasias, which consisted of strings of scale-passages, turns, and shakes, upon successions of chords which are for the most part completely incoherent. Few things could be more instructive, in respect of the fact that our modern music is purely the fruit of cumulative development of artistic devices, than the entire absence of idea, point, and coherence in these early works, which are often the productions of composers who were great musicians and masters of all the resources of refined choral effect. The movements were possibly effective in great churches, from the wild career of the scale-passages in treble, bass, or middle parts, which often rushed (no doubt in moderate tempo) from one end of the instrument to the other. Almost the only structural device which these early organists mastered was the effect of alternating passages of simple imitation, like those in choral music, as a contrast to the brilliant display of the scales. Further than this in point of design they could not go, except in so far as mere common-sense led them to regulate their passages so as to obtain different degrees of fulness in different parts of the movement, and to pile up the effects of brilliant display and gather them all into one sonorous roll of sound at the conclusion. Crude as these works are in design, they were a definite departure in the direction of independent instrumental music on a considerable scale, and were the direct prototypes of the magnificent organ works of J. S. Bach. In fact, the branch of organ music has always continued to be more nearly allied to the great style of the choral epoch than any other instrumental form. The first great representative organist, Frescobaldi, was born in the palmy days of choral music, and made his fame while it was still flourishing; and though the resources of harmonic music were a necessary adjunct to bring this branch to maturity in later days, their ultimate predominance did not obliterate the traces of the earlier polyphonic style so completely as was the case in violin and harpsichord music, nor did their concomitants entirely obscure the time-honoured dignity of the early contrapuntal traditions. In other branches of instrumental music harmonic conditions necessitated the development of an absolutely new style and new methods of art. In organ music the old methods and something of the ancient style were retained, and were only modified by the new conditions so far as was necessary to make the design of the movements systematic and intelligible in general and in detail.

It remains to consider shortly the essential artistic methods and principles of this great era of art. The prevailing influence which regulated all things in every department of art was fitness for choral performance. There was practically no solo singing, and, as has been pointed out above, the feeling of musicians for instrumental effect was extremely crude and undeveloped. Harmony was primarily the result of voices singing melodious parts simultaneously; and the highest skill was that which could weave good vocal parts so as to obtain beautiful and interesting successions of chords. In the conception then formed of good vocal parts only the simplest diatonic intervals were admissible, and only the very simplest chords. It was unnatural for voices to assume discordant relations with one another directly, so the only discords allowed were such as were purely transitory, or such as were obtained by the pretty device of holding one or more notes of a harmonious combination while others moved to positions in the scale which made the stationary ones discordant, till they again resolved themselves into the unity of the harmony. All such discords have a double function; they supply contrast,

9

and make that departure from unity which serves as impulse.
They impel the movement onward, because it is impossible to
rest upon discord, and the mind is not satisfied till the source
of disquiet is intelligibly merged in a more reposeful combination.   In a perfect work of musical art there is no absolute
point of repose between the outset and the close.   To make an
entirely satisfying and complete close is to make what follows
superfluous.   The perfect management of such things, even in
early stages of art, is much more subtle than it looks.   A
really great master so adjusts the relative degrees of movement
and repose that each step has its perfect relation to the context and to the whole.   Every discord must have its resolution;
but till the moment of complete repose which brings the work
to conclusion, each resolution is only so far complete as to
satisfy the mind partially.   The problem is so complicated and
delicate that it is quite beyond the powers of mere calculation;
and its difficulty—combined with hundreds of other artistic
problems of similar delicacy—accounts for the great length of
time that human instinct has taken to arrive at the status of
modern music.   The difficulty also accounts for the variety of
standards which are presented at different periods in musical
history which are more or less mature in their way.   The great
composers of choral music dealt in the very simplest and
slenderest materials.   They reduced the prominence of their
points of repose to a minimum by using extremely few discords, even of the gentle kind above described; and they
obtained variety by making use of the more delicate shades
of difference in the actual qualities of various concords, whose
resolutions were not so restricted; and they evaded the feeling
of coming to an end in the wrong place, by keeping their voice
parts constantly on the move, and by avoiding the formulas of
their conventional cadences in those parts of the scale which
suggested complete finality.

It was natural that the representatives of typically different
races should adopt artistic methods which led to somewhat
different results.   The Netherlanders, who took the lead so
prominently in the fifteenth century, always had a taste for
ingenuities and for subtleties of artistic device.   It was the

Netherland composers who carried the homogeneous form of
the canon to such extremes of futile ingenuity; but it was
also their great composers who achieved all the most arduous
part of the early development of their craft, and handed it on
to the Italians to complete. In the end the work of the
Netherlanders is the most characteristic, but that of the
Italians most delicately beautiful; while the English school,
which followed both, is far more comprehensive in variety,
definiteness, and character, though never attaining to the
extraordinary finish and perfection which is met with in
Palestrina's work at its best. In the greatest triumphs of
Palestrina, Vittoria, and Marenzio, the smooth, easy, masterly
flow of separate voice parts seems naturally to result in perfect combinations of sound; in Lasso's work it is easy to see
the deliberate ingenuity which contrives some weird unexpected successions, and makes chords melt into one another
in ways which have a touch of magic in them; and Josquin
and Hobrecht, notwithstanding the disadvantages of a less
mature state of art, suggest the same attitude. With Byrd
and Gibbons there is a touch of English hardness and boldness;
and in others of the same school, a bright and straightforward
freshness which is peculiarly characteristic. The English
school came to its best days so late as compared with foreign
schools that it is no wonder that its works show many traits of
a later order of musical art than do the purest Italian examples.
But the same premonitions of a great change are also plenti-
fully shown in the works of the adventurous composers of
Venice, especially those of the great Giovanni Gabrieli; who,
besides producing many superb examples of the true old choral
style, endeavoured to introduce the element of direct expression both by harmony and figure, and tried effects of instrumental accompaniment which belong to a different order of art
from that of the pure choral era, and made many experiments
which were among the precursors of the great change which
brought the period of pure choral music to an end.

In a general survey of the aspects of this important period
of art, the condition of homogeneity and indefiniteness appears
to be universal. This is especially the case in respect of the

structure of musical movements. The only form in which a
definite principle of procedure was maintained from beginning
to end was the canon (which the old masters called Fuga), in
which different voices sang the same melody throughout the
movement a little after one another (see p. 97). The device
has occasionally been made interesting by clever treatment, in
spite of its drawbacks; but this does not nullify the fact that
it is inherently mechanical and inartistic by reason of its
rigidity and monotony. Of definite principles of design beyond
this elementary device these early composers had but few.
Their treatment of musical figures and melodic material is
singularly vague. The familiar modern practice of using a
definite subject throughout a considerable portion of a movement, or at certain definite points which have a structural
importance, is hardly to be met with at all. The voices which
entered one after another naturally commenced singing the
same words to phrases of melody which resembled each other.
But composers' ideas of identity of subject-matter were singularly elastic, and even if the first half-dozen notes presented
similar contours in each voice part successively, the melodic
forms soon melted into something else, and from that point
the movement wandered on its devious way without further
reference to its initial phrases. A few cases occur in which
composers use a well-defined figure throughout in constant
reiteration artistically disposed; but such are accidents of the
composer's mood, and any system in such things was quite
foreign to their aims. The same is the case with all principles
of structure either in general or in detail. Occasionally composers produced striking effects by sequences, and by giving
parallel passages to different groups of voices or balancing
choirs; but such devices were not of general application.
Occasionally also the beginning and end of a movement were
made to correspond; but that, too, was extremely rare. The
common modern practice of repeating phrases at long intervals
apart is an abstract musical conception, and its systematic
use in art is the result of the development of instrumental
form in later times.

In no respect is the universal absence of definiteness and

variety more noticeable than in the actual musical material or
"subjects." Throughout the whole range of the old sacred
choral music these are almost without decisive significance.
It is true that composers adopted such innocent devices as a
long descending scale-passage to express the descent into hell,
and a formula which might be traced into a cross for the
"crucifixus," and a slow passage of simple reiterated chords
to express the awe of the worshipper at the thought of the
incarnation, and so on in parallel cases; but the position
occupied by subject-matter and figure in their scheme of art
is altogether different from that which it occupies in the
modern scheme. The subject, indeed, barely stands out from
its context at all. It is as though the art was still in too
nebulous a state for the essential elements to have crystallised
into separate and definite entities. This is chiefly the result
of the absence of rhythm, without which every melodic contour
is to a certain extent wanting in complete definiteness and
force. In the matter of expression again the same absence of
definiteness and variety is noticeable, partly in consequence of
the limited and uniform nature of the scales. As each complete piece of music was subject to the rule of some special
mode, all the sentiments contained in it were restricted by
the characteristics of the mode employed. If it was what a
modern musician would call minor in character, the musical
expression for the "Gloria" had to be got out of it as well as
that for the "Miserere." And though the use of accidentals
modified modal restrictions to a certain extent, the modifications were not sufficiently general to obviate the fact that in
detail a piece of music had to follow the rule and character of
the mode rather than the sentiment of the words. Indeed, this
is so far the rule that the attempt to introduce direct expression into the scheme at the expense of modal purity was
among the immediate causes of the rapid decay and collapse
of the whole system of the old art.

In close connection with the limits of expression were the
limitations of the actual chord material or harmonies. No
great force of expression could be obtained without more
powerful dissonance than the scheme allowed. The scheme

was based on consonant harmonies; and the discords, which were mild in character and comparatively rare in use, were no more than artificial modifications of the chain of concords. The incisive striking upon a discord without preliminary was a thing quite alien to the style; and nothing is more decisive as a sign of the approaching end of pure choral music than the appearance of even the slightest and mildest discord without artificial preparation.

In the general aspect of music of the choral time the same homogeneousness prevails. Sacred music, by the end of the period, was subdivided into mass music, motets, hymns, psalms, and many other titles; but as far as style was concerned the distinctions were more nominal than real, for the difference between one and the other was very slight indeed. The main subdivision of the period was into sacred and secular music. But the higher class of secular music was very much like sacred music in methods, and not very different even in style; while the branches of lighter secular music, which differed most from the highest artistic forms in their more rhythmical character and harmonic structure, were as yet limited both in range and development.

The chief points which were gained in this period were a very fine and delicate perception of the qualities of chords when sung by voices, and wonderful skill in manipulating the melodic progressions of the separate voice parts so as to obtain very subtle gradations of variety in the succession of these chords. While they were achieving these matters, composers unconsciously developed a feeling for the classification of such chords in connection with certain tonal centres. The almost universal practice of the "musica ficta" which entailed the modification of the modes by accidentals, brought the effect of tonality more and more into prominence, especially in the cadences; and by these processes the basis was formed for the new departures which ensued; and with the help of the insignificant attempts at instrumental music, which were made even while the art of unaccompanied choral music was at its highest perfection, the materials which formed the groundwork and footing of the structure of the latest modern art were supplied.

CHAPTER VI

THE RISE OF SECULAR MUSIC

WITHOUT taking into consideration the many external causes
which influenced and modified the character of various arts
about the end of the sixteenth century, it might have been
foreseen that a new departure in music was inevitable on
internal and artistic grounds alone. The range of the art
had been extremely limited so far; and though its limitations
had conduced to the development of singularly perfect results,
such advantages could not prevent men from wearying of
apparent monotony, and becoming restive under restrictions
which seemed to be hindrances to the fullest expression of their
musical ideals. A reaction, such as in analogous situations
in ordinary life drives men accustomed to ease and refinement of surroundings to court hardship, danger, and priva-
tion, drove men of the highest taste and refinement, and
such as were most thoroughly in touch with the spirit and
movement of their age, to cut themselves adrift from the
traditions of a perfectly mature art — to cast aside the
principles which the accumulated observations and efforts of
past generations had brought to an admirable practical issue
—and adopt a kind of music which was formless, crude,
and chaotic.

The higher type of conservative mind instinctively feels
that such wellbeing as society enjoys, and all the wealth of
artistic technique, and the skill by which men achieve all
they do well, are the fruits of the experiences and intelligent
efforts of previous generations. To a mind so constituted
a sweeping rejection of the judgment of ancestry is like
cutting away the very ground upon which things are built;

and the immediate result of sweeping reforms generally justifies conservative forecasts. To the conservative musician of the early days of the seventeenth century the projects of the enthusiasts who founded modern music must have appeared, as radical reforms generally do, to be based on misconceptions—an outrage against all the best grounded principles of art, and the offspring of brains which were childishly regardless of the most obvious consequences. The reformers, with the hopefulness characteristic of enthusiasts, thought they could dispense with all the fruits of past experience, and develop a new art on the basis of pure theoretic speculation. They gave up the subtleties of polyphonic writing and the devices which were natural to choral music; the beautiful effects obtainable by skilful combinations of voice parts; the traditions of a noble style, and the restrictions which made it consistent and mature; and they thought to make a new heaven and a new earth where secular expression should be free and eloquent without reference to past artistic experience as a guide to the artistic means.

But they had to adopt unconsciously much that their predecessors had built up for them. It was as often happens in revolutions, when new constitutions have to be built out of the wisdom of those whose heads have been cut off. Even the earliest experiments were based upon a crude application of chord effects of which they could have had no conception without the development of choral polyphony which their predecessors had laboriously achieved. Their first experiments were essentially steps made in the dark; and the first results that they achieved had the usual aspects of such steps in reform, and look purely infantile and absolutely ineffective by the side of the artistic works which they were meant to supersede. But nevertheless the event proved the reformers to be perfectly right. For unless they had ventured as they did, and had been as blind as reformers sometimes need to be to immediate consequences, the ultimate building up of the marvellously rich and complicated edifice of modern art could never have been achieved. The conservatives were perfectly right in foreseeing that the methods of the new art would immediately bring the old art to ruin. The reformers were equally right in judging that it was necessary to make that great sacrifice in order that art might obtain a new lease of vitality.

The objects of the earliest reformers, such as Cavaliere, Caccini, Galilei, and Peri, were very innocent. They had no idea of making astonishing effects, or of attracting attention by meretricious effrontery. They aimed, with a sobriety which was artistic at least in its reticence, at devising means to combine music and poetry, so that the two arts should enhance one another. They tried to find some simple musical way of declaiming sonnets, poems, and plays with a single voice, accompanied by such gentle instruments as lutes and harpsichords. The idea was not totally new, for theatrical representations with music and a kind of declamation had been attempted before; solo music of a kind had been practised by troubadours, trouvères, and various independent secularists; while instrumental music—which was such an important element in their scheme—had long been cultivated on a small scale, chiefly in short dance movements, but occasionally also for crude experiments more of the nature of abstract art. But nevertheless they had to begin almost from the beginning, and find out the requirements of their art as they went on. At first they seem to have had no idea that any kind of design or even musical figures were required. They thought it sufficient for the solo voice to declaim the poetry in musical sounds whose relations of pitch imitated the inflections of the voice in ordinary declamation; and they were satisfied with an accompaniment which consisted of nothing more than simple chords, such as they had grown accustomed to hear in the music of the Church and in the simple instrumental music of the early days. Though the composers of some of the early dances had already suggested the principle of design by grouping related and contrasted chords, the intelligence of these speculative enthusiasts was at first scarcely so far advanced as to lead them to imagine that a similar practice was advisable in music associated with words.

Each individual chord as a lump of harmony served to support
the voice for the moment; and the utmost their dormant
sense of design seemed to demand in regulating the order of
the harmonies was that, in passages which were specially
unified by a complete verse of the poetry, the same chord
should appear at the beginning and at the end of the phrase.
The development of sense for chord relationship had progressed far enough in the days of the great choral music
to make men perfectly alive to the effect of the familiar
dominant and tonic cadence; and this the composers of the
new style used with great frequency, thereby conclusively
defining the actual ends of passages; but the general structure of the passages themselves remained incoherent, because,
apart from the cadence, composers did not recognise the
essential importance of the apposition of the dominant and
tonic chords as a means of design. The very necessity of
a principle of contrast in the new scheme of art remained
to be found out by long experience. In an art so hedged
about with limitations as the pure choral art had been, such
a principle of contrast was not needed, and the peculiar
properties of the old ecclesiastical modes always acted as a
hindrance to its discovery. And the obstruction did not
cease even when the new music had begun, because the
habits and associations of all kinds of music, both secular
and sacred, had been formed under the influences of the
old modal systems; and these had sunk so deep into men's
natures, and had so coloured their habits of thought, that
they could only shake themselves free and find their true
path by slow degrees. As long as men's minds were influenced by the conventions of the modes, they constantly
made the harmonies move in directions which rendered
nugatory the one chord which was necessary as the principal
centre of contrast; and definiteness of design of the harmonic
kind was thereby rendered impossible. The essence of design
in harmonic music of the modern kind is that groups of chords
and whole passages shall have a well-defined and intelligible
connection with certain tonal centres, and that the centres
round which the successive passages are grouped shall have

definite and intelligible relations of contrast or affinity with one another. The simplest dance tune or street song is now constructed upon such principles no less than the greatest masterpieces. But the early experimenters had no experience of such effects, and jumbled up their chords together incoherently. They thought of little beyond varying their order, and supplying a support to the declamation of the voice. The result is that not only each portion of music set to line and verse, but the whole plan of the works, is indefinite in structure, and has next to no principle of necessary cohesion beyond the occurrence of cadences. The course of the early operas wanders on through pages of monotonous recitative, varied only here and there by little fragments of chorus or short dance tunes, which are almost as innocent of melody or design as the recitative itself.

This obvious condition of homogeneity appears not only in the structure of these works, but also in the expression; for whether poignant anguish or exuberant joy is the theme, there is hardly any variety in the style of the music, which has therefore hardly any function beyond formalising the declamation. In Rinuccini's little drama of Euridice the familiar story is relieved of its poignancy, and a good deal of its point, by the success of Orpheus in winning back his lost love from the Shades. Consequently the composers had to set both the expression of despair at receiving the news of her death, and of joy at bringing her back to life; and from the manner in which they addressed themselves to this object much may be learnt. Two important settings of the little drama exist, both of which saw the light in 1600. The best of the two is that by the enthusiastic amateur Jacopo Peri, which was performed at Florence to grace the wedding festivities of Henry IV. of France and Maria Medici. It was not the first work of its kind, but it is the first of which enough remains in a complete state to afford safe inferences as to the aims and methods of the new school; and the manner in which Peri treated the two highly contrasted situations above alluded to is very

instructive. The following is the passage which was then
held adequate to express the poignancy of Orpheus' feelings
over his loss:—

The following is the music in which he expresses his joy at
bringing his lost bride back to the light of day:—

sel - ve fron-do - se   Gio - i - te ama-ti

col - li   e d'ogni   in - tor - no

Ec - co rim-bom - bi dalle   valle   as-co - se.

The texture of the two passages is obviously very similar;
but it is well not to overlook the points which show some sense
of adaptation to the respective states of emotion.   Both passages afford fair opportunity to a competent singer to infuse
expression into the ostensibly bald phrases.   And, besides
this, they lend themselves very happily to the requirements
of the situations, and show the justness of the composer's
instinct in those respects in which artistic technique is not
very essential.   For the phrases which express bereavement
and sorrow are tortuous, irregular, spasmodic—broken with
catching breath and wailing accent; whereas the expression
of joy is flowing, easy and continuous, and unusually well
defined and regular in form, approaching as nearly to the
types of modern harmonic art as was possible in those days.
Such general points as these can be effected by intelligent
beings without much training or experience; but the details

are carried out crudely and baldly, for the day was still far off
when men learnt how to make anything artistically appropriate
of the instrumental accompaniment.

There is very little in the works of the other representatives of this new departure which indicates views or skill in
any special degree superior to Peri's.   Caccini's setting of the
same drama of Euridice is in general character very like Peri's.
It has the same monotonous expanses of recitative with accompaniment of figured bass, and similar short fragments of chorus,
consisting of a few bars at a time, written with quite as obvious
a lack of sense for choral effect.   Perhaps the most noteworthy
point is that, being one of the earliest solo singers of repute,
and the father of a famous *cantatrice*, he introduced roulades
and ornamental passages for the singers; thereby devising
some of the first formulas, and prefiguring even in those early
days the tasteless and senseless excesses of vain show which
disfigure certain types of modern opera.   The following passage is from Caccini's Euridice :—

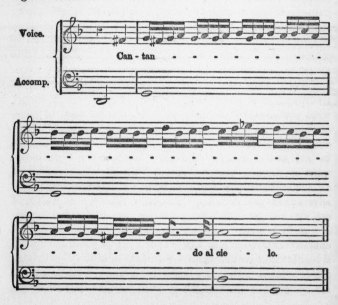

It is noteworthy that these flourishes usually occur close to the end of verses and phrases, just as simpler ones do in the old German folk-songs. Caccini wrote a book about the "Nuove Musiche," in which he described the objects of the reformers ; and in this work he gave some examples of settings of short poems for a solo voice, which serve as almost the earliest examples of consciously contrived solo-songs with instrumental accompaniment, as distinguished from folk-songs. These also serve to emphasise the very slight sense which the composers had of the need for design, or of the possibility of obtaining such a thing by the distribution of the successions of chords. What remains of Emilio Cavaliere's work is similar in character, and shows almost as vague a sense of design. The bass solo which serves as an introduction to his one Oratorio is the finest piece of work left by this group of composers, and is a very noble and impressive monument of the man, of whom we know but little beyond the fact that the invention of recitative is attributed to him by his fellow-composers. To judge from this example, he must have been of larger calibre than they were. Here and there he even shows some sense of modulation as a means of effect, and of consistent use of tonality ; but in texture and artistic treatment of detail he is almost as backward as the rest of his contemporaries.

Though there were a few composers who held by the old traditions, most of the men of marked powers and energy were attracted by the new methods, and by the escape it afforded them from the drudgery of musical education. They soon became conscious of new requirements and possibilities in their line of work, and the early homogeneous experiments were by degrees improved upon. The most noteworthy of all the representatives of the style was Monteverde, whose adventurous genius found a congenial field in such a state of art, and who gave the impress of his personality to a branch of histrionic music which has maintained certain well-defined characteristics from that day till this. It may well be doubted if Monteverde would ever have succeeded in a line of art which required concentration and logical coherence of musical design. He seems to have belonged to that familiar type of artist*

who regard expression as the one and only element of importance. He had been educated in the learning of the ancients,
but had early shown his want of submission to the time-
honoured restrictions by using chords and progressions which
were out of place in the old choral style. He had endeavoured
to introduce effects of strong expression into an order of art
which could only retain its aspect of maturity by excluding
all such direct forms of utterance. A decisive harshness
breaking upon the ear without preliminary was shortly to
become a necessity to musical mankind; but to the old order
of things it was the omen of immediate dissolution. The
methods of choral art did not provide for dramatic force or
the utterance of passionate feeling; and under such circumstances it was natural that Monteverde should misapply his
special gifts, which were all in the direction of dramatic expression. The new departure, when it came, was his opportunity. He was not ostensibly a sharer in the first steps of
the movement; but directly he joined it he entirely eclipsed
all other composers in the field, and in a few years gave it
quite a new complexion. For whereas the first composers had
not laid any great stress on expression, and showed but little
gift for it, Monteverde's instinct and aim was chiefly in
that direction; and he often sought to emphasise his situations
at all costs. His harmonic progressions are for the most part
as incoherent as those of his predecessors, and, as might be
expected with his peculiar aptitudes, he did very little for
design. But he evidently had a very considerable instinct for
stage effect, and realised that mere monotonous recitative was
not the final solution of the problem nor even the nucleus of
dramatic music. It is true he introduces a great quantity of
recitative; but he varies it with instrumental interludes which
now and then have some real point and relevancy about them,
and with passages of solo music which have definite figures of
melody and apposite expression, and with choruses which are
more skilfully contrived and to a certain degree more effective
than those of his predecessors. By this means he broke up
the homogeneous texture of the scenes into passages of well-
defined diversity, and interested his auditors with contrast,

variety, and conspicuously characteristic passages, which heighten the impression of the situations, as all stage music should.

His ideas of instrumental music were very crude, but nevertheless immensely in advance of such as are indicated by the works of his predecessors. Where they had been satisfied with a single line and figures to indicate to the lute players and cembalists the chords they were to use, he brought together a large band of violins, viols, lutes, trumpets, flutes, trombones, a harpsichord, and other instruments, and in special parts of his works gave some of them definite parts to play, and distributed them with some sense of effect and relevancy. His experiments sometimes look childish, but in several cases they are the types which only wanted more experienced handling to become permanent features of modern orchestral music. His instinct led him to make his work more definite and alive in detail than the earlier experiments had been; and though it was too early for the articulations of the structure to become distinct, his style of work is a very clear foreshadowing of the state which was bound to ensue. He was especially conspicuous as the first composer who aimed decisively at histrionic effect, and he originated the tradition which passed through Cavalli and Lulli into France and ultimately made that country its home; while Italy fell under the spell of a different theory of art, and became the special champion of design and beauty of melody.

The immediate source of this important change in the course of musical development in Italy was a reaction from the crude speculativeness of the new style in favour of a revival of the old methods of choral art; and its fruit was an endeavour to adapt what was applicable of those methods to the new theories. The change which came over the new music was so rapid and complete, that it proves that humanity took very little time to realise that something more was wanted than mere moment-to-moment setting of the words of a poem or the scenes of a play. Men who were masters of the technique of the old choral art, such as Giovanni Gabrieli at Venice, tried to apply it in new ways in conformity with the

10

spirit of the new theories; introducing singular experiments of a realistic character, and some remarkable experiments in expression by harmony. This type of art was carried by his interesting pupil, Schütz, into Germany, and by him the first advances were made in the direction of that peculiarly earnest, artistic, and deeply emotional style which is the glory of German music. Each of these and many others contributed their share to the progress of the movement; but circumstances combined to give peculiar prominence to Carissimi, whose experience and genuine feeling for the old artistic methods gave him a good hold upon the artistic possibilities of the new, and helped his judgment to distinguish between what was mere experimental extravagance and what was genuinely artistic expression. He had not the inventiveness or the force and character of Monteverde; but he had more sense of beauty, both in respect of form and sound, and a better artistic balance. This may have been owing to the fact that he did not write for the stage, and was therefore less tempted to trespass in the direction of crude expression. His most important works are in the line of oratorio, and can hardly have been intended (as the earliest oratorios were) to have been represented with scenery and action. In these oratorios he shows a decided revival of the sense for choral effect; but at the same time it is noteworthy that the effect produced by his choral writing is very different from the old style. The sense for harmonic design is conspicuously perceptible, and it is obvious that he tries to apply his skill in part writing to the ends of expression. The choruses are often constructed on bold and simple series of chords, and the figures written for the voices strongly resemble passages which are familiar in Handel's choruses—both florid and plain. In his solo music Carissimi is much more refined and artistic than Monteverde; and though he falls behind him in strength of emotional character, he reaches at times a very high degree of pathos and tenderness, and has a good hold on many varieties of human feeling. The greater part of his solo music is recitative, but it is of a more regular and definite type than that of his predecessors, and often approaches to clear melodic outlines; while there are plenty of examples of solo music in which the reiteration of a characteristic phrase in contrasting and corresponding portions of the scale gives the effect of completeness of design. Thus the art of choral music sprang into new life through the impulse to express dramatic feeling in terms of harmonic design as well as of counterpoint, while solo music gained definition through the same impulse to make it at once expressive and intelligible in form.

But instrumental music still hung fire. For that Carissimi seemed to have but little instinct. Possibly he concentrated so much of his artistic impulse on choral music that his mind was distracted from giving attention to the possibilities of purely instrumental effect. By comparison with his skill in vocal effect his instrumental experiments seem too often very crude and tame, and even inferior to Monteverde's in point. But it may be judged that the feeling for instrumental effect was developing among musicians; for Cesti and Stradella (who were younger contemporaries of Carissimi) both show a very considerable skill for that time in writing string accompaniments to their solos and choruses, using the kind of figures which are familiar to the world in Handel's works. Both these composers, moreover, show a very great advance in feeling for design in vocal melody. Cesti's little arias and melodies from cantatas and operas are often as completely modelled and as definite, both in contours and periods, as the best of Handel's. They are not developed to the extent of similar works of the later age : but as far as they go they show a very keen instinct for balancing phrases, distributing cadences, dovetailing passages, presenting musical figures in various aspects, and contriving good stretches of thoroughly vocal melody. Stradella's genius was of a different cast from Cesti's, and found its natural expression in a different type of sentiment. He had a very remarkable instinct for choral effect, and even for piling up progressions into a climax; and his solo music, though apparently not so happy in varieties of spontaneous melody as Cesti's, aims equally at definiteness of structure. His work in the line of oratorio is specially significant; as he stands comparatively alone in cultivating all the natural resources of that form of art—on the lines which Handel adopted later—at a time when his fellow-composers were falling in with the inclination of their public for solo singing, and were giving up the grand oppor tunities of choral effect as superfluous. Indeed, the branch of oratorio had to wait for representatives of more strenuous nations for its ultimate development. But in other respects Italy continued as much as ever to be the centre of musical progress. The Thirty Years' War and its attendant miseries crushed all musical energy out of Germany, and the Civil War in England delayed the cultivation of the new methods there, while in France the astute craft of Lulli obtained so exclusive a monopoly of musical performances, that he extinguished her own composers in his lifetime, and left native musical impulse paralysed at his death.

The career of this Italian Lulli illustrates very decisively the manner in which artistic developments follow the lines of least resistance, by the simple process of submitting to be guided by the predilections of the public for whom the works of art are devised. Lulli was transplanted into France and into the service of the Court in early years; and he had ample time and opportunity for discovering what French tastes were, and for applying his versatility to meet copious demands which afforded excellent prospects of profuse remuneration. Lulli was undoubtedly made to perceive very early that French taste ran in the direction of the theatre, and more especially in favour of dancing and spectacular effect in connection with it. He had to provide ballet airs for the King and the Court to dance and masquerade to, and plentiful practice developed in him a very notable skill in knitting these dance tunes into compact and definite forms, and varying their character so as to get the best effect when they were grouped in sets. The necessity for meeting the artificial requirements of these masquerades (which were like the English Court masques) taught him how to plan scenes with due sense of effect. It is even possible that he was put in the way of the scheme he adopted by the French themselves; as Cambert, the native composer whom he extin-

guished, had used the same plan in his operatic works which
Lulli afterwards stereotyped on a larger scale. In the vocal
solo part of his work Lulli had opportunity to study the
latest and most popular models when Monteverde's famous
pupil Cavalli came to Paris to conduct some of his operas
for Court festivals. The Italians had not up to that time
given much attention to ballet music, so Cavalli had not been
called upon to develop his talents in that direction. But to
make his works acceptable to the French public ballet was
indispensable; so young Lulli was called upon to fit out
Cavalli's work with the necessary tunes, and through being
associated with him in this manner he gained the opportunity of studying his methods in respect of recitative, declamation, and treatment of the vocal portions of his works.

Under these circumstances Lulli developed a scheme of
opera which was more mature and complete than any other
of his time. The texture of his work on the whole is
crude and bald, but the definition of the various items which
go to make up his operatic scheme is complete as far as it
goes, and he certainly made up his very astute mind as to
the character which each several portion and feature of his
work required to make it effective.

In the first place, the plan of his overture is thoroughly
distinct, and very happily conceived as an introduction to
what follows. It begins almost invariably with a broad and
massive slow movement, which serves as an excellent foundation, and is followed by a quick energetic movement in a
loosely fugal style, prefiguring the type of Handel's overtures
to operas and oratorios. The play itself usually begins with
an introductory scene, often mythological, which comprises
choruses, dances, and such other features as obviously imply
spectacular display and much grouping of people on the stage,
and lend themselves to a good deal of musical sound and animation. The drama proper is interpreted mainly in accompanied recitative, interspersed with frequent snatches of
ballet and a few definite pieces for solo; and most of the
acts end with choruses and massing of crowds on the stage
to give weight and impressiveness to the final climax.

Lulli shows excellent sense of relief and proportion in the general planning and laying out of the musical elements in the scenes, and in regulating the relations of the respective acts and scenes to one another; and he is conspicuously successful for his time in shaking himself free from the ecclesiastical associations of the modes, and adopting a thoroughly secular manner. Where modern methods were wanting or undeveloped, as in his overtures, he had to fall back on the methods of the old choral art and write in fugal or contrapuntal style; but it is clear that he was not very solidly grounded in the traditional "science" of music, and was therefore all the more free to work out his scheme in the harmonic style and with more of the spirit of modern tonality. His instinct for orderliness and system in the laying out of his musical material was in advance of his age; but as the realisation of principles of design was still very backward, he had to use such means of definition as came in his way. He was among the first to make a notable use of what is called the aria form, which consists of three well-defined sections, the first and last corresponding in key and musical material, and the central one supplying contrasts in both these respects. It is essentially the simplest form in music, and might well be called primary form, but in connection with opera it has gained the title of aria-form through its much too frequent and much too obvious use. The conventions of opera were not sufficiently stereotyped in his time for Lulli to use it as persistently as his successors did, and he fortunately experimented in other forms which are more interesting and more elastic. One, of which he makes frequent and very ingenious use, is the time-honoured device of the ground bass. This is a procedure which aims at unifying a whole movement or passage by repeating the same formula of notes in the bass over and over again. It is attractive to a composer of any real capacity; for the developing of contrast, diversity of sentiment, and variety of harmony and melody upon the same framework requires a good deal of musical aptitude. The reason why Lulli and other composers of his time, such as Stradella and Purcell, made such frequent use of it was that the principles of real harmonic form of the modern order—based upon classification of harmonies—were still unsettled, and they had to adopt principles of design which, like canon and fugue, belonged to homogeneous types, and did not in themselves imply an inherent principle of contrast. But the fact that Lulli used it, and other principles of like nature, shows how decisively the human mind was waking up to the need of clear design and coherence in art, which the early experimenters in opera and cantata had regarded as superfluous.

Lulli's type of opera was an immense advance upon the first experiments in plan, in definiteness of expression and rhythm, and in variety of subdivision into component ballet movements, choruses, instrumental interludes, arias, recitatives, and so forth; and though the plan of the drama was very artificial, and was mechanically subservient to stage effect, the character of the music followed the character of the story from moment to moment very successfully, and there is singularly little of superfluous ornament or of passages introduced for the purpose of pure executive display. Indeed the dignity and expressiveness of most of the declamatory portions of these works are creditable alike to Lulli and to his audiences. The operas are mainly defective in the very limited sense of instrumental effect which they imply; in the monotony of the full accompaniments, the absence of artistic refinement and skill of workmanship in detail, and in the general stiffness of style. The nucleus of Lulli's band was a set of strings; probably violins at the top and a group of viols for lower and inner parts, accompanied by a harpsichord, which was played from figured bass. These instruments are used in a very mechanical manner to supply dull harmonies, without attempt at figuration or any process to lighten or enliven the bass and filling in. The strings are supplemented occasionally by trumpets, flutes, hautboys, and other familiar wind instruments to increase the mass of sound, and to supply variety of colour on special occasions. But the obviousness of these occasions shows that musicians had but little craving or taste for variety of colour as yet. The hautboys serve to give local colour to rustic scenes, and the

trumpets and drums are called in to illustrate martial ones,
and so forth. But less obvious occasions call for no distinctive
use of instrumental colour, and there is no delicate adjustment
either of mass of sound or special tone for artistic ends. The
whole group of strings plays constantly together in a monotonous and mechanical manner—extremely homogeneous—
in all movements which are "accompanied;" and recitatives
and solo movements have only bass with figures, from which
the accompanist at the harpsichord supplied the details. It
is especially this weakness and ineffectiveness in instrumental
matters which would make even the best of Lulli's operas
unendurable to a modern audience. He was also necessarily
backward in feeling for the actual effects of modulation and
for its value as an element of form, for the principles of
modern tonality were still undeveloped ; but in many respects
his work is very noteworthy, and not only indicated principles
which great composers afterwards adopted as the bases of
further developments, but established a form of art which has
served as the groundwork for the later development of the
French grand opera; while his theatrical instinct gave an
impetus to the order of essentially histrionic music, and established a type which has survived and sometimes even flashed
into brilliant conspicuousness in modern times.

Almost completely outside the direct course of musical
evolution stands the unique and highly individual genius of
Purcell. The sources of his artistic generalisations can be
traced, as is inevitable even with the most pre-eminently
"inspired" of composers; but isolation was entailed by the
peculiarly characteristic line he adopted, and the fact that
almost all the genuine vitality dropped straight out of English
art directly he died ; while none of his remarkably English
achievements penetrated so far afield as to have any sort of influence upon the course of musical progress on the Continent
Purcell was imbued with the solid traditions of the music of
the English Church composers; but he was equally in touch
with the methods of the most advanced composers of the new
style, especially in its French phase as illustrated by Lulli.
He was also saturated with the characteristic English tunes

of his day, and possessed an instinct for the true relation
between the accents of the language and the accents of musical
melody and declamatory recitative, which has never been surpassed by any composer of the same nationality. Applying
the views of art which were in the air in a typically English
way, he produced characteristic effects of harmony in both
choral and instrumental music, which were without parallel
till J. S. Bach began to enlarge the musical horizon in that
respect. In his solo music, he endeavoured to follow the
meaning of the words in declamatory passages with the
utmost closeness; resorting with almost too much frequency to
obvious realistic devices. But the elaborate scenes and grandly
expanded movements for solo voices in his opera and theatre
music are so full of variety and force as to be still almost un-
surpassed in their particular line. The airs and songs which
he introduced into the same works have a specially tuneful
ring, which is much more pointed and individual than anything to be found in similar productions by his contemporaries
on the Continent. The tunes of the foremost Italian Opera
composers of his time have a family likeness about them which
is rather conventional and monotonous, charming as some of
the tunes are; but Purcell's songs are like so many strongly
diverse forms cut in clear crystal, each ringing with individuality. In much of his instrumental music, such as the
dance tunes in his theatre music, he shows much greater
skill and point and lightness of hand than Lulli, and a much
nearer approach to genuine instrumental style than almost
any composer of his time in any form of instrumental music
which was then cultivated. But England lay far from the
centres of musical activity, and the general course of musical
evolution went on in Europe with hardly any reference whatever to his remarkable artistic achievements.

It is important to realise how early national predispositions
show themselves in music. They are often more decisively
apparent in an early and immature state of art than at later
periods; because the special success and prominence of any
one nation in things artistic causes other nations which are
more slow to develop to imitate their devices and methods in

the intermediate state of art, and thus to belie their own true
tastes for a time, till they have attained sufficient skill to
utter things consistent with their own natures, and shake off
the alien manner. As early as the seventeenth century both
Germany and England showed the tendencies which are
evidently engrained in their musical dispositions, and which
have been carried by the Germans to very extreme lengths.
The real bent of both nations is the same. In respect of
external beauty they are neither of them so keen in appreciation, or so apt in creative faculty, as Italians, and during
the period in which beauty was the principal aim of art they
had to follow the lead of the more precocious nation. But
though the resources of art were not adequate to the ends
of characteristic expression, the natural instinct of the
northern nations in that direction is shown in a great
number of instances. It appears mainly in two aspects. One
is the use of curious daring roughnesses and harshnesses in
chords and progressions, and the other the use of simple
realistic devices to identify the music with the spirit of the
words. Thus Heinrich Schütz in his choral works frequently
contrived strange chords for the purpose of immediate expression. In his setting of the first Psalm the words, "in the
counsel of the ungodly," are expressed as follows:—

The late English phase of the madrigal period affords instructive illustrations of racial tendencies, for composers aimed
at characteristic expression of the words far oftener than the
great Italian masters had done; and they often showed a
tendency towards the realistic expression which Purcell carried
to such an excess. Purcell was indeed the greatest musical
genius of his age, but his lines were cast in most unfortunate
places; for the standards and models for the new style, and
the examples of what could and what could not be done,

ere so deficient that his judgment went not infrequently
stray; and in trying to carry out his ideals according to the
rinciples of the "new music," he sometimes achieves a
marvellous stroke of real genius, but occasionally also falls
into the depths of bathos and childishness. The experiments
hich he made in expression, under the same impulse as
chütz in church choral music, are often quite astounding
a crudeness, and almost impossible to sing; while in secular
olo music (where he is generally successful) he frequently
dopts realistic devices of a quaintly innocent kind, for lack of
esources to utter otherwise his expressive intentions :—

that pants . . . . for breath

Or again

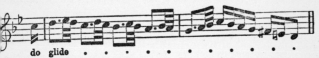

do glide . . . .

Precisely in the same spirit Schütz describes the angel
escending from heaven at the resurrection as follows :—

Der En - gel des Her-ren steig vom Him - mel her - ab

And when he rolls away the stone from the sepulchre he does
t in this wise—

Und wäl - - - - - - - zet den Stein

In Italy, after Cavalli's time, the tastes of the nation soon
influenced the course of operatic development, and impelled it

into a different path from that taken by French and Englis
opera. The tendency which is most apparent at this time is th
outcome of the growing feeling for simplicity and clearness o
form, and distinctness and amenity of melody. The Italiar
gravitated away from strong direct dramatic expression, an
indeed from immediate expression of any kind, and endea
voured merely to illustrate situations as they presented then
selves by the general sentiment of an entire movement or a
entire passage of melody; thus breaking away altogether fro
the path which Monteverde had chosen, and leaving it for othe
nations to follow up to important results. The mission of th
Italians at this time was undoubtedly to lay the foundations o
modern harmonic art, and to establish those primary relation
of harmonies which are the basis of the modern principles o
musical design. A certain native easy-going indolence seem
to have directed them into the road they chose, while th
development of melody of the operatic type (which in itse
is equivalent to linear design) sprang from the gift and i
stinct of the nation for singing. As the century progresse
composers became more skilful in the management of thei
instrumental accompaniments, and began to see more clearl
how to lay out the plan of their operas as wholes, organisin
the acts into well-defined portions, consisting of instrumenta
preludes (called either overtures or sinfonias), interlude
recitatives, airs, and even fairly developed choruses. Th
most important results obtained in these respects are summe
up in the works of Alessandro Scarlatti, who became the mos
prominent composer of his time in secular vocal music an
church music, and no mean master of instrumental music o
the kind which was practised in those days. But the mos
notable part of his contribution to the progress of his art i
in the department of opera; and by a singular fatality hi
method of procedure, though excellent in itself, had a mos
injurious outcome. For his cultivation of the form of th
aria caused him, though a man of real genius and of hig
artistic responsibility of character, to do more than an
one to establish that prominence of the "prima donna" i
opera which has in after times been one of its most fata

impediments. He, of course, had no idea of the evils to
which his practice would lead. The operatic form was still
young, and its field was not yet sufficiently explored to make
it clear in what directions danger lay; and Scarlatti was led,
mainly by his instinct for musical design, to ignore obvious
inconsistency in the dramatic development of the plays which
he set, in order to obtain a complete musical result which
satisfied his own particular instinct and the tastes of his
Italian audiences; and he thereby opened a door of which
vanity and levity were not slow to take advantage.

The history of opera from first to last has been a constant
struggle between the musical and the dramatic elements;
which has resulted in an alternate swaying to and fro, in
course of which at one time the musical material was formalised and made artistically complete at the expense of dramatic
truth, and at another the music was made subservient to the
development of the play. Now that the methods and material
of art have developed to such a marvellous degree of richness
and variety, it is easy to see that nothing short of the utmost
profusion of artistic resources can provide for the adequate adjustment of the requirements of both the literary and musical
elements in such a combination. In the early days it was
inevitable that one of the two should give way, and owing to
the peculiarities of the Italian disposition, it was not on the
musical side that the concessions were made. Scarlatti aimed
at making the units of his operatic scheme musically complete,
and he succeeded so far that his independent solo movements,
called arias, are often beautiful works of art. But the drama,
under the conditions which he established, became merely the
excuse for stringing a number of solo pieces together, and for
distributing them so as to illustrate contrasting moods and
types of sentiment. The story of the drama may be dimly
felt in the background in such works, but it would be the last
thing about which the amateur of Italian opera would have
concerned himself much in those days. Apparently even the
spectacular effect was more considered, because it was less
likely to interfere with the composer's unaccommodating attitude. It soon followed that the interests of the individual

singers became the most powerful influence in regulating th
scheme, and the type of art became thoroughly vicious an
one-sided. The public concentrated so much attention on th
soloists that opera became a mere entertainment in whic
certain vocalists sang, as at an ordinary concert, a series (
arias which were carefully adapted to show off their particula
gifts. There was a great deal of management required, an
the skill of the composer was taxed to devise various types (
passages suitable to the several performers. He had to tak
his soloists with their special gifts as so many settled quantities
and work out a scheme which admitted of their appearing i
a certain order, as regulated by their popularity, money worth
or personal vanity; and out of these quantities, whose orde
was thus mainly prearranged for him, he had to obtain a
effective distribution of types of sentiment and style. It wa
like making patterns with counters of different shapes; an
though the process was a mechanical one, it was a field fo
the expenditure of a good deal of ingenuity, and one no
unprofitable to the musical art, because it necessitated th
development of so many varieties of melodic figure and voca
phrase.

Scarlatti fell in with the necessities of the situation so com
pletely that he poured out opera after opera in which all th
solo pieces were in the same form, and that the simplest con
ceivable. The principle of statement, contrast, and restate
ment so completely answered his requirements that he di
not even take the trouble to write out the restatement; bu
after writing out in full his first section, and the section which
established the principle of contrast, he directed the first
section to be repeated to make the aria complete, by the
simple words "da capo." These arias were interspersed with
passages of recitative, which, from the musical side of the
question, served as breathing spaces between one aria and
another, and prevented their jostling one another; while on
the dramatic side they served to carry on the plainer parts of
the dialogue. It is noteworthy that both his recitative and
his instrumental ritornels are less characteristic than Monteverde's had been. Being a practical man, he realised that the

public did not care much about them, and he did not care to
expend effort where it was almost sure to be wasted. All the
Italian composers soon gave up attempting to put any expression into their recitatives, and made them as near as possible
mere formalised declamation—sometimes not even declamation, but formalised talk. Moreover, the progressions of the
accompanying chords became as aimless and empty as the progressions of the voice, so that the effect depended solely upon
the skill of the singer in delivery; and this retrograde tendency produced as its natural result one of the most detestable conventions in all the range of art; which has helped to
kill works which contain many grand and beautiful features,
because the amount of senseless rigmarole with which they are
mated is positively unendurable.

Scarlatti exerted himself occasionally in writing ensemble
movements, but the only department in which he made as
important a mark as in his arias was in his overtures. The
progress made in instrumental performance, and the attention
which music for violins was beginning to attract, gave him
the opportunity to improve the status of certain instrumental
portions of his work. Some of his overtures are bright,
definite, and genuinely instrumental in style. He generally
wrote them in three or four short movements, distributed in
the order which is familiar in modern symphonies. When he
used three movements, the first was a solid allegro, corresponding to the first movement of the average modern
sonata; the second was a short slow movement aiming at
expression; and the third a lively allegro; and this scheme
came to be universally adopted even till the time of Mozart,
who wrote his early opera overtures in this form. When four
movements were written the scheme was practically the same,
as the first was merely a slow introduction. These little
symphonies were generally scored, with a certain amount of
skill and elasticity, for a group of stringed instruments, with
the occasional addition of a few wind instruments, such as
trumpets. As the principles of harmonic form were still
undetermined, the style was necessarily rather contrapuntal;
but the feeling for tonality is always conspicuously present

in the general outline of the movements. There is nothing
in them of instrumentation of the modern kind, and the
movements are short and compact; but the nucleus, such
as it was, served as the foundation upon which the scheme
of modern symphony was based. In course of time these
opera overtures (which often went by the name of "symphonies") were played apart from the operas to which
they belonged, and then similar works were written without
operas to follow them; and as the feeling for instrumentation
and the understanding of principles of development and of
harmonic design improved, the scheme was widened and enriched and diversified till it appeared in its utmost perfection
in the great works of Beethoven.

In the pure instrumental line the works of the early Italian
violinists form a very important historical landmark. The
development of the art of violin-making to the unsurpassable
perfection attained by the great Italian violin-makers, such
as the Amatis, Guarnerius, Stradivari, and Bergonzi, naturally
coincided with a remarkable development of the technique of
violin-playing. The crude experiments of earlier generations
in dance movements, fantasias, variations, and movements
copied from types of choral music, were superseded by a
much more mature and artistic class of work, in which the
capabilities of the violin for expression and effect were
happily brought into play. The art gained immensely for
a time through composers being also performers, for they
understood better than any one what forms of figure and
melody were most easily made effective. They made a good
many experiments in diverse forms, and ultimately settled
down to the acceptance of certain definite groups of movements whose order and arrangement approved themselves to
their instincts. The scheme is in the main always the same,
consisting of dignified animation to begin with, expressive
slow cantabile for the centre, and light gaiety to end with.
And it may be noted in passing that this is also in conformity
with that universal principle of design which it seems to
be the aim of all music to achieve; and almost all modern
works in which several movements are grouped together are

mainly variations of it, or outcomes of the essential artistic necessity of contrast and restatement. The names the violin composers gave to their works were various. A Sonata da Camera was mainly a group of dance movements, essentially secular in style; a Sonata da Chiesa was a group of abstract movements in more serious style, generally comprising a fugue or some other contrapuntal movement, derived ultimately from the old choral music. Concertos were variable in their constituents, and were written for more instruments. The modern sonata was an outcome of all three, and of the general development of instrumental expression and technique, which also went on under the names of Suites, Lessons, Ordres, Partitas, and many other titles. Corelli's works stand at the head of all these types, and indeed of all modern instrumental music, for hardly anything written before his time appeals to the modern hearer as being sufficiently mature to be tolerable; and though in point of technique his range was rather limited, he managed to produce works which in their way are complete, well-balanced, and perfectly adapted to the requirements of instrumental performance. The appearance of crude helplessness and uncertainty which characterises the works of earlier composers is no longer perceptible, and his compositions rest securely upon their own basis. This was indeed an extremely important step to have achieved, and can hardly be overrated as indicating an epoch in art. All music whatever which was of any dimensions, except rambling fantasias, organ toccatas, and contrapuntal fugues, had hitherto been dependent on words for its full intelligibility. Real artistic development, independent of such connection, had not been possible till men changed their point of view and developed their feeling for tonality and for the classification of harmony.

Corelli's methods are ostensibly contrapuntal, but it is noteworthy that his is not the old kind of counterpoint, but rather an artistic treatment of part-writing, which is assimilated into chords whose progressions are adapted to the principles of modern tonality. He uses sequences for the purposes of form, and modulations for purposes of contrast and balance,

11

and cadences to define periods and sections, and other characteristic devices of modern art; and though the traces of the old church modes are occasionally apparent, they are felt to be getting more and more slight. There is more of art than of human feeling in his work, as is inevitable at such a stage of development; but his art as far as it goes is very good, and the style of expression refined and pleasant.

There is no need to overrate the absolute value of Corelli's works as music to establish their historic importance. The fact that they are the earliest examples of pure instrumental music which have maintained any hold upon lovers of the art implies that men's instincts do not endorse the methods upon which earlier works were constructed. His works therefore mark the point where imperfect attempts are at last replaced by achievement.

Corelli's contemporary, Vivaldi, who was a more brilliant executant than Corelli himself, had even keener sense for harmonic principles; and though his work has not the substance, nor the uniform interest, nor the smoothness of part-writing, nor, finally, the permanent popularity of Corelli's work, it was extremely valuable at the moment for supplying various types of instrumental passages and for helping to establish the feeling for harmonic design. In his concertos and sonatas the harmonic plan is clear even to obviousness, and there is much less of contrapuntal and free inner development than in Corelli's works; but they are more characteristically fitted out with typical figures of harmonic accompaniment, brilliant *fiorituri*, and passages which show a high instinct for instrumental effect. From Corelli and Vivaldi sprang that wonderful school of Italian violinists and composers who did more than any others to give the modern harmonic system of design a solid foundation, and to establish those principles of development which have been refined and elaborated by many generations of instrumental composers up to the present time.

Among other lines of progress later events made the development of organ music of peculiar importance. As has before been pointed out, organ music obtained an independent status sooner than any other branch of instrumental music, probably because organists were afforded such frequent opportunities of experiment in solo-playing in connection with the services of the Church. Many of the kinds of work in which they experimented led to nothing particular, but their imitation of choral works led to the development of fugue, which is one of the most important and elastic of all forms of art. The immediate source of the method of its construction was the manner in which the voices in choral movements entered one after another singing the same initial phrase at the different pitches which best suited their calibre—the tenor taking it a fourth or fifth above the bass, and the alto a fourth or fifth above the tenor, and the treble at the same distance above the alto, or *vice versâ*. In the old choral music the initial phrases were usually rather indefinite, and but rarely reappeared in the course of the movement. But when the same process was adopted for instrumental music without words, composers soon felt the advantage of making the initial phrase characteristically definite, and common-sense taught them the advantage of unifying the movement throughout by making the initial phrase, as it were, the text of the whole discourse. Then again common-sense equally taught them that mere repetition of the initial phrases in the same order and at the same pitch was wearisome; and they soon found the further advantage of associating the principal phrase or subject with contrasting subordinate phrases, and of making the order and pitch of subsequent reiterations of the initial phrase afford contrast by varying from the first order of statement. Then as their feeling for tonality grew stronger, they realised the advantage of making the course of the movement modulate into new keys, and of presenting the initial phrases or subjects, and the subordinate figures or counter-subjects, in relation to new tonics. Thus the general aspect of the fugue came to resemble some of the simpler forms of harmonic music, by beginning in one key, passing to extraneous keys by way of contrast, and ending by bringing the course of the progressions round to the original key, and by recapitulating the initial phrases or subjects prominently to round the whole movement into completeness.

The fugal form had an advantage over pure harmonic forms through its enabling composers to dispense with the cadences which defined the various sections, but broke up the continuity of the whole. But it was a disadvantage, on the other hand, that the methods of using the subjects were so inviting to musicians of an ingenious turn of mind that the form became vitiated by sheer excess of artifice, in the manipulation of subjects and counter-subjects, and interweaving of strands into all manner of curious combinations; while the possibilities of pure contrapuntal device were discussed up and down to such an extent, that most composers who used the form forgot that all this artifice was superfluous, except as a means to express something over and beyond their own ingenuity. In the end the elastic capabilities which it possessed for variety of expression, and for effective general development based upon the use of well-marked subjects, attracted many of the greatest composers; and not only served for toccatas, movements of sonatas, and even dance suites, but was readapted for choral purposes, and became one of the most effective forms for choruses possible, and far better adapted for genuine choral effect than the so-called sonata forms. It was not indeed till the resources of music were developed all round to the very highest pitch that any better form for choral music was found; and then finally the old pure type of fugue gave way to forms of art which are more elastic still. The early organists, from the two Gabrielis, Swelinck, and Frescobaldi onwards, served the art nobly in the fugal and kindred forms; devising types of figure and traits of style which were well suited to the instrument, and contriving many schemes of design, which were worked out in course of time, till they became noble types of complete and expressive art.

Music for the harpsichord and clavichord rather lagged behind for a time, as, for domestic purposes, neither was so attractive as the violin; and in the early part of the century they still had a formidable rival in the lute. Works for these instruments began to be produced very early in the century, but of these all except rare and exceptional specimens by Orlando Gibbons and Byrd are chiefly interesting on account of their containing the crude foreshadowings of later developments of technique. The first nation to make successful mark in this line were the French, especially the famous Couperin, who had a very lively sense of the style which was best suited to the instrument, and developed a happy knack of writing tuneful and compact little movements which he grouped, with great feeling for contrast and consistency, into sets called Ordres, which are much the same as the groups more familiarly known in later times as Suites. His prototypes were probably the sets of little movements for lutes, such as those of Denis Gaultier. He was evidently a man of considerable musical gifts of a high order, but he sacrificed more dignified lines of art in concession to the French popular taste for ballet tunes. He was one of the first to write tuneful little movements of the kind which became so popular in later days; and it is noteworthy that he, as well as the earlier lutenists, and his later compatriot, Rameau, foreshadowed the taste of the French for illustrating definite ideas by music, and for making what may be called picture-tunes, in preference to developing the less obvious implications of pure self-dependent music, in lines of concentrated and comprehensive art.

The progress of this somewhat immature period shows the inevitable tendency of all things from homogeneity towards diversity and definiteness. In its widest aspects art is seen to branch out into a variety of different forms. The difference in style and matter between choral movements and instrumental works begins to be more definite and decisive. The types of opera, oratorio, cantata, and of the various kinds of church music become more distinct, and are even subdivided into different subordinate types, as was the case with Italian and French opera. Instrumental music, from being mainly either imitations of choral music, or vague toccatas and fantasias, or short dance tunes, established a complete independent existence, and began to branch out into the various forms which have since become representative as sonatas and symphonies. The treatment of instruments began to be individually characteristic, and the style of expression and of figure appropriate to different kinds began to be discerned. In the works themselves the articulation of the component parts attains more and more definiteness and clearness of modelling, and methods were found out for making each movement more logical and coherent. Among the most important achievements of the time is the final breaking away from the influences of the old modes, which made the design and texture of the older works so indefinite. The earliest phases of the developing feeling for tonality of the modern kind, which implies a classification of harmonies and an adoption of systematic harmonic progressions, already gave the new works an appearance of orderliness and stability which marks the inauguration of a new era in art; while the use of definite principles of rhythm enabled musicians to make their ideas infinitely more characteristic and vivid, and caused the periods and sections of the movements to gain a sense of completeness and clearness which was impossible under the old order of things.

CHAPTER VII

COMBINATION OF OLD METHODS AND NEW PRINCIPLES

THE development of principles of design in music must inevitably wait upon the development of technique. Very little can be done with limited means of performance; and the adequacy of such means is dependent on the previous perfecting of various instruments, and on the discovery of the particular types of expression and figure which are adapted to them. One of the reasons why instrumental music lagged behind other branches of art was, that men were slow in finding out the arts of execution; and even when the stock of figures and phrases which were adapted to various instruments had become plentiful, it took composers some time to assimilate them sufficiently, so as to have them always ready at hand to apply to the purposes of art when composing. It was this which gave performers so great an advantage in the early days, and accounts for the fact that all the great composers of organ music in early days were famous organists, and all the successful composers of violin music were brilliant public performers. In modern times it is necessarily rather the reverse, and some of the greatest of recent composers have been famous for anything rather than for their powers as executants.

But though form is so dependent upon technique of every kind, the development of both went on in early days more or less simultaneously. The management and disposition of the materials and subjects used by the composer is all part of the business of designing, and while the violinists and organists were devising their types of figure they learnt to fit them together in schemes which had the necessary general good effect as well as the special telling effect in detail; and all branches of art contributed something of their share towards the sum total of advance in art generally. But the various methods and resources of art were developed in connection with the different departments in which they were most immediately required. Composers found out what voices could do and what they could not do in writing their church music, oratorios, cantatas, and so forth. They studied the forms of expression and melody best suited for solo voices in operas and cantatas, and they studied the effects and forms of figure which were best adapted to various instruments, and found out by slow degrees the effects which could be produced by various instruments in combination when they were trying to write sonatas, suites, concertos, and overtures. Each genuine composer then as now added his mite to the resources of growing art when he managed to do something new. And in those days, when the field had not been so over-cultivated, it was easier to turn up new ground, and to add something both effectual and wholesome to the sum of artistic products than it became in later times.

It must not be overlooked that all branches of art became more and more interdependent as musical development went on. Opera and oratorio required instrumental music as well as solo and choral music, and instrumental music had to borrow types of melody and expression as well as types of design from choral and solo music. Hence it followed that each department of music could only go ahead of others in those respects which were absolutely within its own range; and there were several occasions in the history of art when a special branch came to a standstill for a time because the development of other branches upon which it had to draw for further advance was in a backward state. This was mainly the reason why opera, which was cultivated with such special activity in the seventeenth century, came practically to a standstill for some time at the point illustrated by Scarlatti and Lulli. The actual internal organisation of the component parts, such as the arias, improved immensely in style and richness and scope as men gained better hold of principles of melodic development; and

Handel and Hasse and Buononcini, and many others, improved in that respect on the types of their predecessors. But the general scheme of opera stood much where it was, and the best operas produced in the next fifty years (even those by Handel) are not in the least degree more capable of being endured as wholes by a modern audience than those of Lulli and Scarlatti.

As has before been pointed out, the early representatives of the new style of music had been extremely inefficient in choral writing, because they thought that the methods and learning of the old school were superfluous for their purposes. But in the course of about fifty years musicians found the need of again studying and gathering the fruits of the experience of earlier generations, and something of the old choral style was revived. However, by that time men's minds were thoroughly well set in the direction of modern tonality and harmonic form as distinct from the melodic modes and essentially contrapuntal texture of the earlier art, and the result was that the old contrapuntal methods were adapted to new conditions when they came into use again; and this made them capable of serving for new kinds of expression and effect. The old methods were resumed under the influence of the new feeling for tonality. Composers began anew to write free and characteristic parts for the several voices in choral combinations, but they made the harmonies, which were the sum of the combined counterpoints, move so as to illustrate the principles of harmonic form, and thus gave to the hearer the sense of orderliness and design, as well as the sense of contrapuntal complexity. And it is not too much to say that their attitude soon changed the principle of their work. Where formerly they had simply adapted melody to melody, they now often thought first of the progression of the harmony, and made separate voice-parts run so as to gain points of vantage in the successive chords. In the old state of things counterpoint sometimes appeared, chiefly by accident, in the guise of harmony; in the new style simple harmonic successions were made deliberately to look like good counterpoint.

This was partly the result of the peculiar disposition of the

Italians. They attained to very considerable skill in manipulating voice-parts smoothly and vocally, but they were not particularly ardent after technical artistic interest or characteristic expression. Their sense of beauty shows itself in the orderliness and ease of their harmonic progressions, and in the excellent art with which general variety is obtained. But as usual a certain native indolence and dislike of strenuous concentration made them incline too much towards methods which lessened the demands upon the attention of audiences. They preferred that the design of an enormous number of movements should be exactly the same, and commonplace and obvious as well, rather than that they should have any difficulty in following and understanding what they listened to. The result was favourable to the establishment of formal principles in choral music, but it put a premium on carelessness in the carrying out of detail and in the choice of musical material; and the result was that composers got their effects as cheaply as they could, and too often fell into the habit of writing mere successions of chords without either melody or independent part-writing, trusting to the massive sound of many voices in chorus for their effect. But, granting these drawbacks, it may well be conceded that the Italians were pioneers in this new style of choral writing, as they were in most other things; and both in the direction of harmonic form in choral works and in the new style of counterpoint they did invaluable service to art.

Another new feature of this phase of choral music was its combination with instrumental music. In the old order of things the instruments had sometimes doubled the voices, but very little attempt had been made to use the instrumental forces as independent means of effect. The new mode of combining voices and instruments made a very great difference to the freedom with which the voices could be treated, and to the effect of form and expression which could be obtained. But at the same time it is important to note that the instrumental element was still very much in the background, and did not in any sense divide the honours with the choral effects. The instrumental forces were accessories or vassals, not equals.

Even the most responsible masters were forced by the backwardness of instrumental art to adopt a contrapuntal style for their orchestral works, and to write for their several instruments as if they were so many voice-parts; and when they attempted variety of colour they used it in broad homogeneous expanses, such as long solos for special wind instruments. The sense for variety of colour was undoubtedly dawning, but as yet composers had to produce their impression with very moderate use of it.

The result was a paradoxical vindication of the inevitable continuity of artistic as of all other kinds of human progress. For although the first beginnings of the new movement were prominently secular, and diverged from the traditions of church music, the first really great and permanent achievements in the new style were on the lines of sacred and serious art, because it was in that line alone that composers could gain full advantage from the old traditions. And whereas the early representatives of the new style had cast aside the study of choral methods, it was in their choral aspects that these oratorios were specially complete and mature. But it did not fall to the Italians to bring these new experiments to full fruit.

It was indeed the first time that the Teutonic temper found full expression in the art which now seems most congenial to the race. Through various causes German progress in music had so far been hindered. While the Netherlands, England, Italy, and even France, had each had important groups of composers, Germany had as yet had but few and more or less isolated representatives. But now that social conditions had quieted down, and the spirit of the nation had better opportunity to expand, her composers rose with extraordinary rapidity to the foremost place, and in their hands comparatively neglected forms of art, such as the oratorio and church cantata, reached the highest standard of which they have proved capable. All the German composers undoubtedly learned much of their business from Italian examples; and it is noteworthy that on this occasion, as on many others the composers who were the most popularly successful adopted

altogether Italian principles, merely infusing into their work
the firmer grit and greater power of characterisation which
comes of the stronger and more deliberate race. But by far
the greatest and most important results were obtained where
the Teutonic impulse for characteristic treatment was given
fullest play; and where the resources made available by the
combination of old contrapuntal principles and the principles
of the new kind of art were applied to the end of lofty and
noble expression.

The difference of result which is the outcome of difference
of method and disposition is illustrated to the fullest degree
in the familiar oratorios of Handel on the one hand, and in
Bach's "Passions" and the best of his church cantatas on the
other. The Italian development of oratorio had been stunted
and perverted through the lack of interest which audiences
took in the choral portions of such works; which appears to
have caused composers of about Handel's time to give up
writing choruses of any importance in their oratorios, and to
lay stress mainly upon arias and solo music. The situation
affords a noteworthy instance of the influence of circumstances upon products. For in his first oratorios, which were
written in Italy for Italian audiences, Handel hardly wrote
any choruses at all, and those which he did write are of
the slightest description. But when, some years later, after
plentiful experience of English tastes, he began writing for
London audiences, he at once adopted the familiar scheme,
in which the most prominent and the most artistically important features are the numerous grand choral movements.
But it so happened that the English of that time had lost
touch with their own native traditions of style, and had
become thoroughly Italianised; it therefore naturally followed
that Handel adopted an Italian manner in his choral writing,
as he had done previously in his operatic works. This was
entirely consistent with all the previous part of his career,
for ever since he had left Hamburg and his native country
in his youth, every new line he took up showed invariably the
influence of Italian methods and Italian musical phraseology.
He was so saturated with musical Italianism of all kinds that

actual phrases of Corelli, Alessandro Scarlatti, Stradella, Carissimi, and others constantly make their appearance in his works ; while the texture of his instrumental movements—such as slow introductions and fugues—closely resembles similar movements by Corelli and Scarlatti, and the style of his choral music closely resembles the facile, smooth, and eminently vocal style of the Italian masters, as exemplified in various kinds of church music of the new kind. Where he improved upon their work so immensely was in the use of the resources of artistic technique for the purposes of expression, and in the greater vitality of contrapuntal texture. As has been frequently pointed out, the Italians cared very little for expression in the music itself, though they liked to have it put in by the performers. Intrinsically it was sufficient for them if the music was melodious and vocal in solos, and if the counterpoint in the choruses conveyed a pleasant sense of orderly form in the progressions of the harmonies. Now both English and Teutons have always had a great feeling for direct expression in the music itself; and when in immature times they could not get it in any other way, their composers tried to get it by obvious realistic means. Italians had tried realistic expression now and again, but always in a half-hearted and ineffectual manner; and they always ended by dropping it. But to genuine Teutons and English such intrinsic expression is a necessity, and it is the force of their instinct for it which has enabled the former to carry to their highest perfection all the forms of the art which the Italians initiated, but had not sufficiently high artistic ideals or sufficient persistence of character to bring to maturity.

This it is which makes so great a difference between Handel's choral work and Italian choral work ; and the same is the case with his arias and other solo music. The fact is so familiar that it hardly needs emphasising. He not only gives in his choruses the direct expression of the feelings of human creatures, whose places the singers might be said to take, in exultation, mourning, rage, devotion, or any other phases of human feeling; but he makes most successful use of them for descriptive purposes, and for conveying the impression of tremendous situations and events. This latter feature in his work may have been somewhat owing to his English surroundings, as the German bent is to use music more for the expression of the inward emotion and sentiment than for direct concrete illustration. But this descriptive phase was a part of the development of the artistic material of music which had to be achieved, and as it might not have been done so thoroughly under the influence of any other nation, it is fortunate that Handel did his part of the work under English influences, for the thoroughly Teutonic part of the work was assuredly as perfectly done as is conceivable by J. S. Bach.

Bach also was a close student of Italian art, as he was of the methods of all skilful composers of whatever nation; but nevertheless his circumstances and constant Teutonic surroundings made him take, in his most genuinely characteristic works, a thoroughly Teutonic line. The circumstances of his career were peculiar, as his life was divided definitely into periods in which he specially studied different departments of art. In his earliest days, at the period in man's life when impressions most easily become permanent, he was most particularly occupied with organ music, with organ style, with the technique and methods of all the greatest organists whose performances he could contrive to hear, and the compositions for the organ of various schools which he could find opportunity to study. Fortunately the organists of that day were exceptionally worthy of their instrument. They did not try either to make it gambol, or to mince trivial sentimentalities, but to utter things that had dignity and noble simplicity, and to produce those majestic effects of rolling sound which were peculiarly suitable to the great vaulted buildings which were the natural homes of their art. Bach's musical organisation became well steeped in organ effects, and the phraseology which was most appropriate to the instrument became the natural language for the expression of his musical ideas, and remained so for the rest of his life, though tempered and enlarged by the wide range of his sympathetic studies in every branch of composition. Together with organ music he heard and absorbed the church music of his country; and the peculiar mystic sentiment, full of tender poetical imagery and personal devotion, which was then characteristic of Teutonic Christianity, took firm hold of his disposition.   Unlike Handel he remained all his life in one small part of Germany, always amid thoroughly Teutonic influences; and the result was that when in the latter part of his life he addressed himself more particularly to the composition of great choral works, the Italian influences are but rarely apparent; and all the details, the manner, the methods, and the type of expression are essentially Teutonic.   Great as was his contrapuntal skill, it was in no sense the contrapuntalism of the Italians; for it may be confessed that his voice-parts are by no means smooth, facile, or even vocal.   The origin of the style of his vocal part-writing was the kind of counterpoint that he had learnt from studying and hearing organ works when young.   He had a marvellous instinct for choral effect of many kinds, in no way inferior to Handel's, though so extraordinarily different in texture.   But where Handel aimed at the beauty of melodic form, Bach strove for characteristic expression.   Where Handel used orderly progressions of simple harmony, Bach aimed at contriving elaborate interweavings of subtly disposed parts to give the effect of the subtlest shades of human feeling.   Where Handel used the most realistic means to convey the hopping of frogs, or the rattling of hailstones, or the rolling of the sea, or the buzzing of flies, Bach attempted to express the inner feelings of human creatures under the impress of any exciting causes.   It must not be supposed that either composer was restricted to these particular lines, for Handel at times succeeded better than most composers in uttering the inner spirit of man's emotions, and Bach at times adopted realistic methods; but the larger portion of Handel's choral work tends in the one direction, and of Bach's in the other.   Nowhere is the difference of their attitude better illustrated than in their use of recitative.   Handel, accepting the conventions of Italian art without hesitation, ruined an enormous number of his works by the emptiest, baldest, and most mechanical formulas; while Bach, dissatisfied with anything which had not significance, endeavoured by the contours and intervals of his solo part, by the progressions and harmonies of his accompaniment, and by every means that was available, to intensify from moment to moment the expression of the words. Bach's recitative was consequently extremely difficult to sing, but the intrinsic expression of the music is as strong as it can be made in such a form. Handel's recitative may be easy to sing, but, with rare and noble exceptions, it means next to nothing, and the formulas often suit one set of words as well as another.

Bach's feeling for melody was not so happy as Handel's. His Teutonic attitude is shown again in the fact that he sought for richer, deeper, and more copious expression than can be achieved by conventional treatment of regular melody with simple secondary accompaniment. Solo music indeed was not the most congenial form for the expression of his ideas, and faithfully as he tried to achieve a perfect scheme and principle of procedure, he never made sure of a satisfactory result. He aimed at something which is a little beyond the capacity of a formal solo movement to express, and the soloist is often sacrificed to the exigencies of artistic development. He could not rest satisfied with the apparent superficiality of Italian treatment of melody, and but rarely even attempted to produce a suave or ear-catching tune. When the mood he wished to illustrate lent itself to melodic expression, he produced exquisitely touching or innocently joyous fragments of tune, which lay hold of the mind all the more firmly because of their characteristic sincerity, and the absence of any pretence of making the thing pleasant and agreeable at the expense of the truth of the sentiment. The only respect in which he fell conspicuously under the spell of convention was in following, without sufficient consideration, the principle of repetition indicated by the too familiar direction "da capo." It is as though, when he had carried out his artistic scheme with all the technical richness and care in detail he could master up to a certain point, he felt he had done what art required of him, and wrote "da capo al fine," without consideration of the length to which it would carry his

movement; and thereby impaired some of his happiest in-
spirations through want of the practical observation that even
a good audience is human. And it may be confessed that
though his artistic insight, power of self-criticism, and variety
of inventiveness were almost the highest ever possessed by
man, his fervently idealistic nature was just a little deficient
in practical common sense. He worked so much by himself,
and had so little opportunity of testing his greatest works by
the light of experience in performance, that he sometimes overlooked their relation to other human beings, and wrote for
the sheer pleasure of mastering a problem or developing to its
full circuit a scheme which he had in his mind.

In instrumentation both of these giants among composers
were equally backward, though their aims and methods, and
the results they achieved, were very different. They were
necessarily restricted to the standard of their time at the
beginning of their careers, and Handel did as little as it is
possible for a great master to do in adding to the resources
of the instrumental side of music. He tried interesting
experiments, occasionally, even in his earliest works, but his
mind was not set on making much use of new resources, or on
using colour as an enhancement of expression. His mastery
of choral effect and gift of melody, and power of portrayal by
vocal means, were sufficient for his purposes; and the instruments served chiefly to strengthen and support the voices, and
to play introductory passages to the arias and choruses, and
simple marches and dance tunes, which were written mainly
for stringed instruments in the contrapuntal manner. He
looked to the present, and finished up much as he began.
Bach, on the other hand, looking always forward, gives proofs
of much more purpose in his use of instrumental resources.
He used a great variety of instruments of all kinds, both
wind and strings, though not so much to increase the volume
of tone in the mass as to give special quality and unity
of colour to various movements. The days when composite
colouring and constantly altering shades of various qualities
of tone are an ordinary feature of the art were yet very far
off; and he never seems to have thought of adopting any-

12

thing like such modern methods of variety. But as far as his unique principles go, they are at times singularly effective. He realised the various expressive qualities of the tone and style of hautboys, flutes, solo violins, horns, trumpets, viole da gamba, and many other instruments; and with the view of intensifying the pathos, or the poignancy, or the joyousness, or the sublimity of his words, he found suitable figures for them and wove them with the happiest effect throughout the whole accompaniment of a movement. The device was not new, for it was the first method that composers adopted in trying to make use of variety of orchestral colour; but Bach's use of it for the purposes of expression was new, and was an important step in the direction of effectual use of instrumental resources. To the object of obtaining great sonority from his instrumental forces Bach does not seem to have given much of his mind. Both he and Handel relied so much upon the organ to fill in accompaniments and supply fulness of sound, that it does not seem to have struck either of them as worth while to look for any degree of richness or volume from combinations of orchestral instruments. In loud passages neither of them attempt to dispose the various instruments in such a way as to get the best tone out of them; and when played in modern times, under modern conditions, the wood wind instruments are often totally drowned by the strings. The proportions were very different in those times, but even if the old proportions of wind and strings were restored, many contrapuntal effects in which flutes or hautboys have to take essential parts on equal terms with violins, would be quite ineffective.

Their scheme of oratorio and church music being what it was, the backwardness of instrumental effect was but of small consequence. The means they used for their effects were essentially choral forces and solo voices, and these were amply sufficient for the purposes they had in hand. Instrumental music and the arts of instrumentation have been developed almost entirely under secular conditions. In such works as Handel's and Bach's, which illustrated mainly religious aspects of human feeling and character, the absence of subtle sensuous excitements of colour was possibly rather an advantage than otherwise. Whatever lack of maturity is observable in both is felt, not so much in the lack of instrumental effect, as in the crude recitative of Handel and in the overdoing of contrapuntal complexity in places where it is not essential in Bach. Their works are mature without instrumentation, and even the exquisite skill of Mozart's additional accompaniments to Handel's work cannot disguise the fact that the phraseology of modern instrumentation is out of touch with the style of the older masterpieces.

In considering the aspects of their great sacred choral works it is of importance to note the circumstances which called them into existence. Both composers came to the writing of such works quite at the end of their careers, when their mastery of their art was most complete; and they brought the fruits of their experience in all branches of art to bear upon them. Moreover, the circumstances of their respective careers had great influence upon the quality of the products. Handel had all through been a practical public man, constantly in touch with the public, and constantly watching their likes and dislikes, and catering for his supporters accordingly. He began as a subordinate violin-player in Keiser's Hamburg Opera-House, where his abilities soon caused him to be promoted to the position of accompanist on the harpsichord; which was excellent training for an opera composer, and taught him the ins and outs of that branch of public entertainment. This short preliminary was soon succeeded by brilliant successes as a composer in Italy, and these in turn led to his long and brilliant career as an opera composer in England, which lasted some twenty-six years. Then, finally, the accident of having an opera-house on his hands in Lent, on days when opera performances were not allowed, led to his trying the experiment of setting sacred dramas for performance on the stage of his theatre. These differed from the operas in their more serious and solid character, the absence of action, and the introduction of grand choral movements. But he began this experiment purely as a business manager, and did not attempt to write complete new works, but merely patched together choruses and other numbers out

of earlier works, giving them new words and adding some
new movements to make the whole pass muster, and calling
the patchwork by a scriptural name. The success of the
experiment encouraged him to proceed to compose or patch
together more works of the same kind; and a strange illustration of his attitude towards oratorio at first is afforded by
the fact that the grandest and most impressive of all his
works is actually a piece of patchwork; for " Israel in Egypt "
contains a most surprising number of old movements which
may have been early compositions of his own, and also a very
large quantity of musical material which was unquestionably
by other composers. He transformed some of the borrowed
materials into extremely effective choruses, and wrote other
new choruses which are among his finest achievements; and
the greatness of his own work has carried the second-rate
work along with it. But his procedure shows that he did not
treat the form of oratorio at first as a responsible conscientious
composer might be expected to do, but as a man who had to
supply the public with a fine entertainment. It cannot indeed
be doubted that though he was capable of rising to very
great achievements, and was capable of noble and sincere
expression, he thought a great deal of the tastes of a big
public, and not very intently of refinements of art, or originality of matter or of plan. His disposition was not so much
to work up to any exalted ideals of his own, as to feel sympathetically what was the highest standard of taste of the
public for which he was constantly working, and to supply
what that demanded. This must not be taken to mean that
he habitually wrote down to a low standard of public taste.
Composers who persuade themselves to do that generally take
a very low view of their public, and write even worse than
they need. Handel had on the whole very good reason to
think well of his public, notwithstanding their unwillingness
to listen to " Israel in Egypt " without some sugar-plums in
the shape of opera airs to relieve its austere grandeur. They
thoroughly appreciated others of his works, and the reception
accorded to the " Messiah " was sufficient to encourage him to
put all his heart into his later works of the oratorio order.

Thinking so much of the big public may therefore have been no great drawback to him; and some of the thanks for the lofty standard of his achievements are due to the good taste and sense of the people for whom he catered. His position made him practical, and helped him to that definite and wholesomely direct style which was congenial to his English audiences; and though they may be also answerable for a certain amount of commonplace and complacency in his work, they deserve credit for encouraging him in the line of choral work, which resulted in the achievement of those effects of genuine grandeur, simple dignity, and cosmic power which mark his culmination as one of the great eras of art.

The circumstances which led to Bach's great choral works were absolutely different, and account for a great deal of the marked difference in the product. The contrast in the circumstances of the two composers is noticeable from their earliest years. When Handel was absorbing the influences of an opera-house, Bach was listening to the great organists of his time. When Handel was practising Italianisms in every branch of art, Bach was studying mainly the ways and tastes of his own people. Moreover, the relation of a composer to his surroundings is of supreme importance, and Bach's position in relation to "the public" was most peculiar. By comparison with the public nature of Handel's career Bach's life seems like that of a reflective recluse. So far from catering for a public, throughout the greater part of his life he hardly knew what an audience was, and he had next to no opportunities whatever to feel the public pulse. But in any case he could hardly have brought himself to see his art through other people's eyes; for it was his nature to judge solely for himself, and he laboured throughout his life with simplicity and singleness of heart to come up to his own highest ideals in all branches of art, and to satisfy his own critical judgment without a thought of the effect his work would have upon any but an ideal auditor. His principle of study is most happily illustrative of the manner in which all musical progress is made. For he early adopted the practice of studying and copying out the works of composers who excelled in all the different branches of art, and of endeavouring to improve upon their achievements. Sometimes he actually rewrote the works of other composers, and oftentimes he deliberately imitated them both for style and design ; and wherever he recognised an artistic principle of undoubted value and vitality, he as it were absorbed and amalgamated it as part of his own artistic procedure. He ranged far and wide, and studied the methods of Italians, Frenchmen, Netherlanders, and Germans—writers of choral music and of organ music, of violin music and of harpsichord music. And not only that, but he always sedulously criticised himself, and recast, remodelled, and rewrote everything which new experiences or a happier mood made him feel capable of improving. This would have been impossible in the busy public life of Handel, and was not in that composer's line. Bach's was a far more individual and personal position. He wanted to express what he himself personally felt and approved. Handel adapted himself to feel and approve what the public approved.

It naturally followed that Bach's style became far more individual and strongly marked, and that he went far beyond the standard of the musical intelligence of his time ; and the inevitable consequence was that his most ideally great and genuine passages of human expression were merely regarded by his contemporaries as ingenious feats of pedantic ingenuity. A man could not well be more utterly alone or without sympathy than he was. Even his sons and pupils but half understood him. But we do not know that he suffered from it. We can only see plainly that it drove him inwards upon himself, and made him adopt that independent attitude which is capable of producing the very highest results in men who have grit enough to save them from extravagance and incoherence. He wrote because it interested him to write, and with the natural impulse of the perfectly sincere composer to bring out what was in him in the best form that he could give to it; and his musical constitution being the purest and noblest and most full of human feeling and emotion ever possessed by a composer, the art of music is more indebted to him than to any other composer who ever lived, especially for the extension of the arts of expression.

The peculiar services he did in the branch of pure instrumental art must be discussed elsewhere. The services he did to choral art, especially in his Passions, the B minor mass and smaller masses, the great unaccompanied motets and the various cantatas, are equal to Handel's, though on such different lines. The effect of the isolation in which his work was produced was no doubt to make it in some respects experimental, but it ensured the highest development of the art of expression and of the technique which serves to the ends of expression. To the same end also served the Teutonic aspect of his labours. The oratorios of other nations were not part of religious exercises, nor the direct expression of devotional feeling. They had merely been versions of lives of famous scriptural heroes or events, set to music partly in narrative and partly in dramatic form. But the Germans had fastened with peculiar intensity of feeling on the story of the Passion, and set it again and again in a musical form, as though determined to give it the utmost significance that lay in their power. The plan was to break up the story into its most vivid situations and intersperse these with reflective choruses and solos, which helped the mind to dwell intently and lovingly upon each step in the tragedy. It was essentially a devotional function in which every one present took a personal share. Even the audience, apart from the performers, took part in the noble chorales—so characteristic of the Teutonic nature— which were interspersed throughout. Many poets and many composers tried their hands at this curious form of art, Bach himself several times; and the crown was put on the whole series finally by the famous Passion according to St. Matthew, which Bach wrote and rewrote towards the end of his career for performance at Leipzig.

It is not necessary to emphasise further the difference between Bach's treatment of great sacred choral works and Handel's. The oratorios of the latter were nearly all dramatic or epic, and the subjects were treated as nearly as possible histrionically. There are portions of Bach's Passions which treat the situations with great dramatic force, but in the main they are the direct outcome of personal devotion, and in them the mystic emotionalism of the Teutonic nature found its purest expression.   Thus in the works of the two great composers the types of musical utterance which represent epic and narrative treatment on the one hand, and inward immediate feeling on the other, were completely realised on the largest scale that the art of that day allowed. Handel's direct and practical way of enforcing the events and making his story vivid by great musical means has given great pleasure to an immense public, and as it were summed up the labours of his predecessors into a grand and impressive result. Bach, with higher ideals, produced work which was often experimental, and even at times unpractical; but he used the sum of his predecessors' work as his stepping-stone, and did much greater service to his art. He appeals to a much smaller public than Handel, and is totally unacceptable to shallow, worldly, or unpoetical temperaments; but he has given much higher pleasure to those whose mental and emotional organisation is sufficiently high to be in touch with him, and there are but few of the greatest composers of later times who have not felt him to be their most inspiring example.

CHAPTER VIII

THE CLIMAX OF EARLY INSTRUMENTAL MUSIC

ALTHOUGH the principles of design upon which modern self-dependent instrumental music is based had hardly dawned upon the minds of men till the eighteenth century was nearly half spent, the latest instrumental music of the early period, written almost entirely upon the same general principles as choral music, is not only historically important, but has more genuine vitality than a very large proportion of the music which has come into existence since the cultivation of pure harmonic music has so greatly enlarged the resources of composers. The situation is parallel in many respects to the earlier crisis of Palestrina and Marenzio. There is less of the sense of immaturity in their work than in the work of Lulli and Scarlatti of nearly a century later; and there is far less of immaturity in the instrumental works of Bach and Handel and their fellows than in the works of Galuppi or Paradisi, or even in the early works of Haydn. Maturity is a relative term altogether. If a man's ideas are worth expressing, and are capable of being expressed completely within the limits of his resources, his productions may be in a certain sense completely mature at almost any epoch in the progress of artistic development. If Palestrina had introduced discords more freely and treated them with less reserve, and had aimed generally at a stronger type of expression, the balance of his work would have been destroyed; he would have gone beyond the limits which were then inevitable for completely artistic work. Part of his greatness consisted in his feeling exactly where the limitations of his kind of art were, and achieving his aims within the field of which he was complete master. The position of the composers in Bach's time was much the same; and part of his own particular greatness consisted in seeing within what particular range the technical resources of art, which preceding development had placed in his hands, were most fully available.

It is very necessary to keep in mind the fact that different types of artistic procedure representing different epochs frequently overlap. Just as in the arrangements of society a monarchy may be thriving successfully in one country, while its neighbour is trying experiments in democratic institutions; so in art it constantly happens that a new style has broken into vigorous activity before the old style has produced its greatest results. And there is a further parallel in the fact, that as the theories and practices of the republican country may filter into the country where the more conventional form of government still prevails, so the new ideas which are beginning to be realised in other departments of artistic energy often creep into the heart of an old but still active sytem, even before it has come to full maturity. Even the strictest representatives of an ancient and well-developed style try occasional experiments on revolutionary lines. The bounds of the old order were transgressed before Palestrina's time, and many men began to have clear ideas of harmonic form of the sonata order long before John Sebastian Bach put the crown on the old style of instrumental music. Bach himself tried experiments in this line, and did his utmost to master and gauge the value of the new style, by copying, rearranging, rewriting, and imitating the works of prominent representatives of the new school. But it is clear that he was not satisfied with the results, and that the style was not congenial to him. His peculiar gifts would not have found sufficient means for employment on the simple lines of harmonic form as then understood, and the necessity of submitting to uniform distribution of the various parts of his design would have hampered him in the experiments in modulation and harmonisation which are among his greatest glories.

So it came about finally that he attempted but little of a sonata order, but concentrated his powers on works of the old style—the toccatas, canzonas, fantasias, fugues, suites

partitas, and other varieties; and his work in those lines
sums up the fruitful labours of all his predecessors, and provides the most perfect examples of all the older forms. The
essence of the being of the old instrumental forms was the
polyphonic texture in which every part or voice is on equal
terms with every other one. There is no despotic tune with
subservient accompaniment, nor strict conventions as to the
distribution of chords according to their tonalities. The use
of chords as artistic entities had undoubtedly become quite
familiar, but it was not on any principle of their systematic
distribution that works were designed. They were of secondary
importance to polyphonic elaboration of musical figures; by
the interweaving of which, like the strands of a rope, the
works were made coherent and interesting.

Of all the forms of instrumental music which were characteristic of this phase of art, the fugue is the most familiar and
the most perfectly organised. It was the form in which Bach
most delighted, and the one which gave him fullest variety of
scope and opportunity for expression. Its beginnings have
already been sketched. The earliest forms were obvious imitations of choral music adapted for the organ or for sets of viols.
The type of choral work which was imitated was extremely
indefinite as far as the musical ideas were concerned, and the
musical "subjects" were not necessarily reiterated in the
course of the movements. But when the form came to be
used independently of words, the barrenness of mere meandering counterpoint soon became apparent, and characteristic
musical figures became more definitely noticeable, and were
frequently reiterated in the course of a work to give unity
to the whole. The early composers who speculated on these
lines called their works by all sorts of names—canzonas,
ricercari, fantasias, and so forth; and they were very unsystematic in their ways of introducing their "subjects." But
experience led them by degrees to regulate things with due
attention to symmetry and better distribution of their
materials. By degrees the aspect of the form became sufficiently distinctive for theorists to take note of it, and the
simplicity of the conditions of procedure led them to imagine

that an artistic scheme might be very successfully devised by mere speculation, without regard to the existing facts of art and they contrived such a multiplicity of directions to show composers how to expend their superfluous inartistic ingenuity according to the letter of their law, that men in general came to think that the fugue form was invented for nothing else but to enable pedants to show how clever they are. As a matter of fact, the rules were devised without consideration of the necessities of the case, and it naturally follows that hardly any of the finest fugues in the whole range of the musical art are strictly in accordance with the directions of the teachers on the subject; and if it had not been for Bach and Handel this most elastic and invaluable form would have become a mere dead formality.

The essence of the form in its mature state is simply that the successive parts shall enter like several voices, one after another, with a "subject"—which is a musical phrase of sufficiently definite melody and rhythm to stand out from its context and be identifiable—and that this subject shall give the cue to the mood of the movement at the outset and re appear frequently throughout. Artistic interest and variety of effect are maintained by the manner in which the voices or parts sometimes sound all at once, and sometimes are reduced to a minimum of one or two. Climaxes are obtained by making them busier and busier with the subject; making it appear at one time in one part, and at another time in another, the voices or parts catching one another up like people who are so eager in the discussion of their subject that they do not wait for each other to finish their sentences. Subordinate subjects are made to circle round the principal one, and the various ideas are made to appear in different relations to one another, sometimes high and sometimes low, sometimes quick and at other times slow, but always maintaining a relevancy in mood and style. And the course of the movement simultaneously makes a complete circuit by passing to subordinate keys, which allow of constant change in the presentation of the subject, and ultimately comes round to the first key again and closes firmly therein. All sorts of devices had been contrived for giving additional effect and interest to the scheme and in Bach's time fugue became the highest representative form of the period of art.

It had been first used for the organ—the association of the instrument with choral music in church services ensured that—and many of Bach's predecessors obtained more effective results in this form than any other that they attempted. Many attempts had been made before Bach's time to adapt it also for harpsichord and for stringed instruments, so that Bach had plenty of models to improve upon, according to his wont, in each department of art.

It ought not to be overlooked, moreover, that his predecessors in the line of organ music were an exceptionally high-spirited group of composers. It is difficult to find a finer or more true-hearted set of men in the whole range of the art than such as Frescobaldi, Froberger, Swelinck, Kerl, Reinken, Buxtehude, Pachelbel, Kuhnau, John Michael Bach, and many others of the same calling and similar musical powers. Each one of them had contributed a considerable number of items of their own both to the materials of art and to the solution of the problems of their manipulation. Bach's own work has thrown theirs into the shade, but the world which has forgotten them is under great obligations to them all. For though their work never reaches the pitch of equal mastery which satisfies the fastidious judgment of those who have enjoyed maturer things, it was only through their devoted pioneering that the musical revelation of the personality of Bach in instrumental music became possible.

In the passionate eagerness to express his thoughts as well as was conceivably possible, Bach studied the works of every man who had distinguished himself in any branch of art. And with the true instinct which is so like concentrated common-sense, he took each department of art in turn, and always at times when he had opportunities to test his own experiments in similar lines. At one time he devoted himself to organ music, at another to secular instrumental muic, at another to choral music. As has been pointed out elsewhere, the organ period came first, and coloured his style for the rest of his life.

The organ is obviously not an instrument which is capable of much expression in detail, but it is undoubtedly capable of exercising great emotional effect upon human beings, partly through its long association with feelings which are most deeply rooted in human nature, and partly through the magnificent volume of continuous sound that it is capable of producing. The latter quality supplies in a great measure the guiding principle for its successful treatment by a composer; and the effect of the most successful works written for it, depends in great measure on the manner in which the crises of voluminous sound are managed. The fugue form happens to be the most perfect contrivance for the attainment of these ends. For it completely isolates the text of the discourse, which is the principal subject; and the successive entries of the parts necessarily make a gradual increase of general sonority. Looking at fugue from the sensational side, the human creature is made to go through successive states of tension and relaxation; and the perfection of a great master's management lies in his power to adjust the distribution of his successive climaxes of sonority and complexity proportionately to the receptive capacities of human creatures, beginning from different points, and rising successively to different degrees of richness and fulness. The difficulty of the operation lies in the necessity for building up the successive effects of massive complexity out of the musical ideas. A great master like Bach is instinctively aware that appeals to sensation must be accompanied by proportionate appeals to higher faculties. It is only in the crudest phases of modern theatrical music that mere appeals to sensation are dignified by the name of art. In modern opera climaxes of sound are often piled up one after another without doing anything but excite the animal side of man's nature. The glory of Bach's management of such things is that the intrinsic interest of the music itself is always in proportion to the power and volume of the actual sound. Indeed the volume of the sound is sometimes made to seen.

tenfold greater than the mere notes sounding would warrant, by reason of the extraordinary complexity and vitality of the details out of which it is compounded. Moreover, Bach has such a hold upon the resources of his art, that when he has to reduce the number of notes sounding to a minimum, the relation of the passage to its context prevents the interest from flagging. It was in such circumstances that his predecessors had often failed. They could often write several pages of fine, rich, and noble music, but never held the balance so perfectly but that at some time or other the movement seems to fall to pieces. Bach at his best manipulates all his resources so well that even his quietest moments have some principle of interest which keeps the mind engaged, and his final climax of sound and complicated polyphony comes like the utmost possible exultation, taking complete possession of the beings who hear with the understanding as well as the senses, and raising them out of themselves into a genuine rapture.

Of course Bach did not restrict himself to such types of procedure. There are plenty of works which are mainly intellectual from end to end, relying on the beauty of some melodic phrase or the energy of some rhythmic figure to supply what is necessary on the side of feeling. In such works a characteristic subject is taken as a *thesis*, and presented in every possible light with byplay of subordinate *theses*, like little commentaries, which are often beautifully expressive melodic figures, and are all welded together into a complete whole by the endless resource and acute instinct of the composer.

The style of the organ works is eminently serious at all times, as befits the character of the instrument. But Bach uses subjects with regular dance rhythms, as well as those of the choral type ; and those which are most popular are generally the rhythmic fugues. In the toccatas, fantasias, and preludes he is but rarely rhythmic to any pronounced extent. He finds figures which have a natural animation without too much lilt, and welds them into great sequences, which have a coherence of their own, from the point of view

of tonal design, without having anything of the sonata character about them. The sonata mood and type of form is
conspicuously absent, and most happily so. That grew up
under secular conditions, and the style represents totally
different habits of mind and manner from those which were
natural to the men who cultivated the old polyphonic forms.
Bach succeeded in finding forms for himself which in relation
to his polyphonic methods are completely satisfying to the
mind, and which admitted of wide range of modulation and
variety and system in the presentation of subjects without
foregoing the advantages of clearly recognisable part-writing.
He had complete mastery of all genuine organ devices
which tell in the hearing;—the effects of long sustained
notes accompanied by wonderful ramifications of rapid
passages; the effects of sequences of linked suspensions of
great powerful chords; the contrast of whirling rapid notes
with slow and stately march of pedals and harmonies. He
knew how the pearly clearness of certain stops lent itself to
pasages of intricate rhythmic counterpoint, and what charm,
lay in the perfect management of several simultaneous melodies
—especially when the accents came at different moments in
the different parts; and he designed his movements so well
that he made all such and many other genuine organ effects
exert their fullest impression on the hearers. He rarely
allows himself to break into a dramatic vein, though he sometimes appeals to the mind in phases which are closely akin to
the dramatic—as in the great fantasia in G minor, the toccata
in D minor, the prelude in B minor. He occasionally touches
on tender and pathetic strains, but for the most part rightly
adopts an attitude of grand dignity which is at once generous
in its warmth and vigour, and reserved in the matter of
sentiment.

His work in this line seems to comprise all the possibilities
of pure organ music. Everything that has been written since
is but the pale shadow of his splendid conceptions; and
though the modern attempts to turn the organ into a sort
of second-rate orchestra by means of infinite variety of stops
are often very surprising (and very heterogeneous), they

certainly cannot compare with his work for intrinsic quality
or genuine direct impressiveness. The organ is naturally
associated with types of thought and emotion which are
traditionally referred to a religious basis; and the later
development of purely secular music has hardly touched its
true field.

In the line of orchestral music, such as orchestral suites and
concerti grossi, Bach's achievements are often supremely de-
lightful—vigorous, vivacious, and characteristic. But they are
not of any great historical importance. The backward state
of the arts of instrumentation tells against them, as does
Bach's natural inclination to treat all the members of his
orchestra on equal terms as so many counterpoints. On the
other hand, his work for harpsichord and clavichord is of
supreme importance; for in this line again he put the crown
on a special type of development, and made the final and most
perfect exposition of the varieties of the suite form, and of the
old instrumental fugue, as well as of all those varieties of types
of toccata and fantasia which were especially characteristic of
the polyphonic period.

In connection with these lesser keyed instruments his objects
were necessarily different from those which he had in view
in organ composition. No volume of sound nor sustainment
of tone for any length of time was possible. While the organ
had ancient associations and great echoing buildings to lend
enchantment to the performance, the lesser keyed instruments
were chiefly confined to the intimate familiarities of domestic
life. Bach's favourite instrument, the clavichord, admitted
of some tender expression and delicate phrasing; but the
harpsichord, with a certain noble roughness of tone, admitted
of hardly any expression and of no great variety of volume.
Here indeed was a great temptation to subside into purely
intellectual subtleties. But there was an amount of human
nature about Bach which prevented his wasting his time in
ingenious futilities. Considering how infinitely capable he was
of every kind of ingenuity, it is surprising how few examples
there are in his works of misuse of artistic resources. He was
incessantly trying experiments, and it was natural that he

13

should test the effect of pure technical feats now and then, but the proportion of things which are purely mechanical to those which have a genuine musical basis is very small. He exercised his supreme mastery of such resources very often, as in the canons in the Goldberg Variations, but in most cases the mere ingenuity is subordinate to higher and more generous principles of effect. Exceptions like the Kunst der Fuge and Musikalisches Opfer were deliberately contrived for definitely technical purposes, and hardly come within the range of real practical music.

Among the most important of his clavier works are the several groups of suites and partitas. These are sets of dance tunes grouped together in such a way as to make a composite cycle out of well-contrasted units, all knit together in the circuit of one key. The idea of grouping dance tunes together was of very old standing; and composers had tried endless varieties, from galliards and pavans to rigadoons and trumpet tunes. But by degrees they settled down to a scheme which was in principle exactly the same as that of the distribution of sonata movements in later times—having the serious and more highly organised movements at the beginning, the slow dances in the middle, and the gay rhythmic dances at the end. Many composers had succeeded admirably in this form, especially Couperin, who generally fell in with the taste of his French audiences by adding to the nucleus a long series of lively picture-tunes which savoured of the theatrical ballet. Bach took Couperin for one of his models, and paid attention chiefly to the most artistic part of his work, and set himself to improve upon it. The form in which he cast his movements is always on the same lines. They are divided into two nearly equal halves, the first passing out from the principal key to a point of contrast, and closing there to emphasise it; and the second starting from that point and returning to the point from which the movement began. This is all that the movements have of actual harmonic form, though they frequently illustrate an early stage of typical sonata movements, by the correspondence of the opening bars of each half, and of the closing bars of each half. The texture of all the movements—even of the lightest—is polyphonic. The two first movements of the suite are generally an allemande and a courante, which are often very elaborate in intricacy of independent counterpoint. The courante was also made additionally intricate by curious cross rhythms. In these movements Bach is more often purely technical than in any other branch of his work; and though very dignified and noble, they are occasionally rather dry. On the other hand, the central movement (the sarabande) almost always represents his highest pitch of expressiveness and interest; and it is, moreover, the movement in which he is least contrapuntal. There are sarabandes of all kinds. Some are purely melodic, some superbly rich in harmonisation, some gravely rhythmic, and some are treated with beautifully expressive counterpoint. In almost all of them Bach strikes some vein of very concentrated expression, and maintains it with perfect consistency from beginning to end. After the central expressive point of the sarabande the light and gay movements naturally follow. A suite was held to be complete which had but one of such merry movements (a gigue) at the end. But as a sort of concession to human weakness very light and rhythmic movements were commonly admitted directly after the sarabande, such as the bourrées, gavottes, minuets, and passepieds. In such movements Bach was wonderfully at home. In perfect neatness and finish of such rapid, sparkling little movements, no one has ever surpassed him; and he contrived them throughout in the terms of perfect art. For they are not of the modern type of dance tune with dummy accompaniment, but works in which everything sounding has vitality, most frequently in the form of busiest and merriest two-part counterpoint. The final gigues also are nearly always contrapuntal, and often almost fugal. But they are by no means severe. Such examples as the gigue of the G major French suite and the F major English suite are sufficient to prove that uncompromisingly artistic methods are by no means inconsistent with most vivacious gaiety.

By the side of Bach's suites may suitably be mentioned the two sets of suites by Handel, though they are not of anything like equal artistic importance. The second set are indeed for the most part so poor and inert that they have almost dropped out of notice altogether. They were probably written just to supply a demand engendered by the great success of the first set, which are vastly superior in every respect, and have maintained a lively popularity even till the present day. Both sets are, however, very peculiar examples of the order of art to which they profess to belong, which may by some people be regarded as a merit. They comprise combinations and distributions of movements, which are not frequently met with in suites, such as long series of variations, and very effective fugues; and they are obviously better calculated to win popular favour than such austere and conscientious types as those of J. S. Bach, but the details are much plainer and the materials less concentrated and interesting. The same qualities are noticeable in all Handel's various ventures in the line of instrumental music such as his effective and popular organ concertos, some very attractive violin sonatas, the very unequal grand concertos and similar compositions and pasticcios for orchestral instruments, and the long chaconnes for harpsichord alone. Handel was too great a genius to be able to help breaking out occasionally into something remarkably fine and attractive, even when he was not putting his heart into what he was doing. But the public nature of his career is indicated in this as in other departments of his work, both in respect of its advantages and its drawbacks. The artistic level is not consistently as high as Bach's, and the influence of Italian modes of thought has the effect, in this range of art especially, of making a great part of his instrumental music more justly classifiable with the works of the early harmonic style, to be considered in the next chapter, than with the distinct group which represent the "climax of early instrumental music."

Of all the works with which Bach enriched the world, the one which is most cherished by musicians is the Collection of Preludes and Fugues which is known in England as the "Forty-eight," and in Germany as "Das wohltemperirte Clavier"—which means "The clavichord tuned in equal temperament." The very name of this work brings forward a point which is of great moment in the story of the art, namely, the final settling of the particular scale which serves for all our later music; which has already been shortly summarised in Chapter II.

In choral music wide diatonic intervals are so far preferable to semitones that in the early days, when all music was choral, composers found a very limited number of flats and sharps sufficient for all their requirements. Modulations from one key to another were not thought of in the way in which they are now, for men were very slow in arriving at a clear understanding of the principle of tonality or definition of key. But when instrumental music began to be cultivated, and men developed a sense for identity and variety of key, and began to use modulations as a basis of design as well as a means of effect, they were brought face to face with a perplexing problem. It is a familiar paradox of acoustics that if a series of fifths are tuned one on the top of another, the notes at which they arrive soon begin to be different from notes at the same position in the scale which are arrived at by other methods of tuning. Thus, if starting from C, the notes G, D, and E are successively tuned as perfect fifths, the E is not the same E that would be produced by tuning a true third and transposing it by the necessary octaves. And the same happens if the fifths are tuned one on the top of another till they appear to arrive at the same note from which they started. B♯, according to modern ideas, is the same as C, but if theoretically in tune it would be practically out of tune, and many of the other sharps and flats which coincide on the keyboard are in the same category. This was of course no great obstacle as long as composers only wanted to use B♭, E♭, C♯, F♯, and G♯. The old methods of tuning made these possible without modifying the essential intervals, such as the fifths and thirds. No provision was made for the other accidentals, because they were not required until music had gone a long way beyond the limits of the ecclesiastical modes. But by Bach's time the feeling for the modern system of keys and of major and minor scales was quite mature. All composers perfectly understood the status of the various notes in the scales, at least instinctively, and modulation from one key to another had become a vital essential of art. No music was possible without it. But it still took some time for music to expand so far as to make modulation to extraneous keys seem a matter worth contending for. Cautious conservatives would not be persuaded that any modification of the old system of tuning was wanted; but the more adventurous spirits would not be gainsaid. They found that they required to assume A♭ to be the same as G♯, and D♭ as C♯, and the fact that the chords which resulted from their experiments were hideously out of tune in the old method of tuning would not stop them. It became more and more obvious that modulation must be possible, for the purposes of the new kind of art, into every key represented by a note in the system. Otherwise there would be blanks in particular directions which would inevitably make the system unequal and imperfect. In other words, it was necessary that all the notes in the system should stand on an equal footing in relation to one another. Bach foresaw this with such clearness that he tuned his own instrument on the system of "equal temperament," and gave his opinion to the world in a most practical form, which was this series of preludes and fugues, major and minor, in every key represented by a note in the system. Till his time certain extreme keys had hardly ever been used, and his action emphasised the final crystallisation of the modern scale system, which makes it as different from the system used by the musicians of the Middle Ages as the heptatonic system of the Persians is from the pentatonic system of the Chinese. In all cases the scale is an artificial product contrived for particular artistic ends. The old scale, with a limited number of available notes, was sufficient for the purposes of the old church music, because the aims of the art were different. The growth of modern instrumental music brought new aims into men's minds, and they had to contrive a new scale system to satisfy them. The division of the octave into twelve equal intervals, to which Bach in this objective way gave his full sanction, is now a commonplace of every musical person's experience. Some people imagine that it was always so. But in reality the existing system is only a hundred and fifty years old, and was resisted by some musicians even till the present century.

The two books of preludes and fugues represent an extraordinary variety of artistic speculation on Bach's part. They have much the same standing in his artistic scheme as the concentrated lyrical pieces of Chopin and Schumann have in modern times. The system of design upon which the modern pieces are devised had yet to be developed, and the only well-established and trustworthy form for concentrated expression of abstract ideas was the fugue. As the fugues in this collection belong to various periods in Bach's life, they naturally illustrate purely technical as well as expressive aims; but there are very few that have only technical interest. Most of them obviously illustrate such states of feeling and of mood as music is especially fitted to express, and they do so in terms of the most perfect and finished art. There are fugues which express many shades of merriment and banter (C minor, C♯ major, B♭ in first book; F minor in second book). Strong confident fugues (D major, first book; A minor, second book); intensely sad fugues (B♭ minor and B minor, first book); serenely reposeful fugues (E major and B major, second book); tenderly pathetic fugues (G♯ minor in both books). In every case his subject gives him his cue, and the treatment of harmonisation, modulation, counterpoint, design, and general tone, follows consistently the mood which the subject indicated. Bach's objects were absolutely different from those of the theoretical writers on fugue. He aimed at designs which are more akin to the devices of harmonic form, making different parts of the work balance with one another in style, by special characteristic runs, or special sequences—anything which gives an additional value and interest to the mere technicalities of the treatment of the subject. He never makes the mistake of writing a fugue in sonata form, which is little better than a forcing together of incompatible types of style. From the point of view of polyphonic writing the fugues are as pure as they can be made, but his frequent use of sequences and similar devices gives an additional sense of stability to the design without distracting the mind from the true objects of the form. The fugues have the reputation of being the most important part of the work, but in reality the preludes are fully as interesting, and even more unique. They are very varied in character, and many are evident experiments in compact little forms, the schemes of which Bach worked out for himself. Several of them exist in more than one version; which seems to imply that he gave them much consideration, and revised them several times before he was satisfied. No collection of equal interest and variety exists in the whole range of music. Some of the preludes are of the nature of very carefully considered extemporisations. The art of preluding was very much practised in those days, and consisted mainly of stringing together successions of chords in the guise of arpeggios, or characteristic figures devised on the frame of an arpeggio. Successions of harmonies had not as yet got stale by conventional usage, so Bach employed his gift for contriving beautiful and neat little arpeggio figures to make complete movements out of chord successions, which range through dreamy modulations without ever losing coherence, or falling out of the rational order required to make a complete and compact unity. A happy extension of this typical prelude-device is to break off the arpeggios and add a coda, which serves as a peculiarly apt contrast. Both the preludes in C♯ major are happy in this respect, especially the one in the second book. Another development of the same type, but in a much more impulsive and expressive style, is that in D minor in the first book, in which the characteristic progressions of harmony are so directed as to arrive at quite a passionate climax just before the end. Following the same line again, the figures corresponding to the arpeggio forms of the chords are sometimes made specially definite as musical figures, and a whole movement is developed out of various phases of the same compact musical idea (D major in first book). In such ways device was built upon device to make new types of movements. Of quite a different order is the wonderful prelude in E♭ minor in the first book, which is a highly emotional kind of song, with a most remarkable succession of interrupted cadences at the end, which exactly illustrate the longing mood of the principal idea. Of similar type is the highly ornamental solo rhapsody in G minor in the first book, which might be a beautiful violin piece with a compactly consistent polyphonic accompaniment. A few are dance movements in disguise (A♭ in first book). One is either an imitation or an arrangement of a typical orchestral movement of the period with violin and trumpet passages interchanging (D major in second book). A very few are on the lines of a modern sonata movement, though the style is so different from that of the sonatas of that century that the relationship is barely recognisable (F minor in second book). A few are studies based on short but beautifully expressive figures which make the movement coherent by their constant interchange (B minor in second book). The variety is so extraordinary that it is impossible to give a full account of them; and every individual movement is a finished piece of workmanship, perfect in design and full of refined expression; and few things in the range of art are so full of suggestions of fresh possibilities on quite unconventional lines in the treatment of harmonic expression, melody, and rhythm. The preludes and fugues as a whole have been subjected to the closest scrutiny by numberless musicians of the keenest intelligence for the greater part of a century, and they bear the test so well that the better men know them the more they resort to them; and the collection is likely to remain the sacred book of musicians who have any real musical sense as long as the present system of music continues. In their particular phase of art, they appear to touch the highest point imaginable.

Bach was fortunate in occupying a unique position at the end of the purely polyphonic period, before the influence of the Italian opera had gained force enough to spoil the fresh sincerity of the style. The moment the balance swung over to the harmonic side, and men thought more of the ease of the progressions of the harmony than of the details of the polyphonic texture, work on his lines became almost impossible. The change is curiously illustrated by the difference between the ring of such a work as his "Chromatische Fantasie," and of the experi ments on the same lines by so true a composer as his son, Philip Emmanuel. The first is one of the greatest movements ever written for a keyed instrument; the latter soon reveal a mechanical emptiness, when the formulas and types of phrase of an Italian pattern are given in ecstatic fragments, which are utterly inconsistent with the formal Italian style. It is perhaps possible, on the other hand, to write something new on the lines of the toccata; but in his particular polyphonic treatment of the form Bach's work is so high and noble that it entirely forbids all hope of advance beyond his standard. People have very rarely attempted toccatas of his kind again. The modern type is of a totally different order, for some curious convention seems to have grown up that a toccata is a movement in which rapid notes must go on from beginning to end. Bach's works were founded on the types of the old organists, and it was a very congenial style to him— as he revelled in the grand successions of powerful harmonies, and the contrasts of brilliant passages, and the varieties of all possible imitative passages, and expressive counterpoint. Indeed he had a gift for rapid ornamental passages almost unequalled by any other composer; for with him they never suggest mere emptiness and show, but have some function in relation to the design, or some essential basis of effect, or some ingenious principle of accent, or some inherent principle of actual melodic beauty which puts them entirely out of the category of things purely ornamental. Thus even into the merest trifles he infused reality. The same genuineness and sincerity look out from every corner of his work, and—art having been happily at the right stage for his purposes—give the world assurance of artistic possessions which the passage of time and more intimate acquaintance only render the more lovable.

CHAPTER IX

THE BEGINNINGS OF MODERN INSTRUMENTAL MUSIC

It would have been an eminently pardonable mistake for any intelligent musician to have fallen into, in the third quarter of the eighteenth century, if he concluded that J. S. Bach's career was a failure, and that his influence upon the progress of his art amounted to the minimum conceivable. Indeed the whole course of musical history in every branch went straight out of the sphere of his activity for a long while; his work ceased to have any significance to the generation which succeeded him, and his eloquence fell upon deaf ears. A few of his pupils went on writing music of the same type as his in a half-hearted way, and his own most distinguished son, Philip Emmanuel, adopted at least the artistic manner of working up his details and making the internal organisation of his works alive with figure and rhythm. But even he, the sincerest composer of the following generation, was infected by the complacent, polite superficiality of his time; and he was forced, in accepting the harmonic principle of working in its Italian phase, to take with it some of the empty formulas and conventional tricks of speech which had become part of its being, and which sometimes seem to belie the genuineness of his utterances, and put him somewhat out of touch with his whole-hearted father.

The fact of J. S. Bach's isolation is so obvious that it is often referred to and accounted for on the ground that he was so far ahead of his time. It is true that his gift for divining new possibilities of combination, new progressions of harmony, and new effects and procedures of modulation, was so great that his contemporaries could not keep pace with him. The very plenitude of his inventiveness exhausted their faculties before they got to the point of following his drift; and succeeding generations plodded on for a long time before they came up with him, and ultimately grasped that he aimed not at pure technical ingenuities as ends in themselves, but at infinite variety of artistic devices as means to expression. This, however, is not a complete explanation of the situation, but only an individual example among the more widely acting causes which governed the progress of art. The very loftiness of Bach's character and artistic aims prevented his condescending to do some of the work which had to be done before modern music could be completely matured; and the supremacy of Italian music, both operatic and otherwise, in the next generation, and the simultaneous lowering of standard and style, was as inevitable as a reaction as it was necessary as a preliminary to further progress.

Handel and Bach had carried the art of expressive counterpoint to the utmost extremes possible under the artistic conditions of their time, which were limited to the combination of polyphonic writing with the simplest kind of harmonic form. The harmonic element is still in the background in their work because so much energy is expended upon the details of the complex choral and contrapuntal expression. As long as composers aimed chiefly at choral effect, they were impelled to individualise the parts out of which the harmony was composed, to make them worthy of the human voices; aiming rather at melodic than rhythmic treatment. And though they submitted to certain general principles of harmonic sequence, the principle of systematic harmonic design was more or less a secondary consideration. But after Handel and Bach there did not seem much to be done in the line of polyphonic expression. Genuine secular influences began to gain strength, and with them the feeling for instrumental music; and men began to feel their way towards a line of art which could be altogether complete without the ingenuities of counterpoint or the words which formed a necessary part of vocal utterance. As has been pointed out, an instinctive desire for harmonic design and for clear definite distribution of harmonies had been in the air for a long time. It is as though there had been a wrestle for supremacy between the two principles of treatment. Composers who belonged to the same class as Handel and Bach looked upon the independent and equal freedom of motion of all parts (which is called counterpoint) as the essence of good style; and the massing and distribution of the harmonies as secondary. The two great masters carried their feeling for contrapuntal effect into every department of art. Even in their arias the principle is often discernible. For though they generally only wrote out the voice part and special instrumental parts, and left the harmonies to be supplied from figures by the accompanist, yet in a large proportion of instances even the bass part moves about quite as vivaciously as the melody; as, for instance :—

It is true that the use of harmony in the lump was early attempted in solo arias and recitatives, and examples, such as "Comfort ye," may be quoted to show that Handel could use harmonic methods of accompaniment with effect; but by far the larger proportion of the solo movements in his operas and oratorios have accompaniments which are contrapuntally conceived; and Bach's impulse was even more strongly to make all parts of his scheme equally alive and individual.

But as soon as their work was done the index swung over

and the balance went down on the harmonic side. Counter
point, and interest in the subordinate parts of the music,
became of secondary importance (or even less), and clearness
and intelligibility of harmonic and melodic progressions became the primary consideration. Composers made a show of
counterpoint now and then, but it was not the real thing. The
parts in ostensibly contrapuntal works of the time immediately
following Bach and Handel are not in the least interesting or
alive. They are mechanically contrived to have the appearance of being busy, and serve for nothing more; and it was
no great loss when such pinchbeck was undisguisedly replaced
by the conventional figures of accompaniment which became
so characteristic of the harmonic period even in the palmy
days of Mozart and Haydn. But such traits and contrivances
had to be found out like everything else, and in the time
at present under consideration they were not in common
use. Indeed as far as the Italian share of the work of
developing harmonic form goes, the early period contem
poraneous with Handel and Bach is the purest and most
honourable. That most remarkable school of Italian violinists
and composers who began with Corelli and Vivaldi forms
as noble and sincere a group as any in music; and to them,
more than to any others, the credit of establishing the
principles of harmonic form on a firm basis for instrumental music is due.

The great Italian violin-makers had, in the course of the
seventeenth century, brought their skill up to the highest
perfection, and put into the hands of performers the most
ideally perfect instrument for expression that human ingenuity
seems capable of devising. Their achievement came just at
the right moment for artistic purposes, and Italian musicians
of the highest gifts took to the instrument with passionate
ardour. In the violin there is so little intervening mechanism
between the player and his means of utterance that it becomes
almost part of himself; and is as near as possible to being an
additional voice with greater compass and elasticity than his
natural organ of song. To the Italian nature such an instrument was even specially suitable, and as the inartistic

sophisms, to which Italians have proved so lamentably prone to succumb, had not yet darkened the musical horizon, their instinct for beauty of form and melody led them under its influence to very notable achievements. Corelli's style was noble and healthy, but the range of his technique was limited. In that respect his great successors—many of them his pupils or their pupils in turn — progressed by leaps and bounds. Men like Veracini, Tartini, Geminiani, Locatelli, Le Clair and Nardini, possessed with the passion to attain some ideal joy that their instrument seemed to promise in possibility, soon brought their department of art to almost the highest pitch of perfection. The congenial nature of their instrument seems to have inspired them to find out with extraordinary rapidity the forms of melody and figure, and the kinds of phrasing and expression that suited it; and adding contrivance to contrivance, they soon learnt the best way to overcome the mechanical difficulties of stopping and bowing in such a way as to obtain the finest tone, the purest intonation, and the greatest facility and fluency of motion.

But what was still more notable and important was their successful development of a scheme for musical works which could be completely intelligible on its own account, without either systematic dance rhythm or contrapuntal devices or words to explain it. The speed with which they advanced towards an intelligent grasp of the principles necessary for such a purpose of design is very surprising. It was probably due to the fact that they were all performers, and performers on a solo instrument. The central idea in the violin soloist's mind was to make his effect by melody, with subordinate accompaniment; that is, melody supported by simple harmonies, and not melody as only the upper part of a set of equal independent parts. The solo violin has been forced—and forced with success—to play contrapuntal movements; but it may be confessed, without disrespect to J. S. Bach, that counterpoint is not its natural mode of expressing itself, and that its resources of expression could not have led to the development of the typical Italian solo sonata if the accom

paniment had been on equal terms with the solo instrument. It is naturally a single-part instrument—a singing
instrument with great capacity for enlivening and adorning
its *cantabile* with brilliant passages. It was therefore imperative for the player-composers to find a form which
should not depend for its interest upon contrapuntal ingenuities and devices—a form which should mainly depend
upon distribution of melodious passages, supported by systematic and simple harmonic accompaniment. The opportunities for testing their experiments being plentiful, they
soon found and established a solution of the problem; and
their solution forms the groundwork of the development of
those principles of design which ultimately served Haydn,
Mozart, and Beethoven in all their greatest and most perfect works.

The types which served these composers for models were the
Sonate da Chiesa and the Sonate da Camera of the Corellian
time. Their instinct impelled them to develop movements
which were not purely dance tunes, but of wider and freer
range; which should admit of warm melodic expression without degenerating into incoherent rambling ecstasy. They had
the sense to see from the first that mere formal continuous
melody is not the most suitable type for instrumental music.
For, as was pointed out in the first chapter, there is deep-rooted
in the nature of all instrumental music the need of some
rhythmic vitality, in consonance with the primal source of
instrumental expression. And for instrumental music, pure,
continuous, vocal melody, undefined by rhythm, is only temporarily or relatively endurable; even with such an ideal melodic
instrument as the violin. These player-composers, then, set
themselves to devise a scheme in which to begin with the contours of connected melodic phrases (supported and defined by
simple harmonic accompaniment), gave the impression of definite
tonality—that is, of being decisively in some particular key,
and giving an unmistakable indication of it. They found
out how to proceed by giving the impression of leaving that
key and passing to another, without departing from the
characteristic spirit and mood of the music, as shown in the

"subjects" and figures; and how to give the impression of
relative completeness by closing in a key which is in strong
contrast to the first; and so round off one-half of the
design. But this point being in apposition to the starting-
point, leaves the mind dissatisfied and in expectation of fresh
disclosures. So they made the balance complete by resuming the subjects and melodic figures of the first half in
the extraneous key and working back to the starting-point;
and they made their final close with the same figures as
were used to conclude the first half, but in the principal
key instead of the key of contrast. This was practically
the scheme adopted in dance movements of suites; but
the great violinists improved upon the suite type by much
clearer definition of the subjects; and by giving them a
much wider range, and making them represent the key
more decisively. As time went on they extended the range
of each division of the movement, and made each balance
the other more completely. They also lengthened the
second half of the movement by introducing more extensive
modulations in the middle of it, and thus introduced a
new and important element of contrast. How this simple
type of form was extended and developed into the scheme
uniformly adopted in their best movements by the three great
masters of pure instrumental music must be considered in
its place.

This was the highest type of harmonic design used by the
early composers of sonatas. They also used simpler ones like
the primitive rondo, which is the least organised and coherent
of forms; and the aria type, which is the same in principle
of structure as the familiar primitive minuet and trio. As
instrumental art was still in a very experimental stage the
character and order of the movements which they combined
to make a complete group or sonata varied considerably; but
the general tendency was towards the familiar arrangement
of three movements:—1. A solid allegro; 2. an expressive
slow movement; 3. a lively finale—to which was often most
suitably appended a slow and dignified "introduction," to begin
the whole work. The reasons which made men gravitate

14

towards this grouping of movements appear to be obvious.
The slow introduction was particularly suitable to the noble
qualities of the violin, and was the more needful in violin
sonatas, as it not infrequently happened that the first allegro
was in a loose fugal form, following the model of the canzonas
in Sonate da Chiesa; and as that would necessitate beginning
with only a single part sounding at a time, it was not sufficient
to lay hold of the audience's attention at once. Whereas a
massive full-sounding introduction insists upon being heard.
Moreover, the instinct of the composers was right in adopting
a serious style to put the audience in proper mood for what
was to follow. It is a familiar experience that when people
are appealed to on trival and light grounds they can with
difficulty be brought to attend to anything serious afterwards. The principal allegro movement which follows the
introduction always tends to be the most elaborately organised of all the movements, and to appeal to the intellectual side of the audience. In this the composer puts
forth all his resources of development and mastery of
design. The intellectual tendency was illustrated in the
early days by the fugal form in which the movement was
usually cast, as in the Sonate da Chiesa; and when in
harmonic form it was the one in which the design above
described was adopted. Sometimes it was an allemande, as
in the Sonate da Camera, and the suites and partitas and
ordres. The allemande was nominally a dance form, and
was distributed in regular groups of bars in accordance
with the requirements of the dance; but it was always
the most solid and elaborate of all the movements in the
group in which it occurred (except sometimes the French
courante), and it often contained imitations and elaborate
counterpoint. The position of a movement of this character fits with the requirements of an audience, for people
are more capable of entering into and enjoying serious
matters and subtleties of intellectual skill when their attention
is fresh and unwearied.

After the intellectual came the emotional. The slow
movement which follows, not only serves as a marked con-

trast, but appeals to the opposite side of men's natures. The intellectual faculties are, comparatively speaking, allowed to rest, and all the appeal is made to sensibilities by expression. Strange as it may seem, it was in this movement that the Italian violin-composers most frequently failed; and the same is the case with Haydn and Mozart and the whole school of harpsichord-composers; and the full perfection of the slow emotional movement was not attained till Beethoven's time. The reason is that music had to wait for the development of the technique of expression much longer than for the technique of mere design. And it may be noted in passing that nothing marks the difference between extreme modern music and the earlier phases than the different degree and quality of passionate emotion it expresses. But at least these performer-composers aimed at expression in this movement; and when they were at fault and found nothing sympathetic to say, they took refuge—like opera singers and people in ordinary circumstances in life—in ornamental flourishes and such superfluities as disguise the barrenness of invention and feeling under the show of dexterity.

The function of the lively last movement is equally intelligible. It is usually in dance rhythm of some kind, and was always more direct and free from intellectual subtleties than the other movements. It was gay—spontaneous—headlong. At once an antidote and a tonic. Restoring the balance after the excitement of too much sensibility, and calling into play the healthy human faculties which are associated with muscular activity. As though the composer, after putting his auditors under a spell of enchantment, called them back to the realities of life by setting their limbs going.

In short, the sum of the scheme is—

1. The preliminary summons to attention, attuning the mind to what is to follow.

2. The appeal to intelligence; and to appreciation of artistic subtleties and refinements of design.

3. The appeal to emotional sensibilities.

4. The re-establishment of healthy brightness of tone—
a recall to the realities of life.

This is the natural outline of the scheme, which in the
main has persisted from the beginnings of genuine instrumental music till the present day. It has of course been
varied by the ingenuity and insight of really capable composers, as well as by the fatuity of musical malaprops.

Nearly all the violin sonatas of the Italian type were written
by violin players, with the exception of a few by John
Sebastian Bach, Handel and Hasse, and such comprehensive
composers. The quality of these works is, on the whole,
far higher than that of the examples of other forms of
instrumental music of the early time, but very important
results were also obtained by composers of harpsichord
sonatas.

Keyed instruments did not find so much favour at this time
with Italians. The superior capabilities of the violin for
cantabile purposes attracted the best of their efforts, and met
with most sympathy from the public. It remained for
Germans, with their great sense of the higher resources of
harmony and polyphony, to cultivate the instruments which
offered excellent opportunities in those directions, but were
decidedly defective for the utterance of melody. Nevertheless
Italians contributed an extremely important share to the early
establishment of this department of art; and even before the
violin sonata had been cultivated with so much success, the
singular genius of Domenico Scarlatti had not only laid the
foundations of modern music for keyed instruments, but contributed some very permanent items to the edifice. His
instinct for the requirements of his instrument was so marvellous, and his development of technique so wide and rich, that
he seems to spring full armed into the view of history. That
he had models and types to work upon is certain, but his style
is so unlike the familiar old suites and fugues and fantasias
and ricercare, and other harpsichord music of the early times,
that it seems likely that the work of his prototypes has been
lost. His musical character makes it probable that he studied
players rather than composers; for the quality that is most

conspicuous in his work is his thorough command of the situation as a performer. His work, at its best, gives the impression that he played upon his audience as much as he did on his harpsichord. He knows well the things that will tell, and how to awake interest in a new mood when the effects of any particular line are exhausted. Considering how little attention had been given to technique before his time, his feats of agility are really marvellous. The variety and incisiveness of his rhythms, the peculiarities of his harmony, his wild whirling rapid passages, his rattling shakes, his leaps from end to end of the keyboard, all indicate a preternaturally vivacious temperament; and unlike many later virtuosos, he is thoroughly alive to the meaning of music as an art, and does not make his feats of dexterity his principal object. They serve as the means to convey his singularly characteristic ideas in forms as abstract as modern sonatas. The definiteness of his musical ideas is one of the most surprising things about him. For when the development of any branch of art is in its infancy, it generally taxes all a man's powers to master the mere mechanical problems of technique and style. But Scarlatti steps out with a sort of diabolic masterfulness, and gives utterance with perfect ease to things which are unmistakable images of his characteristic personality. In spirit and intention his works prefigure one of the latest of modern musical developments, the scherzo. For vivacity, wit, irony, mischief, mockery, and all the category of human traits which Beethoven's scherzo served so brilliantly to express, the world had to wait for a full century to see Scarlatti's equal again. He left behind him a most copious legacy to mankind, but his successors were very slow to avail themselves of it. The majority of harpsichord composers immediately after his time were more inclined to follow a path that was redolent of the saponaceous influences of opera, and made their works but slightly distinct as forms of instrumental art. His influence is traceable here and there, but it did not bear full fruit till the development of genuine pianoforte playing began.

His sense of design was not so strong as his ideas or his

feeling for effect. His works consist of single movements, which are almost invariably in the same form as the earlier movements of suites, such as the allemandes and courantes; only considerably extended after the manner of the violin sonatas, and singularly free from systematic dance rhythm. He rarely wrote fugues, and when he did they were not particularly good ones, either technically or intrinsically. He was too much of a performer to care much about the conventional ingenuities of fugue, and too much of a free lance to put his thoughts in so elaborate a form; though he often makes a beginning as if he was going to write a serious fugue, and then goes on in a different manner. The harmonic principle of design came to him most naturally, and, as far as they go in that respect, his movements are singularly lucid and definite. But they are not operatic. They are genuine representatives of a distinct branch of art; and the expression of ideas in terms exactly adapted to the instrument by means of which they are to be made perceptible to the human mind.

Of the other Italians who did service in the line of harpsichord music the most deserving of mention is Paradisi. His technique is nothing like so extended as Scarlatti's, and the style is much less incisive; but he shows a very excellent instinct for his instrument, and a singularly just and intelligent feeling for harmonic design. The best of his sonatas (which are most frequently in two movements without a slow movement) show considerable skill in modelling ideas into the forms necessary for defining the key. The design of his best movements is the same as that of the great violin composers; but even more structurally definite. He deserves credit also for devising true sonata subjects, and escaping the temptation of writing fragments of operatic tunes with dummy accompaniments — a rock upon which the Italians, and even some very wise Germans in later times, were very liable to split.

The true centre of progress in the line of the harpsichord sonata soon proved to be in Germany. As has been before remarked, many of Germany's most distinguished composers such as Graun, Hasse, and John Christian Bach, adopted Italian manners to suit the tastes of the fashionable classes; but there were a few here and there who did not bow the knee to Baal; and noteworthiest of these was Philip Emmanuel Bach. Though gifted with little of the poetical qualities or the noble loftiness of idea and expression of his father, he was in a position to do considerable service to his art. He adopted without reserve the Italian harmonic principle of design which had become universal by his time, and adapted to it a method of treating details, and harmonisation, and rhythmic and figurative interest, which was essentially Teutonic. The high intellectual qualities come out both in his scope of harmony, and in the richness and ingenious subtlety with which he manipulates his sentences and phrases. He did so much to give the harpsichord sonata a definite status of its own that he is sometimes spoken of as its inventor. This he obviously was not, but he was for some time its most prominent representative. He owed a good deal to his father's training and example, though more in respect of detail and texture than in style or design. His father had made some experiments in the harmonic style, but on the whole he was rather shy of it, and rarely achieved anything first-rate in it. But his son, taking to it at a time when it had become more familiar and more malleable, was the first to treat it with Teutonic thoroughness. Italian influence is sometimes apparent, but happily it is not often the influence of the opera. Instrumental music had developed far enough for him to express his ideas in a genuinely instrumental style—frequently in figures as compact and incisive as Beethoven's—to make his modulations as deliberately and clearly as Mozart, and to define his contrasting key with perfect clearness, and to dispose all the various ingredients of his structure with unmistakable skill and certitude. His sonatas are usually in three movements—the central one slow and expressive, and the first and last quick. It is characteristic of his Teutonic disposition that he is a little shy of adopting the traditional lightness and gaiety as the mood of his last movement.   But he finds an excellent alternative in forcible vigour and brilliancy.

There is yet another branch of instrumental music which was very slow in developing, but has come in later days to form one of the most conspicuous features of the art.

As has before been pointed out, all the composers of the early part of the eighteenth century, even the giants, had been specially backward in feeling for orchestral effect.   They used instruments of most diverse tone-quality in a purely contrapuntal manner, just as they would have used voices, or the independent parts of an organ composition.   Those methods of using colour which enhance the telling power of ideas, and exert such moving glamour upon the sensibilities of modern human creatures, were quite out of their range.   The adoption of harmonic principles of treatment was as essential to the development of modern orchestration as to the development of forms of the sonata order.   As long as composers were writing accompaniments to contrapuntal choral works they disposed their instruments also contrapuntally; and it was not till they had to write independent instrumental movements that the requirements of instrumentation began to dawn upon them.

The first occasions which induced composers to attempt independent orchestral movements of the harmonic kind were for the symphonies or overtures of operas.   These had been written at first, as by Scarlatti and Lulli, for stringed instruments only, with the occasional addition of trumpet solos. Composers insensibly got into the habit of enhancing the effect of their strings by a few other wind instruments; and before long the group of instruments was stereotyped (as every other department of opera was) into a set of strings and two pairs of wind instruments, such as two hautboys, or two flutes and two horns.   The conventional opera writers had no very great inducement to make their overtures either finished works of art, or subtly expressive, or in any way interesting. for they felt that very little attention was paid to them. They appear to have produced them in a most perfunctory manner, to make a sort of introductory clatter while the fashionable operatic audiences were settling into their places, and exchanging the customary greetings and small talk which are inevitable in such gatherings of light-minded folk. The musical clatter was distributed into three movements, in the same order as the movements of violin sonatas, and in thoroughly harmonic style of the very cheapest description. There inevitably were some composers who could not help putting tolerably artistic touches and lively points into their work, and in course of time the symphonies came to be considerably in request on their own merits, apart from their connection with the operas; and enormous numbers were written both for people to listen to, and also for them to talk and eat to. Composers for the most part saved themselves all the trouble they could. They used musical material of such slight definiteness that it is often hardly to be dignified by the name of ideas; and they also spared themselves the labour of writing in the parts for the various instruments whenever possible. They made the second violins play with the first violins, and directed the violas to play with the basses—which must have caused the viola players to spend a good deal of their time in not playing at all, or otherwise in producing extremely disagreeable effects, when the bass part went below their compass. Moreover, the wind instruments that were sufficiently agile were generally directed to double the violins, or to hold notes and chords while the violins ran about in scales or figures. There was little or no idea of differentiating the various parts to suit the respective instruments, and equally little attempt to use their various qualities of tone as means of effect. The horn parts had the most individuality through the mere accident that they were not agile enough to play violin or viola parts; and composers being driven to give long notes to these instruments, by degrees found out their great value as a means of holding things together and supplying a sort of background of soft steady tone while the other instruments were moving about.

When these "symphonies" or "overtures" came to be played more often apart from the operas, both composers and

performers began to realise that they were wasting oppor
tunities by slovenliness. The process of coming round to
more sensible and refined ways is very interesting to
watch in the successive publications of these very numerous
symphonies. It is like the gradual return of a human being
to intelligence and right-mindedness after being temporarily
submerged in levity. At first the style of the works was
empty and conventional in detail, and it can be guessed that
the players hacked through the performances in a careless
style, which was quite as much as the music and the audience
deserved. There were hardly any indications given for the
most ordinary refinements of performance—such as phrasing,
bowing, or *pianos* or *fortes;* and gradations of more delicate
nature are implied to have been entirely ignored. But as
time went on the directions for expression and refinements
of performance became more numerous; and composers even
began to use mutes to vary the effect, and to see that
hautboys are capable of better uses than mere pointless
doubling of string parts, or playing irrelevant holding notes.
Little by little things crept into a better state of artistic
finish and nicety; the varieties of instruments in the group
were more carefully considered, and their qualities of tone
were used to better purpose; and the style of the passages
was better suited to the capabilities of the instruments. Composers began to grow more aware of the sensuous effect of
colour, and to realise that two colours which are beautiful
when pure may be coarse and disagreeable when mixed. And
so, by degrees, a totally new and extremely subtle branch
of art is seen to be emerging from the chaotic products of
indifference and carelessness. The refinements of modern
orchestration, and those subtleties of sensuous colour-effect
which are among the most marvellous and almost un-
analysable developments of human instinct, took a very
considerable period to mature, and many generations of men
had a share in developing them. But the inherent difference
of nature between the old and new is perceptible even in the
course of one generation. For even in a symphony of John
Christian Bach's there is a roundness and smoothness in the

sound of the harmony, as conveyed by the different instrumental *timbres*, which is quite different from the unassimilated counterpoint of his great father's instrumental style. In the instrumentation of the great masters of the earlier generation the tone-qualities seem to be divided from one another by innate repulsion; but in the harmonic style they seem to melt into one another insensibly, and to become part of a composite mass of harmony whose shades are constantly shifting and varying.

Amongst the men who had an important share in the early development of orchestral music, a Bohemian violinist, named Stamitz, seems to have been most noteworthy. He was leader and conductor of the band at the little German court of Mannheim, and seems to have been fortunate in his opportunities of carrying out reforms. He set his face to organise his band thoroughly, to make his violins play with refinement and careful attention to phrasing, and to obtain various shades of *piano* and *forte*, and all the advantages which can be secured by good balance of tone. He succeeded in developing the best orchestra in Europe, and established a tradition which lasted long after he had passed away, even till Mozart came through Mannheim on his way to Paris, and had an opportunity of hearing what refined orchestral playing was like—probably for the first time in his life—with important results to the world in general.

A similar line was pursued by the Belgian Gossec in Paris, who tried to stir up the Parisians to realise the possibilities of instrumental effect. He in his smaller way followed something of the same line as Berlioz, laying very great, even superfluous, stress on the importance of elaborate directions to the performers.

The position of Philip Emmanuel Bach in this line of art was important, though not quite in conformity with the tendencies of his age. In his best symphonies he adopted a line of his own; similar in principle to the ways of his father in his orchestral suites and concerti grossi. They have an underlying basis of harmonic form, but yet they are quite different in design and style from the symphonies of the Italian order above discussed; and though remarkably vigorous, animated and original in conception, they have not led to any further developments on the same lines. His management of the various instruments shows considerable skill and clear perception of the effective uses to which they can be put; and he treats them with thorough independence and variety. His feeling for orchestration is even more strikingly illustrated in his oratorios, "The Israelites in the Wilderness" and "The Resurrection." In these he makes experiments in orchestral effects which sound curiously like late modern products, and he tries to enforce the sentiment of his situations with a daring and insight which is very far ahead of his time. But in these, as in many other noteworthy attempts, he was considerably isolated, and out of touch with the easy-going spirit of his day. His works, apart from the sonatas, seem to have taken no hold upon his contemporaries, and serve chiefly to illustrate the rapidity with which change of view, and the new conditions of art, helped men to discover the possibilities of orchestral effect. The application of instrumental effect to the oratorio was destined ultimately to give that form a new lease of life, and to lead to new ulterior developments, but Philip Emmanuel's attempt was at that time, as far as public taste was concerned, premature.

The enormous number of symphonies which were produced and published in those days, by composers whose very names are forgotten, proves that public taste was gravitating strongly towards orchestral music; and it is pleasant to reflect that the more composers improved the quality of their art, the more prominently they came into the light of day. When they escaped out of the Slough of Indifference they made progress very fast; and considering how complete is the change of attitude between Bach and Mozart, it is very creditable to the energy and sincerity of musical humanity that this new phase of orchestral art was so well organised in the space of about half a century. But it must be remembered that it was the outcome of a separate movement which began before

the time of Handel and Bach, and was going on, though on
different lines from those they followed, during their lifetime.
Their line of work branched out from the direct line of harmonic music into a special province of its own. The purely
harmonic style was not sufficiently matured to allow of their
expressing themselves fully in it; had it been otherwise a
development like Beethoven's would have come nearly a
hundred years sooner. It was the possibility of combining
the polyphonic principles of the old choral art—painfully
worked out in the ages before harmonic music began—with
the simplest principles of the new harmonic music, which
afforded them the opportunity they used so magnificently.
And while they were busy with their great achievements, it
was left to smaller men to get through the preliminaries of
such forms as the sonata and the symphony—for even such
insignificant business as the devising of an "Alberti bass,"
and of similar forms of conventional accompaniment, had to
be done by somebody. But by the multitude of workers the
requirements of art were brought up to the penultimate stage
ready for the use of the three great representatives of instrumental music.

The main points so far achieved may be here summed up.

The Italians initiated an enthusiastic culture of the violin,
and in a very short time developed the resources of its
technique and the style of music adapted to it. The same
was done simultaneously for the harpsichord by other groups
of composers in Italy, Germany, France, and England. To
supply these typical solo instruments with intelligible music,
composers laboured with excellent success to devise schemes
of design and methods of development, which without the help
of words became sufficient reason of existence and principle
of coherence. At the same time, the growth of feeling for
the effect of massed harmonies placed composers in a position
to develop the possibilities of effect of orchestral instruments
in combination; and before long the growing perception of
the adaptability of various kinds of technique and of the
relations of different qualities of tone to one another, and
of the possible functions of the different instruments in the

scheme of orchestral composition, put things in the right direction to move on towards the accomplishment of the highest and richest achievement in the story of music—the employment of the complicated resources of an immense aggregate of different instruments for the purposes of vivid and infinitely variable expression.

CHAPTER X

THE MIDDLE STAGE OF MODERN OPERA

EVERY form of art has a variety of sides and aspects which appeal to different men in different degrees. A work may entrance one man through the beauty of its colour, while another finds it insupportable for its weakness of design. One man cares only for melody, when another is satisfied with grand harmony; one wants artistic skill, when another cares only for expression. This is true even of symphonies and sonatas, and such pure examples of human artistic contrivance; but in opera the complication and variety of constituent means of effect intensify the difficulties of the situation tenfold, and the chances of satisfying all tastes are necessarily extremely remote, for the elements that have to be combined seem to be almost incompatible. Scenic effect has to be considered as well as the development of the dramatic situations, and the dialogue, and the music. The action and the scenery distract the attention from the music, and the dialogue naturally goes too fast for it. Music, being mainly the expression of states of mind and feeling, takes time to convey its meaning; and in all but the most advanced stages of art the types of design which seem indispensable to make it intelligible require the repetition of definite passages of melody, and submission to rules of procedure which seem to be completely at variance with dramatic effect. If the action halts or hangs fire, the dramatic effect is paralysed; but if a phase of human passion which has once been passed has to be re-enacted to meet the supposed requirements of music, the situation becomes little less than ridiculous. So, in early days it seemed as if people had to take their choice, and either accept the music as the essential, and let the words and scenic appurtenances cease to have any dramatic significance; or to fasten their attention on the action and dialogue, and allow the music to be merely an indefinite rambling background of tone, which was hardly fit to be called music at all. The Italians, who enjoyed the distinction of developing the first stages of the operatic form, were much more impressionable on the musical than on the dramatic side, and as soon as the new secular type of music began to take shape, they gave their verdict absolutely in favour of the former; and the drama rapidly receded farther and farther into the background. The scheme was well devised up to a certain point; but as soon as the typical form of movement known as the aria had been fairly established, the ingenious artifices which had seemed to settle the plan of operations degenerated into mere conventions, and even musical progress in general came to a dead standstill. It was impossible for the music to grow or develop, for there was nothing in the occasion to call for any human expression or human interest. The sole purpose of existence of the opera was to show off a few celebrated Italian singers, who required to be accommodated according to fixed rules of precedence, which precluded any kind of freedom of dramatic action. The only glimpse of life which was apparent for some time was in the little humorous operas which began to come into notice about the beginning of the eighteenth century. The regular singer's opera was a most solemn and sedate function, and hardly admitted of anything so incongruous as humour. Humorous scenes had been attempted, even by Alessandro Scarlatti; but apparently they were considered out of place, and humour in general was relegated to the little musical comedies called intermezzos, or "opera buffa," which were performed in between the acts of the opera seria. From one point of view this made the situation even more absurd. It was like performing "King Lear" and the "School for Scandal" in alternate acts. But the ultimate result was eminently beneficial to opera in general. The composers who took the opera buffa in hand developed a special style for the purpose —merry, bright, vivacious, and pointed, and in its way very characteristic. In the music of the opera seria no attempt was made to follow the action in the music, because action in such situations could have amounted to nothing more than stilted gesticulation. But the composers of the intermezzi tried to keep the scene in their minds, and to accentuate gestures by sforzandos and queer surprising progressions, in accordance with the meaning of the actions, and so to bring all the resources of effect into the closest union. And this is a point of more importance than might appear without paying a little attention to it. As has before been pointed out, music mainly implies vocal expression in melody, and expressive gesture in rhythm and accent; and in the condition into which Italian opera had degenerated, the rhythmic element had for the most part retired into the background. Under the circumstances, the rhythmic animation and gaiety which was adapted to humorous purposes was the very thing that was wanted to reinfuse a little humanity into the formal torpor of opera seria.

The importance of the new departure may be judged by its fruits. A direct result of considerable importance was the French light comic opera, which started into existence after a visit of an Italian opera troupe to Paris in 1752, who performed Italian intermezzi, and aroused much controversy and opposition, mainly on the ground that Italians were not Frenchmen. But the style took root and was cultivated by French composers, who developed on its basis a type of light opera of the neatest and most artistic kind. But of still more importance was its actual influence on opera in general. The style inaugurated by the Italians in intermezzi is the source of the sparkling gaiety of Mozart's light and merry scenes in "Seraglio," "Nozze di Figaro," and "Don Giovanni." Osmin's famous song in the "Seraglio" is a direct descendant of the style which Pergolese so admirably illustrated in "La Serva Padrona;" and so is all Leporello's and Figaro's music. The style indeed was so congenial to Mozart's disposition that it coloured his work throughout; and traces of it peep out in symphonies, quartettes and sonatas, as well

15

as in his operas. And even Beethoven sometimes gives clear indications that he knew such ways of expressing lighter moods.*

The powerful influence which such a slight and rather trivial style exerted upon music in general at that time is clearly owing to the fact that it was the only line of operatic art which had any real life in it. When serious art drifts into formality, and composers and artists show that their efforts are concentrated upon the utterance of mere barren conventionalities, light music, and even vulgar and trivial music, which gives people a strong impression of being genuinely human, is bound to succeed best of the two. The audiences of the comic opera were at least allowed to take some genuine interest, and to get a genuine laugh out of the human perplexities and comic situations, and to feel that there was a reality about them which the heroic complacencies of the opera seria did not possess. As far as solid reforms of the opera seria itself are concerned, the public might have allowed things to go on in the same perfunctory way till the present time. The courtly fashionable people neither wanted nor deserved anything better; and the general reforms had to be forced on the notice of an indifferent world by the irrepressible energy of a personal conviction.

Gluck deserves great homage as a man of the rarest genius. But he deserves fully as much again for the splendid sincerity with which he refused to put up with the shams which the rest of the world found quite good enough to amuse them, and made men wake up to realise that opera was worth reforming. He brought about the first crisis in the history of this form of art, by calling attention to the fact that a work of art is always worth making as good as possible, and that opera itself would be more enjoyable and more worthy of intelligent beings if the dramatic side of the matter received more consideration. He was premature, as it happened, for the resources of his art were not yet fully equal to such undertakings as he

* Quartett in B♭, Op. 18, No. 6, at beginning. Opening scene of Fidelio. Violin sonata in C minor, last movement.

proposed; but at least he succeeded in dispelling a good deal of apathy, and in persuading people that real dramatic music was a possibility.

He himself received his operatic education in the school of Italian opera, and wrote a good many operas on the usual lines, which had good and characteristic music in them, but did not make any great impression on the world in general. The conviction that reforms were necessary was forced upon him by degrees; and he was encouraged by the similar views held by prominent people who were connected with operatic matters, such as even the famous librettist, Metastasio himself. He made several isolated attempts to re-establish the lost element of dramatic effect in opera from 1762 onwards. In 1767 "Alceste" was brought out in Vienna; and to the published edition he appended a preface, which so well expressed his view of the situation that a few of its sentences must necessarily be quoted. He proclaimed his object to be "to avoid all those abuses which had crept into Italian opera through the mistaken vanity of singers and the unwise compliance of composers," and proceeded:—

"I endeavoured to restrict the music to its proper function, that of seconding the poetry by enforcing the expression of the sentiment and the interest of the situations without interrupting the action or weakening it by superfluous ornament. . . . I have been very careful never to interrupt a singer in the heat of the dialogue in order to introduce a tedious ritornelle, nor to stop him in the middle of a word for the purpose of displaying the flexibility of his voice on some favourable vowel. . . . I have not thought it right to hurry through the second part of a song, if the words happened to be the most important of the whole, in order to repeat the first part four times over; or to finish the air where the sense does not end in order to allow the singer to exhibit his power of varying the passage at pleasure.

" My idea was that the Sinfonia ought to indicate the subject, and prepare the spectators for the character of the piece they are about to see; that the instruments ought to be introduced in proportion to the degree of interest and passion in the words; and that it was necessary, above all, to avoid making too great a disparity between the recitative and the air in the dialogue, so as not to break the sense of a period or awkwardly interrupt the movement and animation of a scene," &c.

The Viennese were not so much moved by these considerations, or by his practical exposition of them in the shape of opera, as he had naturally hoped; and ultimately he had to transfer the scene of action to Paris, where conditions were on the whole likely to be more favourable. The French in their national opera had always managed to keep the dramatic side of things more steadily in view than the Italians. Lulli had established the type before described, and his operas held the stage, to the exclusion of nearly all others, for some time after he had departed out of the world. Ultimately Rameau, one of the greatest of all French composers, improved very materially upon Lulli's work by a better handling of his instrumental resources, more lightness and variety and geniality in the music, and a better artistic standard of work all around. He was a man of musically sincere character, with more grasp of harmonic expression than is usual with Frenchmen, and with far more genuinely dramatic perception of the theatrical kind than any other man of his time—for it is noteworthy that he was born two years before Handel. It is highly probable that he had considerable influence upon Gluck; for that composer passed through Paris in 1746, and heard and was impressed by Rameau's work, which was conspicuously different from the average Italian product to which he was accustomed. And though Gluck's own work went ultimately far beyond Rameau's in every respect, whether artistic or expressive, there is a touch of the spirit of Rameau even in his mature and most characteristic works.

Paris then was the most hopeful place for him to get his views on dramatic matters attended to; and though it is obvious that the real evils which he attacked were in the Italian form of opera, and that the natural form of French opera was not so amenable to his criticisms, yet it was better to promulgate them in a place where people might pay a little attention than to address the worse than deafness of indifference.

The summary of his Parisian campaign is that he began by enlisting able literary men on his side, and rousing public curiosity by getting his theories discussed. He then brought out the first practical illustration of his theories in a version of Racine's "Iphigénie en Aulide," in 1774; and followed it up with a revised version of his earlier "Orfeo" under the name of "Orphée et Eurydice," and a revised version of "Alceste" in 1776, and "Armide" in 1777. After this a very estimable Italian composer, Piccini, was brought over from Italy by Gluck's opponents in the hopes of defeating him in a downright contest; and for a while the fervours of the rival partisans divided Paris. Gluck brought out his final manifesto, "Iphigénie en Tauride," in 1781, with great success. Piccini's setting of the same subject was acknowledged to be inferior, and the Gluckists remained masters of the field.

The point which is of highest importance in Gluck's victory, as far as the development of the art is concerned, is the restoration of the element of genuine human expression to its place in the scheme of art. Gluck, like every one else, was forced to accept the work of his predecessors as the basis of his own, and even to retain some of the most conspicuous features of the scheme which he aimed at destroying. He had to write arias on the old lines, for they were the only definite types of design then understood; and Gluck was far too wise to think he could dispense with definite design. He had also to accept the ballet, for it was too vital a part of the French operatic scheme to be discarded without almost certainty of failure. But, in the case of the arias, he did his best to make them as characteristic of the situations as the backward state of the art allowed; and he often replaced them by short movements of very complete and simple form—more like the type of folk-songs—into which he concentrated a great deal of genuine expression. For the ballets he had the justification of the ancients; and he undoubtedly applied them in many cases extremely well. Wherever it was possible they were made part of the action, and became a very effective part of it. As, for instance, the dance and chorus of furies at the threshold of the infernal regions in "Orfeo," and the chorus and ballets of Scythians in "Iphigénie en Tauride." For his treatment of recitative he had the earlier examples of Lulli and Rameau, who had both adopted a free style of expressive declamation with definite accompaniment; often with very successful results. Since their time music had very much enlarged its resources of expression and had become more elastic; and Gluck, while working on the same lines, improved immensely upon their standard in respect of refinement and artistic finish. Moreover, the expressive qualities of his admirable recitatives are very much enhanced by his way of dealing with the accompaniment. He neglected no opportunity to make use of the qualities of his orchestral instruments—as far as in him lay—to enforce and accentuate the situations, and even to intensify the passing moment of feeling implied by the dialogue. Composers were successfully developing the sense of the functions and resources of instrumentation. Even Gluck's rival, Piccini, made some very appropriate effects by using his instruments consistently with the spirit of the situations. But Gluck applied himself to the matter with far more intensity, and far more genuine perception of the characters of the instruments. Indeed it would hardly be an exaggeration to say, that he was the first composer in the world who had any genuine understanding of this very modern phase of the art. Mozart was the first to show real natural gift and genuine feeling for beautiful disposition of tone, but Gluck anticipated modern procedure in adapting his colours exactly to the mood of the situation. A good deal had been attempted already in a sort of half-hearted and formal manner, but he was the first to seize firmly on the right principles and to carry out his objects with any mastery of resources.

The texture of his work is such as might be expected from his training. He shows very little feeling for polyphony, or for the effects which are produced by those kinds of chords which become possible only through the independent treat-

ment of parts. In this respect he was the very opposite of
Bach. His early experiences of choral writing had been in a
bad school; and his choruses, except when animated by some
powerful dramatic impulse, are poor and badly managed, both
for vocal tone and general effect. But his orchestration is
as much more mature than Bach's and Handel's as his choral
writing is inferior. There is no attempt to treat his instruments like voices or counterpoints, nor to use them solely
because artistic effect, apart from dramatic effect, makes it
advisable. The treatment is in every respect harmonic, not
contrapuntal; and his harmonies are extremely simple and
limited in range. But he uses them with such an excellent
sense of proportion that the general result is, even harmoni-
cally, more impressive than the work of modern composers
who have a more copious supply to draw from, but less discretion and discrimination. It may be confessed that in his
efforts to infuse expression into every possible moment he
very much overdoes the use of appogiaturas, till the device
becomes at times a somewhat pointless mannerism; but the
greatness of his genius is emphasised by the fact that he contrived to attain a very high pitch of genuine expression, and
to sustain the general musical character of extensive works, in
conformity with the nature of the situations, at a time when
the resources of expression, especially in the dramatic line,
were very limited. It must also be remembered that the
development of modern instrumental forms of art had only
just begun, and Gluck lacked models of orchestral style as
well as of design. It so happened that the first of Mozart's
symphonies which is really notable from the point of view of
style and design was first performed in Paris in the middle
of the war of the Gluckists and Piccinists. But no great
symphony had been written before, and when Gluck was
formulating his theories and speculating on the possibilities
of musical expression, the art of modern instrumentation
was still in its infancy. Moreover, Gluck had no such natural
gift for the management of general effect as Mozart. His
powers as a composer were developed mainly under the influence of his strong feeling for things dramatic and poetical,

and it was the intensity with which he felt the situations which gave him musical utterance. His orchestration has none of the roundness or balance or maturity of Mozart's. It is unequal and uncertain, and requires humouring in performance to make it produce the effect which is intended. But, like the rest of his work, it is essentially sincere, and its very crudity is sometimes apt to the situations that he required it to illustrate.

His influence upon the history of art in certain directions was great, but not such as might be expected. Upon Italian opera seria he had scarcely any influence at all. It went on its absurdly illogical and undramatic way unmoved. The kind of people who patronised it did not want anything good; they only wanted to be amused. Italian composers were not troubled with convictions as Gluck was, and they have too often liked bad music quite as much as their audiences. Upon French opera the influence of Gluck was more permanent, and his schemes were developed by later composers to grandiose proportions, sometimes with excellent results, sometimes with an unfortunate tendency to emphasise histrionic display, which certainly does not chime with Gluck's refined intentions.

His system was too ideal for the world of his time, and the niche which he occupies is singularly isolated, through the inadequacy of musical means to meet his requirements. His singular energy and clearness of dramatic insight forced a special path for himself out of the direct course of musical progress. It was as though he pushed for himself a special short cut up a very arduous ascent where other men could not follow him. And it was not until music in general had gone by a more circuitous route, which avoided the rocks and precipices, that it finally arrived at a position which made his ideals attainable. No one in his time could pursue the path he had marked out, for no one but himself had sufficient mastery of dramatic expression even to equal his work in that respect, much less to improve upon it.

Though the genuine opera seria of the Italians was not destined to be lifted out of the ruts into which it had fallen for a long while, the scheme which their composers had inaugurated served as the basis upon which composers of the more enduring Teutonic race gradually developed the resources necessary for the achievement of the operatic ideal. Germans had been for some time dominated by Italian influences in every department of art as badly as the Italians themselves; and when Mozart came upon the scene, it is probable that he heard next to nothing in his earlier years which was Teutonic either in style or in name. Italian music reigned supreme in Vienna and Salzburg; and throughout his most impressionable years he constantly imbibed the phraseology, the principles of design, and the artistic methods of Italian composers and their German imitators. He was no reformer by nature, and the immense services he did to art were in no sense either speculative or theoretic, but merely a sort of natural growth; amounting to a general improvement of the texture of things rather than to a marked change either in principles or details. He was gifted with an extraordinarily keen sense of beauty, and with the most astounding natural facility in all things artistic which ever was the lot of man. The inevitable consequence was that he began to see how to improve upon the work of his predecessors in every direction very early; and he was afforded ample opportunities.

Before he was ten years old he had made a triumphal progress through the most important cities in Europe, and had tried his hand at most of the branches of composition; and by the age of twelve he was writing operas for the Italians themselves, and had surpassed most living composers in all departments of artistic workmanship. All his earlier operas were on the usual Italian lines; and though they show his unusual powers in finished modelling of melody, and skilful management of accompaniment, they do not need any special consideration. The first really important mark he made was an indirect result of his visit to Mannheim on the way to Paris in 1777. The town was, and had been for some time, the centre of the best musical activity in Germany; and it was here that Mozart first heard refined and careful orchestral playing, and came into contact with patriotic schemes for developing national art and national opera. The experiences he enjoyed during a rather prolonged stay thoroughly roused him to give his full attention to the possibilities of orchestral effect; and the enthusiasm for thoroughness in all departments of art, which possessed the people of Mannheim, undoubtedly led him to treat the operatic form of art with more consideration for fitness and dramatic effect than it would have occurred to him to do if he had remained entirely under Italian or Viennese influence. The first important fruit in the line of opera was " Idomeneo," which he produced three years later (1781) for the Carnival in Munich, where he had every inducement to exert himself to the utmost, as the taste of the public was better there than in Vienna, and the resources of the orchestra and chorus were very large. His libretto was modelled on an old Italian one which had been used nearly seventy years before; but this did not affect the quality of his work, which is so very much richer and better than any earlier opera of its class that it makes a point of signal importance in the story of the art. To begin with, he used an unusually large orchestra, and he used it in a way which was quite new to the world. He did not aim at characterisation so much as Gluck had done, for in that respect Gluck was speculatively too much ahead of his time. But his method shows far more spontaneous skill, through his keen feeling for beauty and variety of tone; and his perfect use of each several instrument in the way best suited to its special idiosyncrasies gives the effect of security and completeness. Nothing is wasted. No player of a wind instrument merely blows into his pipe to make a sound to fill up a gap, nor do the violin players now and then merely draw out an isolated sound to make a chord complete. Everything is articulate, finished, full of life; and that without adopting a contrapuntal manner, or obtrusively introducing figures that are not wanted and merely distract the attention. Mozart at this early stage shows himself a completely mature master of all the practical resources of orchestration; and in almost every department and every aspect of the work a like fine

artistic sense is shown.   The earlier composers had to concentrate their attention and almost all their skill on the solo
singer's voice part; and the care which they bestowed on
the rest of their work was mainly to keep it in the background.   Mozart's spontaneous instinct for artistic fitness
brought things to their proper level, and simultaneously raised
the standard of interest in every respect.   Even in the matter
of singing and acting the soloist has in this case to share the
honours with the chorus; which is now brought forward not
only to give the requisite mass of tone and scenic animation
to the ends of acts, but to take an important part in the action
throughout.   The chorus becomes a living portion of the
scheme, and is wielded by the composer in a way which shows
that he tried to feel what real people would do in the situations in which he had to put them, and not what mere
theatrical chorus singers would be doing among the wings
and stage properties.   The same story has repeated itself again
and again.   When any scheme like the presentation of a
stage play has been contrived, and there arises a large demand
for new works, men who supply them get into the habit of
thinking of nothing but the artifices of the stage.   They put
the machinery in motion, and all they succeed in presenting
is a property shipwreck, or a stage murder, or the passion of
a prima donna in full sight of an audience.   Mozart showed
a superiority to that weakness of the imagination, most
notably in his comic scenes in the later operas.   But it is easy
to see that in "Idomeneo" too he tried to keep in mind the
reality of the human circumstances of which the stage
machinery is but the symbol.   Mozart never trespassed
through laying too much stress on expression.   It was
necessarily rather the reverse, for he belonged to a formal
period; in which the machinery of art claimed a great
deal of attention.   But within the limits of formality he
often succeeded in infusing true and sincere human expression, and he used his resources of colour, rhythm, and
melody with perfect relevancy to the situations.   In those
respects the distance between his work and that of the
Italian composers of his time is really enormous.   But

there are still a great deal too many of those formalities which are inevitably brought in to hide the gaps made by unsolved problems. The arias are too rigid in form, and the various complete pieces are crudely introduced. The divisions do not assimilate into a well-moulded whole, but are separate items, like the old singers' arias, though so immensely superior to them in intrinsic qualities, and so much more varied in general character. And, moreover, a great deal of the dialogue is set in the insupportable make-shift manner of the middle-period Italian recitative; which makes an almost insuperable blot in any serious work in which it occurs. It passes muster in comic works, because it can be accepted together with other confessions of human weakness as conceivably humorous. But in a work of serious interest it breaks the continuity of things worse than even ordinary speech; for its chaotic inanity is such a perversion of the purpose of music that it becomes far more noticeable than dialogue, which pretends to be nothing more than it is.

Apart from these recitatives, Mozart probably carried expression as far as was then possible within the limits by which he was bound. His instinct for design was too cautious to allow him to venture upon untried methods which might fit more closely to the dialogue and to the progress of the action. He had to repeat his passages, and to take his "tonic and dominant" quite regularly, according to the laws of form as then understood, and to write set melodies on familiar lines. He had hardly any experience of methods of immediate concentrated expression, such as Bach's mastery of harmony and counterpoint enabled him to use. And even if he had known how to achieve such things, the types of procedure would not have fitted into his scheme of art; for they would have betrayed their incongruity, and thrown the balance of style out of gear. Art had to go a long way before such amalgamation was possible. Even Mozart himself was as yet far from the standard of his greatest symphonies; and, far as "Idomeneo" is beyond the standard of any previous Italian operas, and interesting and rich in artistic power and resource, its forma-

lity and inadequacy as a solution of the operatic problem is
indicated by the fact that it is almost totally unknown to the
musical public.

The national desire for genuine Teutonic opera was spreading and growing more eager in Mozart's time; and the
Emperor of Austria took up the cause, and invited him to
write a regular German opera. The principal obstacle was
that a national opera, like anything else in art, had to be
built up by slow degrees; and there was a conspicuous lack
of models for style and plan, and treatment of things dramatic
in a German manner. Keiser's attempts lay too far away in
the past, and were too crude to have much bearing in Mozart's
time; and the only form which had succeeded at all in later
times was the Singspiel, which was little more than a play
with incidental music and songs, very similar to the type
in vogue in England about Purcell's time. These plays had
generally been very slight, and sometimes farcical, so there
was very little in them to serve as a basis for work of a solid
kind. But such as it was, Mozart accepted the form as the
type to follow in his "Entführung aus dem Serail." In the
event very little came of it that was characteristically Teutonic. The music itself is admirable, and every artistic accessory and detail is managed as only Mozart could manage
such things at that time. But the light scenes were in the
Italian buffo style, and the harmonisation and instrumentation and phraseology are all in the style Mozart usually
employed in Italian opera. Every one who understands
anything about art will know that this was inevitable; for
a man can only work on the lines and in the terms he
is master of. The most that Mozart could do was to impart a more genuinely warm and expressive feeling to a
few of the airs, and in no other respect is any Teutonic
flavour discernible. Mozart for the moment elevated the
form of the Singspiel into the regions of loftiest art; but
that was not what a Singspiel audience wanted, and his
work was not characteristically Teutonic enough, either in
subject or style, to enlist the national sympathies; and
though on the whole it succeeded very well, its success was

on the old grounds, and not on the grounds of its being a satisfactory or complete solution of the problem of national opera. Further action in the same direction was postponed, and Mozart resumed the composition of Italian operas. His next effort was the brilliant "Nozze di Figaro," founded on Beaumarchais' play. It came out in 1786, and "Don Giovanni" followed in 1787. These are not on such a grand scale as "Idomeneo," but they have the superior attraction of a great deal of real fun, which is essentially a human element. The stories of both Figaro and Don Giovanni are cynically humorous, and seem scarcely fit to be taken seriously; but it is easy to follow and to be amused by all the escapades and scrapes of the Don and Leporello, and by Figaro and Cherubino and the rest of the merry throng. They are just as much realities as Mozart's merry tunes; and the necessary stage conventions do not jar so noticeably as they would do if the works had often touched upon deeper chords and portrayed stronger and more vital emotions. It is just in those situations where, owing to the exigencies of his story, the composer has to deal with a tragic moment, that the formality necessarily becomes prominent. Real tragic intensity of feeling would be quite out of place in such surroundings; and such sorrows as Elvira's are not in any case capable of being adequately expressed in the old-fashioned form of the aria, with its complacent orderly melody, and mechanical repetition of the same words of sorrow. It is in such situations that the utter inadequacy of the old operatic scheme becomes too conspicuously glaring.

The process of development in the right direction is shown by the way in which Mozart often knits together a number of movements into a continuous series, especially at the end of an act. This was the way in which complete assimilation of the musical factors into a composite whole was gradually approached. In some cases, as in the finales in Figaro, he contrives to make the interchange of dialogue between the characters very rapid for a long time at a stretch, producing an extremely animated effect. But it illustrates the imma-

turity of the operatic form that he still felt it necessary
to repeat his musical phrases again and again to make them
lay hold of the minds of the audience.   The lightness of the
subjects he dealt with necessitated his carrying out every
feature of his scheme very simply and spontaneously, and this
device of phrase repetition he used without the least disguise.
He probably borrowed it from the Italian composers of opera
buffa, and it became so much a part of his system that he
employs it in every class of work, in symphonies and sonatas
as well as in operas.   The result is that the works become
very easy to follow; but the practice cannot be said to be
a characteristic of an advanced state of art.   On the other
hand, Mozart undoubtedly brought his music into very close
connection with the action, especially in comic scenes.   It
sometimes fits so perfectly that it seems as though he had
the whole scene before him, and followed all the by-play and
gestures in his mind while writing.   This also was probably
a development of the methods of the composers of opera
buffa.

Of Mozart's two last Italian operas little need be said.
"Cosi fan tutte" is a comic opera which was written by
order of the Emperor of Austria to an unsatisfactory libretto,
which made the success, which the real brightness of the
music might have otherwise obtained, completely impossible.   "La Clemenza di Tito" was an opera seria of the
old kind written for a coronation at Prague to an old
libretto by Metastasio, which had been set by most of the
earlier stock composers before it came to Mozart's turn,
and did not contain any elements which could inspire him
to fresh achievements.

His last operatic work was far more important, for once
again it made him the representative of the German aspiration to have a national opera.   On the previous occasion the
experiment had been made under the auspices of the Austrian
Emperor and his court; the new one was made for an essentially popular audience.   The invitation came from the actor-
manager Schikaneder, who had been catering for the Viennese
public for some time with fair success.   He conceived the

idea that the German public would be attracted by a magic opera; and to judge from the surprising number of magic operas which have since appeared in Germany, he gauged the Teutonic disposition in that respect very acutely. The play, which Schikaneder himself prepared and called "Die Zauberflöte," is almost unintelligible; but it contained some good opportunities for musical effect, and as the interest of the play was supposed to centre round some mystic secrets of Freemasonry, which at that time were especially interesting to the German mind, it was not altogether inappropriate that it should be unintelligible to the general and the feminine public. Mozart's setting was again mainly Italian in style, but he infused a degree of dignified and noble sentiment into certain parts of the work which was quite unlike what was to be met with in Italian operas; and in the end, between his music and the mystery of the play, the work became a spontaneous success of a pronounced description, and was taken up very eagerly all over Germany.

It can hardly be said, however, that it quite satisfied the aspirations after a national opera, though it was decidedly a step of some importance in that direction. The actual solution of the problem depended on conditions which at that time were unattainable, for the national style for operatic purposes had yet to be found. What little there was of distinctly Teutonic style had not been applied in such a manner; neither had the accessories, such as the appropriate type of harmonisation and of accompaniment, been cultivated sufficiently to be available on such a large scale as opera. German melodic ideas would not fit to the conventional types of harmonic accompaniment used for Italian melody, any more than a Gothic roof and steeple would fit on to an Ionic building. The racial musical instincts of Teutons and Italians were different. The instinct of Italians was all in favour of beauty and simplicity. They cared little for intensely vivid expression of any kind, and their most natural method of utterance was melody, associated with the forms of accompaniment which support a solo voice in the very simplest manner. They were perfectly content to

hear the same formulas again and again. For instance, the
same formulas of harmony, and even of melody, were used for
the last few bars before the cadence in endless different arias
and scenas ; and the same successions of chords served for the
song of the lady bewailing her murdered father and for that
of the gentleman rejoicing over the success of a love suit.
The bent of Germans, on the other hand, was not so much
towards beauty as towards expression and character. Their
very type of beauty was different from that of the Italians.
The Italians looked for beauty of externals, and the Germans
for beauty of thought. The instinct for beauty of thought
comes out analogously in their artists' work. To the eye
there is not much beauty of externals in Albert Dürer and
Holbein, but of expression and thought there is ample to
engage the mind and the sensibilities again and again. So
it was in music from the earliest time, in Schütz's work as in
Bach's and in Brahms'. And though melody was a factor in
the German scheme, characteristic harmony became one also
very early. And as harmony has more power of immediate
expression than melody, the Teutonic nature was drawn
towards it more and more. And as polyphonic treatment
enhances the capacity of harmony for expression, and gives
vitality to its inner details, the Teutonic mind was also drawn
in that direction. Polyphony is melody multiplied, and represents the composite nature of man's character and man's
moods and motives of action in a way that mere single melody
can never do. The Germans having the feeling and instinct
for these higher things, it was clearly impossible for their
ideals of operatic art to be satisfied with such immature conditions as are represented in Mozart's operas, admirable
though the works themselves are as representing the Italian
conception of art. But though Mozart, owing to his circumstances, and the state of art at that time, could not satisfy
the full aspirations of the Germans in their own field, he
raised Italian opera to its highest point. His more earnest
German surroundings, and his experiences at Mannheim, led
his impressionable disposition to the full development of his
marvellous aptitude for orchestration ; to a higher, richer, and

16

more characteristic standard of melody; to a wider range of harmony, and more perfect modelling and management of design, than had ever been attained by Italians. In all these things he enriched the art to an enormous extent, and left it more highly organised in nearly all its various departments than when he took it up.

CHAPTER XI

THE MIDDLE STAGE OF "SONATA" FORM

THE principles upon which self-dependent instrumental music was being developed during the greater part of the eighteenth century were quite new to mankind. Before men developed the capacity for understanding the classification of harmonies in connection with certain tonal centres, such principles were altogether inconceivable. But when once the idea of harmonic centralisation was well established, progress in readiness to grasp the artistic purpose of the composer in disposing his groups of harmony, so as to convey the impression of design, was extraordinarily rapid; as may be judged by the difference in obviousness between a concerto of Vivaldi's and a symphony of Mozart's.

It may be admitted, parenthetically, that there was a considerable falling off of style in instrumental music when it came more decisively under operatic influences. The standard of Tartini and his fellow-violinists is much higher than that of most of their successors; who infused the fashionable style of opera music into their instrumental works, to gratify the feeble taste of their fashionable pupils. But the development of the great branch of instrumental music did not follow in a straight line from Corelli and Tartini and such masters, but was the result of a process of filtration through the minds of all sorts and conditions of composers. Haydn and Mozart, and Beethoven in his turn, were in their younger days influenced by the flood of all sorts of music which came under their notice. And though their higher sense of style and expression rejected the more trivial and superficial things that they heard, their own work became a sort of instinctive generalisation, which was based on the general average of all that attracted their attention. Everything has its degree and proportion in such matters, but great work is always the sum of an immense range of influences, and not the product of the impressions produced by a few isolated pieces of perfection. Thus in painting, if a man study only the manner in which some single master overcomes some special difficulty, his own treatment will probably be only a reflection of that master's work. But if he studies the methods of several, and finds the particular excellences of each, and grasps their principles of application, he has enlarged his own resources; and then he will not merely reproduce the external aspects of the works of one man, but will find out how to express his own individuality in terms which are the fruit of wider understanding of technique.

The special department in which the sum of all sorts of experiments was leading to a satisfactory establishment of principles, in the early part of the eighteenth century, was the extremely important one of harmonic design. Musical instinct was leading men to give the best of their powers to the development of the types of design now familiar in sonatas, and out of a multiplicity of experiments Mozart and Haydn, and their lesser contemporaries, gave their verdict very decisively in favour of a type of movement which looks at first most peculiar and enigmatical; but which not only proved to be most elastic and satisfying in practice, but becomes amply intelligible when the course of its history is taken into consideration.

The aim of composers was first to establish a point of departure; and when that had been sufficiently insisted upon, to set out from it and find an orderly series of contrasts of as many and various kinds as the art allowed; and to dispose them in such a way as to make each step lead onwards, till a circuit was completed by returning to and re-establishing the original starting-point. The first form in which this principle of design is perceptible is the type of ordinary dance tune, which proceeded from a given point to a contrasting point, and after laying sufficient stress upon that point to emphasise the con-

trast, worked back again and re-established the initial position.   When this type arrived at any degree of definite
organisation, the most noticeable feature was the division into
two fairly equal halves, with a close in the key of contrast
at the end of the first half.   Composers aimed at distributing
their materials in such a framework so as to give the strongest
emphasis to the most essential points, and to make the ideas
lay hold of the mind.   The requirements of average human
beings were best consulted by making the beginning of the
first half coincide in musical material with the beginning of
the second half, and the end of the first half coincide with
the end of the second half; since the beginnings and ends
of phrases are always most easily retained by the mind.   The
portions between the beginnings and the endings were
generally rather vague and indefinite, though composers who
had any artistic sense tried to keep the style strictly relevant
throughout, and to maintain any rhythm which had presented
itself definitely at the outset.   The plan of a considerable
majority of movements remained on these lines until the end
of the polyphonic period of instrumental music; and the
movements in the most artistic suites and partitas have very
little more in the way of design.

When harmonic principles came to be cultivated in sonatas,
the same order of distribution of materials was adopted; but
in accordance with harmonic requirements, the passages which
coincided in musical material were lengthened, and made more
definite, both in respect of melody and rhythm.   And at
length the passage in the contrasting key, which had originally
been little more than a cadence, was expanded to a length
fully equal to the passage in the principal key; and it was
frequently marked by a second subject or new idea, which
became the distinguishing feature of the key of contrast.   The
ideas presented in the principal keys were repeated in the
second half of the movement in positions corresponding to the
arrangement of the earlier form; the first idea coming in
the key of contrast at the beginning of the second half, and the
second in the home key at the end.   The portion between the
two subjects in the second half began to expand very early;

both to widen the scope of the modulations, and because composers' instincts told them that there still was a lack of contrast through the exact regularity and definiteness of the main
divisions. They felt that a contrast to this excess of definiteness
was wanted, and they found it in the process of breaking up the
subjects into their constituent figures and distributing them in
progressions which had an appearance of being unsystematic.

By the time the movement had expanded to such proportions, the mere re-statement of the second subject at the end
was barely sufficient to give a comfortable reassurance of
being safe home in the original key. And, moreover, as the
progress of music in general was tending to a much more
decisive recognition of the musical subjects and ideas themselves as the aim and end of things, it seemed strange that the
musical idea, which occupied such prominence by reason of its
appearing at the outset, should be so neglected in the latter
part of the movement. So it became customary to repeat the
first subject as well as the second at the end of all things in
the principal key. Then it appeared that there was too much
of this first subject, so its formal repetition at the beginning
of the second half was dropped, though it still often appears
in its old place even in modern works of the sonata order.

The whole process of development may be seen at a glance
in a mechanical scheme. Taking the letters to represent the
musical material, and the numerals to represent the principal
keys, and the double bar to represent the point where the
movement is divided into two portions, the process was mainly
as follows :—

1st form　.　a^1, transition ending in b^2 ‖ a^2, transition ending in b^1.

2nd form　.　A^1　B^2　‖　A^2　modulations　B^1.

3rd form　.　A^1　B^2　‖　A^2　modulations　A^1　B^1.

4th form　.　A^1　B^2　‖　modulation and development　A^1　B^1.

In the early sonatas both halves of the movement were played twice. As artistic feeling developed, the repetition of the second half was frequently dispensed with, but the repetition of the first half was maintained, mainly to help the mind to grasp firmly the principle of contrast between the two keys. In modern times the repetition of the first half is also commonly dispensed with, because the musical instinct has become so quick to grasp any indication of design that it no longer requires to have such things insisted on; and also because the progress of music towards a more passionately emotional phase makes it noticeably anomalous to go through the same exciting crises twice over. Beethoven's practice illustrates this point very happily; for in the less directly emotional sonatas in which design is particularly emphasised, he gives the usual direction for the repetition of the first half; as in the early sonatas, when the possibility of dispensing with such conventions had not dawned upon him, and in the first movements of such later sonatas as the Waldstein (Opus 53) and the one in F♯ (Opus 78). In movements which are so decisively emotional and expressive as the first movements of the Appassionata (F minor, Opus 57), of the E minor (Opus 90), of the A major (Opus 101), and the E major (Opus 109), the repetition is dispensed with, and the movements are made as continuous as possible from end to end, so as to hide the formal element and guard against the mind's being distracted by it.

The prominence which Italian operatic taste gave to melody and to superficial views of art led people to regard the principle of design as consisting of the exposition of a first tune in one key and of a second tune in a contrasting key, and certain developments based on them to follow and complete the scheme. But in fact the musical subject is one thing and the design is another. The "subject," as it is called, had to have a form of its own to begin with; and though some composers, working under operatic influences, did often write two long continuous passages of melody which successively represent the principal key and the key of contrast, the acuter instinct of true instrumental composers generally aimed at short and incisive figures for their musical ideas, which indicated the spirit and mood of their work in a manner more suited to pure instrumental music, and made them lay hold of the mind quickly; and they completed the musical sentences, which represented each essential key, by repeating the most characteristic figures in different positions in the scale, or with ingenious variations of detail which gave them extra interest.

The necessity for making the essential keys clear led to various interesting and probably unconscious devices. The trick of alternating the characteristic harmonies of tonic and dominant in the subject is so familiar that it requires no discussion. More singular is the profusion of examples of different epochs, in which the principal musical idea is conveyed in terms of the tonic chord of the movement, which is the essential point from which the outset is made. A few examples may be noted in the following works. Scarlatti's Sonata in G major—

the principal allegro movement of Tartini's Sonata in G minor (Didone Abandonnata)—

Paradisi's Sonata in D major, Mozart's well-known Sonata in C minor, Beethoven's Sonata in F minor (No. 1), the last movement of his Sonata in C♯ minor; the first of his Sonata Appassionata, his overture Leonora (No. 3), and Weber's Sonata in A♭. The instinctive object of the composer in all cases is to make the whereabouts of his starting-point very definitely understood. Nearly all the finest subjects in existence have some such principle inherent in their structure.

But the subject itself is not the form, nor until it is repeated is it a necessary factor in the scheme of a design in the abstract. It is the idea or musical fact of melody, or rhythm, or harmony, which conveys the mood or thought which the composer wishes to express. The mould in which the idea is cast is a different thing. The idea may be expressed in terms of the tonic chord, but the tonic chord is not the idea. On the other hand, the tonic chord is a part, and a very essential part, of the scheme of design; and upon its being understood in that sense, the feeling for the design of the movement as a whole depends; but the chord is not an idea till it is vitalised by rhythm or melody. Similarly, the design in a picture does not consist of the subject, but of the manner in which the factors which indicate the subject are distributed. The design in music of the sonata order consists of the distribution of the keys and tonal centres and subcentres, rather than of the so-called subjects, or the order in which they are presented. This point requires to be emphasised, because it is not possible to understand what Beethoven did for art, or the meaning of all that came after his time, without realising the distinction between subject and design.

As a matter of fact, there often are a great number of subjects or typical musical ideas in each of the divisions which are generally spoken of as *the* first or *the* second subject; and in the most mature form of sonata movement there is almost always a special third subject whose function and character is so strongly illustrative of the harmonic principle of design as employed in sonatas, as to call for special notice. The first key is always easily indicated, because it comes fresh to the mind; but the second or contrasting key requires more management and more decisive confirmation, because the impression of the first has to be obliterated. For that reason the second principal idea is generally put into very definite and clear terms of tonality, and is often followed by numerous accessory passages obviously indicative of the key; and finally, when the period which represents the contrasting key comes to an end, the wisest composers confirmed that key strongly by introducing a short new subject of specially attractive

character, which is entirely modelled upon a group of chords
forming a complete cadence. The function of this subject is
essentially to call attention to the particular point in the
design where the division representing the contrasting key
comes to an end; and the harmonic formula on which it is
founded is always peculiarly simple.

The whole scheme of this type of movement, which was
fairly established by the time Haydn and Mozart began their
work, implies the following general intention. The first part
of the movement aims at definiteness in every respect—definiteness of subject, definiteness of contrast of key, definiteness of
regular balancing groups of bars and rhythms, definiteness of
progressions. By the time this first division is over the mind
has had enough of such definiteness, and wants a change. The
second division, therefore, represents the breaking up of the
subjects into their constituent elements of figure and rhythm,
the obliteration of the sense of regularity by grouping the bars
irregularly ; and aims, by moving constantly from key to key,
to give the sense of artistic confusion ; which, however, is
always regulated by some inner but disguised principle of
order. When the mind has gone through enough of the
pleasing sense of bewilderment—the sense that has made
riddles attractive to the human creature from time immemorial
—the scheme is completed by resuming the orderly methods
of the first division, and firmly re-establishing the principal key,
which has been carefully avoided since the commencement.

From the point of view of design every moment and every
step from beginning to end should have its own inherent justification and reason for existence. Each concord must have its
due relation to its immediate context, each discord must have
its resolution, each statement its counter-statement. From the
point of view of the subject or idea persistent interest is given
to every moment by the distribution and coherent relevancy
of the melodies and rhythms employed, by the variety of the
situations and the lights in which the musical figures are
placed, and by the development of such climaxes as are inherent in the very principle of their structure. In the most
perfect movements there can be no moment when the prin-

ciple of design is lost sight of, or the ideas cease to be articulate. But it must be confessed that there have been only
two or three composers in the history of the world who have
had such complete hold of their resources as to produce movements which are entirely perfect from end to end from every
point of view; and even these rarest geniuses sometimes nod.

The opportunities which this peculiar form has offered to
composers are so extraordinarily rich that it has been uniformly adopted for sonatas, symphonies, overtures, quartetts,
and all forms of chamber music, and sometimes for small
lyrical pieces. The development of self-dependent instrumental music almost centres round it, and it gives special
character to the long period of art stretching from the second
quarter of the eighteenth century till the advent of Schumann
and Chopin, and the expressive romanticists of the latter days.
It is especially the type of design used for the first movements
of sonatas and symphonies; as it is peculiarly suitable for the
intellectual and more highly organised kinds of music. It has
sometimes been used also for the emotional slow movements,
but it was more usual to adopt a simpler type of form in them
—something similar to the old type of aria, or to the rondo
form. And this same rondo form was also found suitable for
last movements, as it lends itself happily to light and gay
moods; and the constant alternation of definite tunes gives
easy animation to the general effect. As a rule, the rondo
form is not very suitable to the expression of a very high
order of music; but the artistic ingenuity of composers
managed to make the form interesting by throwing the various sections into groups, and by distributing the subject-matter
so as to give enhanced interest to the rather primitive type of
structure.

By the time that Haydn and Mozart arrived upon the scene
this scheme of instrumental music was fairly established, but
it had been used by most composers before their time crudely,
obviously, and mechanically. While the form was new it was
enjoyable as a novelty, and as a mere piece of mechanical ingenuity, and the perverting influence of the predominating
operatic taste prevented composers from applying any faculties

they might have possessed to the improvement of the details. It was the superior artistic instinct of Mozart and Haydn which led them to give attention to such things, and to develop and organise the system of design to a very high degree of perfection.

The circumstances which impelled the two great composers into their respective courses were simple and fortunate. Though both were Southern Germans and Roman Catholics in religion, their circumstances and early associations were widely different. Mozart being the child of a professional musician of considerable attainments and musical culture, was surrounded by artistic conditions from his babyhood; and most of the music with which he came into contact was of an artistically organised kind from the first, while his studies were always wisely directed by his very sensible parent. But the circumstances were not favourable to the development of personal character, and, as far as his art was concerned, he was almost entirely relieved of the individual struggle to ascertain things and make up his mind about them for himself, which has such important results in developing the individuality of the artistic worker. Haydn, on the other hand, was the son of a rustic wheelwright, a real son of the people —whose first musical influences were folk-tunes, whose experience of artistic music came late, and who had, like Bach and Beethoven, and many others of the great ones, to work out his own musical salvation. And, to emphasise the difference between the two men, where Mozart had been entirely subject to Italian influences from the first, and found his most congenial model in such a type as John Christian Bach —the Italian Bach—Haydn by good fortune or happy instinct took for his model Philip Emmanuel Bach, the only prominent composer in Europe who retained any touch of the old traditions of Northern Germany, and some of the sincere and noble spirit of his father, which spared not to make every detail as characteristic and full of vitality as circumstances allowed. The result is that Haydn is throughout as Teutonic in spirit and manner as it was possible to be in those times, and that most of his work has a high degree of personal char-

acteristic vitality; while Mozart, with more delicate artistic
perception, more sense of beauty, a much higher gift of technique and more general facility, is comparatively deficient
in individuality, and hardly shows any trace of Teutonism
in style from first to last.

The careers of the two composers interlaced very peculiarly,
and at different times they exerted influence upon one another.
Haydn is commonly held to have exerted some influence upon
Mozart at first, and when the latter had progressed rapidly
to his highest achievements and had passed away, his work
undoubtedly influenced Haydn. Though Haydn was twenty-
four years older than Mozart, he did not get well into his
work much before the younger composer; for the circumstances of his life necessarily delayed him. He appears to
have begun writing symphonies at the age of twenty-seven,
in 1759, whereas Mozart began at the age of eight, in 1764;
so their musical periods really coincide more nearly than the
differences of their ages might seem to make probable.

After the severe trials of his youth, Haydn's circumstances
changed, and he thereafter enjoyed advantages such as have
hardly fallen to the lot of any other composer. After a short
engagement to a Bohemian Count Morzin, for whom he wrote
his first symphony, he was engaged for many years as Capell-
meister by successive princes of the wealthy and ardently
musical family of Esterhazy. In their establishment he not
only had every encouragement to write the best music he
could produce in every form suitable to instrumental effect,
but he also had a complete band always ready to play new
symphonies whenever wanted, and an opera-house and an
opera company for which he might (and did) write operas.
Such favourable circumstances account for the wonderful
number of symphonies which he wrote. But it is more to
the purpose to note the wonderful growth of his musical
powers, and even of the standard of his ideas from youth
onwards. His progress is a little epitome of the history of
musical evolution. His early quartetts were of the slightest
description; short, undeveloped, and not very interesting in
detail. His early symphonies were exactly of the standard

adopted by the average composer of such things all over the musical world at that time; and not notably better in the matter of scoring than John Christian Bach's. There is character and force in them, but the management of the orchestral resources is stiff, and the treatment of the wind instruments mechanical. His development was quite gradual, and he did not arrive at anything particularly notable till after Mozart had achieved his greatest work, and had become in his turn the older man's leader.

Mozart, as above indicated, began writing symphonies as well as operas at the age of eight, and some of his early work is skilful, neat, and artistic. But it was not till after his experiences at Mannheim in 1777 and 1778, so often alluded to, that his full powers in the line of instrumental music were called into play. The musical traditions at Mannheim were at that time probably the best in Europe, and their effect upon Mozart was immediate and salutary. For when he moved on to Paris in 1778, in company with some of the Mannheim instrumentalists, he wrote, for performance there, the first of his symphonies which occupies an important place in musical history. For artistic delicacy in detail, general interest, skilful use of orchestral resources, variety in quality and force of tone, no symphony had ever yet appeared which in any way approached to its standard. But even this by no means represents his highest achievement in the symphonic line. The symphony written for Prague in 1786 is a still further advance, and throws the Parisian one into the shade in every respect. The general quality of the musical thoughts is finer, richer, and more interesting; while the purely orchestral effects, especially in the slow movement, are among the most successful things of the kind he ever achieved. And finally the three great symphonies which he wrote in Vienna in 1788 represent the highest level in idea and style and in every distinguished quality of art he ever attained to. They are the crown of his life's work; for in them he more nearly escapes the traditional formulas of the Italian opera than in any other form of instrumental art except the quartetts; and their general standard of treatment and thought is nobler and more genuinely vigorous than that of any other of his works except the Requiem. In management of orchestral effect these latter symphonies must have been a revelation compared with the standard of the works of his contemporaries and predecessors. His treatment of design had also become much more free and interesting. The introduction of short subtle excursions out of his principal keys in unexpected directions; the variations introduced into his subjects on repetition, by altering the scoring and the actual melodic and harmonic details, and many other devices which infuse new interest into the obviousness of familiar procedure, show a much greater concentration of artistic faculty than had been usual with him. The general treatment is harmonic, but of more expressive character than in his operas; and though the designs are often helped out by conventional formulas which were the common property of all composers in those days, the general mastery of design is almost perfect. Haydn commonly receives the credit of establishing the symphony form on a secure basis; and no doubt he did a great deal for it. But the first symphonies which appeared in the world which still justly keep a hold on the affections of average musical people, as well as highly educated musicians, are those of Mozart. Next in importance after his symphonies come his quartetts. In this form Haydn again was the pioneer, but it fell to Mozart to produce the first really great and perfect examples. This most refined and delicate form of art had come into prominence rather suddenly. It was cultivated with some success by other composers besides Mozart and Haydn, such as Boccherini and Dittersdorf. But the quartetts which Mozart produced in 1782 and dedicated to Haydn are still among the select few of highest value in existence. In a form in which the actual possibilities are so limited, and in which the responsibilities of each individual solo instrument are so great, where the handling requires to be so delicate and so neatly adjusted in every detail, Mozart's artistic skill stood him in good stead. The great difficulty was the exact ascertainment of the kind of treatment best suited to the group of four solo instruments.

It was easy to write contrapuntal movements of the old kind for them, but in the new harmonic style and in form of a sonata order it was extremely difficult to adjust the balance between one instrument and another, so that subordination should not subside into blank dulness, nor independence of inner parts become obtrusive. Mozart among his many gifts had a great sense of fitness, and he adapted himself completely to the necessities of the situation; without adopting a polyphonic manner, and without sacrificing the independence of his instruments.

Instrumental music was at this time branching out into so many forms that it is not possible to follow his treatment of all kinds of different work. The least important are his pianoforte works, such as sonatas and variations, most of which were evidently written without his putting his heart into them, probably for amateur pupils. There are, of course, very important exceptions, and some interesting experiments, which clearly indicate a genuinely earnest humour, such as the two remarkable fantasias in C minor.

Haydn in his turn, without being dependent on Mozart or copying his manner, only came to his finest achievements after Mozart's career was over. Then in the year 1791 began the wonderful series of symphonies which he wrote at the invitation of the violinist and concert-manager Salomon for performance in London. These are as much the crown of his fame as the Prague and Vienna symphonies are of Mozart's. The crudity of his earlier orchestral writing has entirely disappeared; and though he never succeeds in getting such a perfectly mellow equal tone as Mozart's, he treats all his instruments with absolute freedom and fitness. The old traditions sometimes peep out again in rather long solos for wind instruments, and long passages for small groups of instruments in contrast to the "*tuttis;*" but everything is highly characteristic, clear, definite, and mature. On the whole, the treatment inclines to be a little more polyphonic than Mozart's; which accounts for the sound of the instruments not assimilating in the mass of tone quite so well. It was more natural for Mozart to think of the harmonies which

supported the melodies in terms of neatly contrived figures of
accompaniment, where Haydn, with Teutonic impulse, would
incline to think of his mass of tone as divided into various
melodic lines. But the shades of difference are so delicate,
and each composer is so far alternately harmonic and contrapuntal in turn, that it would be unwise to lay too much stress
on this point. Mozart achieves a degree of beauty in his slow
movements to which Haydn does not attain; but in the solid
allegros Haydn is more genuinely vigorous than Mozart. In
the minuet movements—which form an important addition to
their scheme—it is difficult to award the palm. Mozart's are
certainly the most popular, but Haydn's dance tunes have
some of the ring that comes of his lineage; which indeed is
apparent through almost all his work. Even to the last there
is a flavour of rusticity about it. His humour and his merriment are those of the simple honest peasant, while Mozart's
is the wit of a man of the world.

The artistic crisis which Mozart and Haydn represent is
so important that the nature of musical advance made by
them in the instrumental line may here be fitly summed up.
Before their time, the only two branches in which first-rate
and mature work of the harmonic kind had been done were
the violin sonatas written chiefly by the great Italian violinists
and their pupils in other countries, and the clavier sonatas.
The scope of movements was small and without much development, and the ideas even in the best examples were rather
indefinite. By the end of their time instrumental art had
branched out into a very large number of distinct and complete forms; such as symphonies, concertos, quartetts, trios,
and sonatas for violin and clavier. The style appropriate
to each had been more or less ascertained, and the schemes
of design had been perfectly organised for all self-dependent
instrumental music. Both Haydn and Mozart immensely
improved upon their predecessors in the power of finding
characteristic subjects, and in deciding the type of subject
which is best fitted for instrumental music. The difference
in that respect between their early and later works is very
marked. They improved the range of the symphonic cycle

of movements by adding the minuet and trio to the old group of three movements; thereby introducing definite and undisguised dance movements to follow and contrast with the central cantabile slow movement. Between them they had completely transformed the treatment of the orchestra. They not only enlarged it and gave it greater capacity of tone and variety, but they also laid the solid foundations of those methods of art which have become the most characteristic and effective features in the system of modern music. Even in detail the character of music is altered in their hands; all phraseology is made articulate and definite; and the minutiæ which lend themselves to refined and artistic performance are carefully considered, without in any way diminishing the breadth and freedom of the general effect. There is hardly any branch or department of art which does not seem to have been brought to high technical perfection by them; and if the world could be satisfied with the ideal of perfectly organised simplicity, without any great force of expression, instrumental art might well have stopped at the point to which they brought it.

CHAPTER XII

THE PERFECT BALANCE OF EXPRESSION AND DESIGN

THE style and intrinsic qualities of music so faithfully reflect the state of human affairs of the time at which it is produced, that it becomes a sort of symbol of the spirit of the world. At the end of the eighteenth century, in things quite independent of art, society in general had arrived at a crisis in secular affairs which inspired men with a fervour of spirit analogous to the fervour of religious enthusiasm which had sprung up at the time of the Reformation. In certain senses the new ardour was akin to the old. For it was the same protest against the conventions and formalities by which the true spirit of things was hidden, and the development of man's nature and aspirations checked and thwarted. The spirit of the old uprising was illustrated in its highest aspect by the sincerity, depth, and nobility of sentiment of J. S. Bach, and by the best utterances of Handel; and the spirit of the modern uprising found its first adequate musical expression in the work of Beethoven.

As has often been pointed out, a period of art in which rich and powerful expression is manifested must necessarily be preceded by a long period in which the resources of design and the methods of artistic treatment are developed. Artistic matters are on no different footing in that respect from the ordinary work of everyday life. Inspiration without methods and means at its disposal will no more enable a man to write a symphony than to build a ship or a cathedral. No doubt a primeval savage might be inspired with feelings very much like those of some modern composers; but the means and the knowledge how to express these feelings in terms of art would be lacking. All artistic effort which is worth anything tends to enlarge such means ; and the whole history of the arts is mainly a continuous effort of artistically-minded human creatures to make the means and the methods for the expression of the inner impulses richer and more perfect. It is a pure accident that when the means become plentiful and the methods very well understood, many men arise who have a great gift for using these means and methods without any of that personal impulse of inner feeling to express themselves which is the primal justification for their employment. The mere management of design is much easier than the management of expressive utterance. Indeed the fact is familiar that the men who have most to say that is worth saying find the greatest difficulty in saying anything at all. A man who has a genuine impulse to say something beyond common thought has generally to enlarge the phraseology of the art or language in which he speaks ; and those who cannot wait for the development of the phraseology required by the nature of their thoughts, must inevitably remain at least partially unintelligible to their fellow-creatures.

In music the case is very clearly illustrated by the results of the many attempts to achieve ideal expression before the means were adequately developed. Human nature is liable to be impatient of the slow development of resources, and often breaks out into resentment at having to wait so many centuries for the consummation of obvious aims. Monteverde, Purcell, and Gluck are types of those eager spirits who are impatient of the slow march of things, and want to find a short cut to their artistic ideals—just as impatient political enthusiasts long to establish a millennium before they have organised their human beings into a fit state to live in it. Such ardent and genuine composers as they were saw rightly that art is not an end but a means, and having much more natural feeling for expression than for the purely artistic side of things, they tried to make sluggish time move faster, and to attain their ideal artistic region without the preliminary of following the long road that led there. The world never-

theless owes them great thanks; for though men may be
deceived in hoping too much and attempting the impossible,
progress would be even slower than it is if no one were
capable of heroic mistakes. Gluck pointed out the danger of
accepting conventions as solutions of artistic problems, and
he kept the vital artistic questions alive.   But the slow
laws of development had to go on all the same, and in
reality it was just as fortunate that Mozart was by gifts,
training, and circumstances a follower of the old methods,
as that Gluck was consumed with a passionate ardour to
have done with them.   At that particular moment in the
history of art the man who was most urgently needed was
not one with a strong personality or marked individuality
of style and feeling, but one who could look at art mainly
from the artistic point of view, and with the highest sense
of beauty of effect devote himself to the special development
of technique.

Mozart, in this case, represents the type of man who is contented with the average progress of things, and finds no necessity to aim at anything more novel than the doing of what
comes to him to be done in the very best manner he can.   His
best manner was the best of its kind, but it was not final.
Even without Gluck and Haydn by his side the necessary
preliminaries would not have been fully completed.   They did
for characteristic style what he did mainly for the organisation of melody, colour, and design.   And when those various
phases of art which they represented had been put into practical shape, the resources of the composer who was to come
were enormously enlarged.

The superiority of Beethoven's point of vantage to Mozart's
is equal to the sum of all the differences between the state of
art when Mozart took up his work at the age of eight, and the
state at which it had arrived at the end of his career.   Besides
the difference in opportunities, there were immense differences
in the type of the man and his circumstances.   Beethoven
came of the more tenacious Northern stock, partly Dutch and
partly German; and he had the good fortune to be obliged to
cultivate self-dependence very early, and to make acquaintance

with J. S. Bach's works at a time when he was sufficiently impressionable to profit by them. His youthful experiences in Bonn were by no means of the smoothest and pleasantest. He had a good deal to endure in his home life that was harsh and unlovely, and he had to endure a good deal of second-rate music while playing in the local opera band. By the former his character was formed; by the latter the most obvious principles of design were strongly impressed into his organisation. Like most artists whose spur is more in themselves than in natural artistic facilities, he was very slow to come to any artistic achievement. It is almost a law of things that men whose artistic personality is very strong, and who touch the world by the greatness and the power of their expression, come to maturity comparatively late, and sometimes grow greater all through their lives—so it was with Bach, Gluck, Beethoven, and Wagner—while men whose aims are more purely artistic, and whose main spur is facility of diction, come to the point of production early, and do not grow much afterwards. Such composers as Mozart and Mendelssohn succeeded in expressing themselves brilliantly at a very early age; but their technical facility was out of proportion to their individuality and force of human nature, and therefore there is no such surprising difference between the work of their later years and the work of their childhood as there is in the case of Beethoven and Wagner.

In Beethoven's nature there was an extraordinarily keen sense for design, but there was also a very powerful impulse towards expression. In his earliest days he seems to waver from one point of view to another. Most of his early works follow the lines which had become familiar, and show little change from the artistic attitude of Mozart or Haydn. But every now and then, even in the early days at Bonn, the spirit of adventure possesses him, and then some surprising feat, prefiguring the achievements of his best days, makes its appearance; such a stroke as the end of the Coda of the Righini variations, which presents a device which he carried out more effectually and for more expressive purposes much

later in the Coriolan Overture. But these sudden revelations
of the spirit that was within him are at first only spasmodic,
and he subsides again after an outbreak of genius into the
grave deportment of the formal period. But from many
indications it can be judged that mere composition as a
purely artistic operation did not come easily to him. Haydn's
want of sympathy with him, and the well-known verdict of
the theorist Albrechtsberger, alike point to the fact that he
was not born to write without an emotional or intellectual
spur. The moment in the history of music appears to have
been reached, when its great resources were ready to be used
for expressive ends of a new type, and Schubert and Weber
were soon due to illustrate the wide spread of new impulses
in other phases; but it was allotted to Beethoven to lead the
van; and unlike them, he was to do his work within the
limits of the old designs of the sonata type, by grasping the
innermost nature of their principles, and expanding them to
the utmost that they would bear.

It is indeed a most characteristic feature of Beethoven's
work that the greater part, and the best of it all, is cast
in the form of the sonata, which Haydn and Mozart had
organised to so high a degree of perfection as pure design.
Beethoven could not have expressed himself adequately within
the conditions of perfect design—which his instincts truly
told him was an absolute necessity of art—without making
use of a form whose principles were fully understood. It was
his good fortune that the sonata form had been so perfectly
organised, and that the musical public had been made so
perfectly familiar with it, that they were ready to follow
every suggestion and indication of the principle of design;
and even to grasp what he aimed at when he purposely pre-
sumed upon their familiarity with it, to build fresh subtleties
and new devices upon the well-known lines; and sometimes
even to emphasise vital points by making progressions in directions which seemed deliberately to avoid them. Beethoven
had a great gift for extemporisation; and there are many
subtle devices in his work that look as if he had tested
the power of his audiences to follow his points by actual

observation. Like Scarlatti, he often seems to play upon his audience, and to anticipate the processes that will be going on in their minds; and so well to forecast the very things that they will expect to happen, that he can make sure of having the pleasure of puzzling them by doing something else. But in order to put into practice all the multitudinous possibilities he could foresee, he had to take a form which his audience would thoroughly understand. And this is one of the many reasons for the preponderance of the sonata type in his works.

This preponderance is most marked in the early part of his career. His first period, as it is sometimes called, extends to about Opus 50, and to about the thirty-fourth year of his life. His first thirty-one works were all of the sonata order, and the majority of them actually solo pianoforte sonatas. He did not attempt orchestral work till he wrote the concertos in C and B♭ which stand as Opus 15 and 19, but of which the latter was the earliest. The famous septuor, which is a large combination of solo instruments, and implies use of orchestral colour, is Opus 20; and the first symphony was Opus 21, and was not written till he was twenty-nine. In this early period there are some very notable outbreaks of the genuine characteristic Beethoven, as before mentioned, and they grow more frequent as his powers grow more mature. The Kreutzer Sonata for violin and pianoforte has all the traits of the completely great Beethoven. Its introduction is one of the things that no one else has approached in its way for both subtlety of design and expression; and the splendid energy and passion of the allegro, and the extraordinary beauty of the theme and variations, are fully up to his best standard of work. After Opus 50 there comes a sudden flood of works which are among the greatest treasures of musical art. The brilliant Waldstein Sonata is Opus 53; close upon it comes the first symphony which is genuinely great in all aspects, the Eroica, completed in 1804; then one of the most impulsive and passionate of the sonatas, that in F minor, Opus 57; then the delicate G major Concerto, with the extraordinary slow movement, instinct with the dramatic spirit of the very

best moments of Gluck; the Rasoumoffski Quartetts, Opus 59;
the B♭ Symphony; the Violin Concerto; the rugged Overture
to Coriolan; the C minor Symphony, which is the concentrated
essence of the individual Beethoven of that time; the Pastoral
Symphony, which breathes most faithfully his ardent love of
nature and woods and all things health-giving to the human
mind; his one opera, "Fidelio;" the noble Concerto in E♭, justly
called the Emperor; the Quartett in E♭; the romantic Seventh
Symphony, and the playful Eighth Symphony, which he called
his little one; and the Trio in B♭, Opus 97. But as his Opus
numbers pass into the nineties a change begins to be discernible in his style, especially in the Quartett in F minor, Opus
95. The warmth of expression, and the spontaneous flow of
energetic thought which mark the middle period, begin to
give way before the influx of moods that are at once sadder,
more concentrated, and more reflective. By that time—about
his fortieth year—troubles of many kinds were beginning to
tell upon Beethoven's sensitive disposition. The iron had
entered into his soul, and it made him dive deeper into human
problems and emotions. Some of the most divinely and
serenely beautiful of all his conceptions belong to this third
period, but they are attended by moods which reveal his
suffering and his determination to endure. There is more
thought and more experience of life in this period; and if less
of geniality than in his middle life, an infinitely wider range
of feeling, characteristic expression, and style. It seems as
if his art had widened out from being the mere expression of
his own wonderful personality, and had become the interpreter
of the innermost joys and sorrows of all human creatures. In
order to find expression for all that he had in his mind, he
had to expand his resources of design and expression even
further than in his middle period, and the result was that
very little of his later music was understood by his contemporaries. Most of it was considered impossible to play. But
this was in reality not because it was more technically difficult than the works of his middle period, but because it
was so much more difficult to interpret. And as Beethoven
was by this time almost totally deaf, he could not show

people how to perform it rightly; and very few people had enough musical intelligence to find out for themselves. In later times the traditions of what is necessary for the adequate interpretation of these works have been so carefully and minutely described, that even people of no intelligence sometimes contrive not to make great artistic conceptions sound like nonsense; and works once thought impracticable are among the most familiar features of everyday concerts.

It is a palpable fact to every one that Beethoven's works sound fuller and richer than those of any composers since Bach. This is partly owing to the warmth and human interest of his ideas, but it is also due to the actual treatment of the instruments he employs. In pianoforte works it is partly owing to the development of genuine pianoforte playing. The manner of playing the harpsichord and clavichord had been to creep and glide over the keys with flat hands and inactive arms. The early pianofortes had but slight fall in the keys, and consequently the traditions of harpsichord playing were transferred to them without much unfitness. But when the keys were deepened to get more tone, new methods became necessary, and the more powerful muscles of wrists and arms were brought into exercise; and though typical conservative minds regarded any effort to change their habits as a species of heresy, the stronger and more practical musicians soon cultivated such heresies with much success. Clementi especially gave much attention to the proper way of dealing with an instrument in which the sound was produced by the blows of little hammers; and Beethoven followed in the same direction. He instantly dissipated the absurd tradition which implied that what was right for the harpsichord was right for the pianoforte. The instrument suited his passionate, vigorous temperament; it lent itself to rich harmonisation, to rhythmic variety; and by the aid of the pedal he managed to produce the floods of tone in which his soul delighted. His contrivances in the latter direction were especially important, as he not only widened the capacities of the keyed instrument, but gave the first impulse to the characteristic softening and clouding of outlines

which is so familiar in the so-called "romantic" style of
recent times. In the orchestral branches of art the enrich-
ment of tone by the gradual increase of varieties of instruments had been going on ever since Alessandro Scarlatti's
time. The nucleus of strings with two pairs of wind instruments, and a harpsichord to fill in the harmonies, which
was usually employed for the small symphonies in the early
part of the eighteenth century, was increased by the end
of it to strings, flutes, hautboys, bassoons, two horns, two
trumpets, and drums. Haydn and Mozart used clarinets
sometimes, but not often ; it was not till recent times that
the mechanism of the instrument was sufficiently perfect to
make it available, and the tone of the old clarinets was
probably thinner and shriller than that of modern ones.
Beethoven used them from the first in all his symphonies ;
in the third symphony (the Eroica) he added a third horn ; in
the massive C minor symphony he added three trombones and
a double bassoon ; and in the last, No. 9, he added a fourth
horn as well. His object was not so much to add to the noise
as to increase the opportunities for variety; and to organise
the actual and relative possibilities of instrumental tone to
the utmost.

The constitution of the orchestra has remained as he established it ever since. The aspirations of modern sensational
composers have not managed to improve upon the actual order
of the instruments, though they have often increased the
numbers; and the wood wind being now somewhat over-
balanced by the great number of stringed instruments used
for large concert-rooms, the only balance of sonority in "forte"
passages is between strings and brass instruments. And this,
combined with the growing taste for brilliancy of colour, has led
to a slight increase in the latter department. Beethoven enjoyed the advantage, over Haydn and Mozart, that the actual
powers and technical efficiency of performers on orchestral
instruments had greatly improved. He could afford to write
more difficult passages, and to use a wider range of sounds.
Even in his first two symphonies he advanced beyond the
earlier masters in variety of effect and in a certain solemn

depth which is very characteristic of some of his moods; and he uses his instruments with more and more distinctness of purpose as he goes on. He knows exactly where the bright sparkling tone of the flute will serve his turn, and where the pathetic tenderness of the hautboy; the liquid fulness of the clarinet has a place in his scheme, and the extraordinary varieties of the bassoon's tones are most familiar to him, in all its grotesque, humorous, plaintive, and even pathetic aspects. The curious human-like uncertainty and mystery of the horns, and their powers of enriching the softer harmonies, are most especially congenial to him. He knows the majestic force of the trombones in the loud passages, and their impressive solemnity in soft passages; and, unlike many later writers, he never makes them odious with vulgar brutish blatancy. He sees all the varieties in their true light. For the tone qualities of the various instruments in his music serve not only for contrast, but, like colours, to excite sensibilities. Mozart occasionally used special instruments to enforce situations, as in the wonderful accompaniment of soft swelling trombones and horns to the voice of the oracle in "Idomeneo;" and in the familiar passages for the brass instruments in "Don Giovanni" and "Zauberflöte." But a large majority of his special effects are for the mere purpose of pure beauty or contrast; and his variety is not very great. For there is a great family likeness in his frequent uses of thirds in double octaves for bassoons and flutes or hautboys, though the effect is quite beautiful enough to be borne very often. Beethoven's use of his resources in this respect is very much more full of variety, and in a very large number of cases it is so absolutely to the purpose, that it seems to be the necessary outcome of the mood which his particular melody, rhythm, or harmony, or the sum of all three of them, conveys at the particular moment.

But, in truth, design, colour, and expression are so closely wedded in his best work that it is difficult to disintegrate them. The expression is great because it comes exactly in the true place in the scheme of design to tell. The colour exerts its full influence, mainly because the expression and the design put the mind exactly in the receptive condition to be fully impressed by it. Even the most limited of instruments can be made to produce an astounding effect through its relation to its context. The whole of the scherzo of the C minor symphony is as near being miraculous as human work can be; but one of its most absorbing moments is the part where for fifteen bars there is nothing going on but an insignificant chord continuously held by low strings, and a pianissimo rhythmic beat of the drum. Taken out of its context it would be perfectly meaningless. As Beethoven has used it, it is infinitely more impressive than the greatest noise Meyerbeer and his fellows ever succeeded in making.

Beethoven's attitude in relation to art and expression naturally led him by degrees to modify the average scheme of the design of instrumental works in accordance with the ideas which he felt he could artistically express. This was one of the features in his works which indicated the direction in which art was destined to travel after his time. But the changes he made were mainly in respect of the general order and grouping of the movements, and not often in the disposal or ordering of their contents. The form of the principal movement (which is commonly known by the name of "binary *") is so wonderfully elastic that he found little

---

* The term "binary" is undoubtedly unhappy if too much stress is laid on the relation of the plan of the modern type of movement to the strict meaning of the classical terms from which it is derived. The form has changed so much that it presents an aspect more like a threefold unity than a scheme consisting of two balanced divisions. But the word still indicates the undoubted lineage of the type, and there are so many qualities of style and distribution which distinguish it decisively from the primary or simple three-limbed structure, which is its most frequent antithesis, that any attempt to re-name or re-classify the type is to be deprecated, as only tending to add fresh confusion to a subject already obscured by superfluous variety of terminology. There are many words in the English language which have changed their meaning, and do not suggest what was originally meant by the syllables from which they are derived; yet every one understands them well enough. And the language would hardly be a gainer if any one attempted to reconstruct it, in order to restore the primitive meanings of familiar words.

occasion to alter it except by strengthening the main pillars of the structure, and widening its general scope, wherever possible—as in the Codas. His early solo sonatas were on the usual plan, but increased to four movements, like Mozart's and Haydn's symphonies. But in later times, when he had attained a more comprehensive view of the situation, he varied the number and order of the movements in all classes of instrumental works, sometimes increasing to five, and sometimes reducing to two. Sometimes beginning with a slow movement, sometimes omitting it altogether. His most important alteration in the general scheme was the introduction of the scherzo in place of the old minuet. The virtue of introducing the minuet after the slow movement lay in the decisive contrast which the rhythmic principle of the dance afforded to the cantabile character of the slow movement. But the choice was was not really a happy one, because the minuet was not naturally a vigorous rhythmic dance, but graceful, flowing, and rather slow and sedate. Mozart and Haydn were both led correctly by their instincts to give their minuets a far more animated and vigorous character than the actual dance motions warranted; and composers ultimately gave up all attempts to pay any attention to the relation of the music to hypothetical dance motions, and took the movement *presto*, and called it by a new name, the scherzo.

The fact that the scherzo had been known long before does not lessen the importance of Beethoven's systematic adoption of it, which gave it its place in modern music. Both by implication and in itself it is one of the most important of the musical features which made their appearance in the early part of this century. That it made such a much better contrast to the slow movement than the minuet is really of secondary importance, though from the purely artistic point of view the improvement is considerable. Very much more important is the meaning of the change in respect of expression. Many people have unfortunately got into the habit of taking " expression " to mean only sentimental expression; and convention has deprived the language of a comprehensive word in order to give it a special bearing. In reference to music, it

must be taken in its widest sense; and at this moment it is
particularly important to take note of the fact; as the essence
of musical progress from Beethoven onwards lies in the
development of infinite varieties of expression. Beethoven's
adoption of the scherzo was like a manifesto on that point.
The scherzo has become one of the most valuable types for
the conveyance of all those kinds of expression which are
not sentimental; and require to be described in terms of
action rather than terms of vocal utterance. In this its
primal dance origin confirms the gesticulatory meaning of the
rhythmic element in music. With Beethoven the scherzo
became the most free of all the movements in the sonata
group. He did not restrict it to the characteristic triple
time of the minuet, but took any time that the situation
required; and so far dispensed with the systematic orderliness
which usually characterised works designed upon harmonic principles, that the plan of such a movement is often as difficult to
unravel as that of any of Bach's merriest and lightest fugues.
In ranging wide and free among human characteristics and
moods this apparent independence of uniformity and rule was
just perfectly apposite; and it is interesting to note that
Mendelssohn's keen insight divined this fact, and that he
struck out an equally informal line in his scherzos with much
success; for the genuine "scherzo" impulse had a very happy
and wholesome effect upon his disposition. But of course he
cannot be compared with Beethoven either for variety or
scope; for nowhere is the subtlety of Beethoven's imagination
or the keenness of his insight more conspicuous; and no form
shows more clearly or variously the character of the man.
His deep interest in everything that concerned the human
creature, without respect of persons or classes, comes out.
Other movements supplied him with the opportunities for
uttering graver sentiments and emotions; here he dealt with
mischief, raillery, humour, fun of every description, in terms
that are like the healthy honest spirits of a child. Indeed
the analogies are generally most likely to be found in
the spontaneous merriment of children, for the veneer of
respectability and responsibility in people of mature years

buries most of the natural expansion in such directions out of sight.

The resources of the pianoforte were hardly adequate to his purposes in this line; and though he wrote some very successful and graphic examples for the instrument, his most brilliant achievements are in the symphonies, quartetts, and trios, where either variety of colour or the crystalline clearness of violin tone afforded him better opportunities.

The element of design is of such pre-eminent importance in his works that it must inevitably be discussed in some detail; since the effect they produce depends so much upon his marvellous concentration and self-control in that respect. Very few people realise the paramount importance of systematic design, and the extent to which it can be carried; for though they cannot fail to see how important it is in small things, they do not follow out their observation to its logical consequences, and see that it is equally important in great. Even people of little intelligence can perceive that when one chord or figure has been going on for a long while, it is a relief to have it changed; and it does not take any great powers of mind to realise that there is a right place and a wrong for the change to come. But even when that much is seen, and it is realised that the proper management of the successions of chords and keys is the basis of modern instrumental design, people still seem to forget that what applies to one little part applies to the whole; and that in a highly organised work of art there is a right place and a wrong for every change of harmony, and for every rise and fall of the melody throughout a long piece of music. The full effect of every great stroke of art in such cases depends upon the perfect control of the motion, direction, and even the colour of every successive moment in the work. Beethoven often makes a stroke which is only intelligible by its relation to some other passage that is some hundreds of bars away in another part of the movement; but he manages it so perfectly that an auditor over whom he has cast his spell can instantly seize his drift. The extraordinary degree of concentration in this respect is such as no other composer has ever approached. With all Mozart's skill in design, his work is often very loose in texture compared with that of his successor. A short discussion of an obvious parallel may help to make this clearer. It so happens that both Beethoven and Mozart used the same root idea—the former in his first sonata, and the latter in the last movement of his G minor symphony. The gist of the idea is an energetic upward leap through a rhythmic arpeggio to a strongly emotional high note.

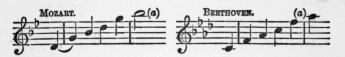

The high note, as the crisis, naturally requires something to round it off. Mozart makes the emphatic point subside into a sentimental harmony; Beethoven cuts it off sharply by an emphatic turn.

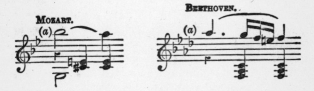

Mozart then simply breaks off and continues the proceedings by a new phrase, which has no striking significance, but is sufficient in relation to the style of the rest of the movement to complete the sentence appropriately.

Beethoven, on the contrary, keeps firm hold of his text; and

18

enforces it by repeating it in another position in the scale, which makes his emotional point rise a step higher.

Then taking his emotional point and its characteristic appendage, he drives it home by repeating it with strong accent, rising higher each time to give it extra intensity.*

And only when the highest point of the crisis is reached does he relax the tension, and a softer and more yielding version of the turn is moulded on to the cadence which concludes his sentence; which therefore stands in its entirety :—

Thus the whole of Beethoven's first sentence is knit together in the closest bonds by insistence upon his emotional point. Mozart, having given his root idea and its counter idea to balance it, repeats them in the same order, but with the order

* Compare the Irish folk-tune on page 79 for the principle.

of the harmony reversed, taking dominant first and tonic to answer it, and so concludes :—

Beethoven, over and above the close consistency with which he uses his idea, unifies the whole passage of eight bars by the skilful use of his bass, which marches up step by step from the leading note next below the tonic starting-point to the dominant above it; thereby helping the mind to grasp the principle of design and to feel the close unity of the whole sentence. In Mozart's passage the alternation of tonic and dominant is easily grasped, and is the means whereby the tonality of the passage is made clear. In Beethoven's passage the alternation of tonic and dominant is equally present and equally regular, but the motion of bass happily disguises it, while it also serves as an additional indication of the structure of the passage. To show the whole artistic purpose and skill of the first twelve bars would require a chapter to itself, for with Beethoven nearly every progression has several aspects. All that can be attempted here is to show how the process is carried on, in such a manner that each step becomes the necessary outcome of the impulse which is expressed at the moment of starting. The end of the first sentence above quoted in full leaves the hearer in the air, as it were; for it ends only on a relatively final chord, the dominant. Further proceedings are therefore necessarily expected; and Beethoven resumes his subject in the bass by way of contrast, and in a position of the scale which for the moment is purposely obscure. He does not wish to reveal his intentions all at once; so the key seems to be C minor, though it is intended to lead to A♭. When the emotional point in the resumed subject-figure is reached, it is immediately pushed on, together with the turn which makes it identifiable, by an unexpected discord. This of course requires its resolution, which is made in such a way as to produce another discord; and so by the necessities of each resolution the music is pushed on step by step till the dominant of the new and contrasting key is reached, and the circuit of this first division of the movement is completed. The root idea has never for a moment been lost sight of; so from both points of view—idea and design alike—no step is without its significance and its bearing. And all the rest of the movement is carried out on the same principles.

To avoid misconception, it is as well to point out that Mozart, in the parallel case above quoted, also uses his materials very consistently, and develops them into new phases; though not with the close concentration even of Beethoven's earliest work.*

Of the almost endless devices and subtleties Beethoven uses to make his design intelligible, the most familiar is a steady progress of the bass by tones or semitones up or down in accordance with the spirit which the moment requires. Where subsidence from a crisis is wanted, it goes down, where extra animation is wanted it rises; and always so as to direct the mind towards the point which it is essential to recognise. One of the most remarkable instances is in the middle of the first movement of the great Appassionata Sonata. The course of events has brought about a point of repose in the key of D♭; and for the purposes of design it is necessary to modulate back to the principal key, F minor, and to concentrate attention upon the chord immediately preceding the step which finally announces that

* It may also be well to point out that the object of this detailed comparison is not to emphasise Beethoven's greatness at the expense of Mozart, but to show the general tendencies of evolution. In this particular case Beethoven's treatment of his subject-matter admits of closer scrutiny than Mozart's. But there are other cases in which Mozart undoubtedly has the advantage; as in the parallel cases of "Batti batti," and the slow movement of Beethoven's quintett in E♭ for pianoforte and wind-instruments.

the rambling and voyaging division of the movement is over, and the principal key reached again. To do this Beethoven makes his bass rise slowly step by step for fifteen bars—from the D♭ below the bass stave to the D♭ next under the treble stave. The whole mass of the harmony rises with it, with increasing excitement, so that the crisis of the emotional aspect of the progression exactly coincides with the point which it is most essential that the mind should grasp firmly in anticipation of one of the most important points in the scheme—the return to the original key and subject. And, by way of contrast to the long-continued motion, the penultimate chord, when arrived at, continues unchanged for eleven bars, the mind being fully occupied with the rattling brilliancy of figured arpeggios. The same kind of sequence transferred to the treble part is to be found in the development portion of the first movement of the sonata in A♭, Opus 110, where the progression drops down step by step for a whole octave; thereby completely unifying the whole of the "development" portion of the movement.

Another device of the same kind is that which makes the whole mass of the harmony move upon a bass constantly shifting by steps of thirds. The most remarkable instance is the introductory movement to the fugue in the sonata in B♭, Opus 106, where the dropping steps of the thirds continue through the whole movement without intermission; supplying an underlying principle of order to all the varieties of mood and expression which occur in it. Another very remarkable instance of the same device is in the middle of the first movement of the sonata in E minor, Opus 90. Some such sequence or principle of order, either on a small or a wide ranging basis, gives coherence and sense of orderliness even to his most elaborately contrived effects of harmonic motion.

His ways of insisting upon his key, without letting it be seen that he is doing so, are many and various. As has been pointed out, he often casts his leading idea in terms of the tonic chord. But he is very fond of suggesting and bewildering at the same time. Thus the principal part of the Eroica subject is made out of the tonic chord of E♭,

but then the whole aspect of things becomes perplexing for a moment by its passing straight out of the key with

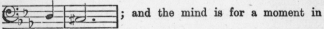 ; and the mind is for a moment in

doubt of its whereabouts. And then Beethoven slips back into his key again as quickly as he went out, as if he made light of his own device. But in reality he has no intention of making light of it. For when the same passage comes back some five minutes later, he knows quite well that his audience will remember it, and thereupon he turns the progression inside out; leaving them even more perplexed and interested than before. Similarly he sometimes begins quite out of the key in order to make the safe arrival at the true starting-point the more striking. Again he sometimes casts even his first subject in the form of a sequence, which leads out of the key immediately, as in the sonata in E minor, Opus 90; but in this case the progressions move by such a logical process that when the circuit is complete the impression of the key is a great deal stronger and more vital than if he had contented himself with alternating tonic and dominant all the while. Both Brahms and Wagner have followed him in this device. Brahms in the Second Rhapsody, and Wagner in the Vorspiel to Tristan. Another way of insisting on the key is the obvious one of emphasising in succession all the principal chords which represent it—tonic, dominant, subdominant, supertonic, &c. Of this there are two exactly parallel cases in works as different as the little G major sonata, Opus 14, No. 2, and the first movement of the Waldstein; where they occur exactly in analogous positions, in the section representing the second or contrasting key.

His subjects themselves very often have some wide principle of general effect besides the mere interest of the details.   It may be a systematic rise of a characteristic figure, as in the subject of the A♭ sonata, Opus 110; or the persistence of a rhythmic nucleus which underlies a more general melodic outline—as in the first sentence of the C minor symphony, or it may be the recurrence of some very striking feature, such as the two fierce blows at the end of the rushing arpeggio in the last movement of the C♯ minor sonata (commonly called Moonlight).   And when there are phases like this he generally extends them, in the development of the subjects, into new situations and aspects.   A happy instance of this is the treatment of the second subject in the last movement of the same C♯ minor sonata :—

Here at the asterisks the accented note successively rises and gains in warmth; and thus it becomes the most striking feature of the subject.   So at the end of the movement Beethoven enhances the passion of it (with great effect also for the purpose of design) by extending the rise and pressing the emotional points closer :—

His power of presenting the same subject in different aspects has a very important bearing on the nature of recent progress of the art.   In his case it is particularly valuable in the development of a movement, as it enabled him to keep true to his initial idea without sameness or mere obvious repetition, and at the same time to add to its interest. He showed this faculty in the highest degree in his variations, a form of which he was quite the greatest master. His treatment indeed makes it one of the most interesting forms of art, while in the hands of composers of less power it is one of the most detestable. With him the theme is a sort of chameleon thought which is capable of undergoing all kinds of mysterious changes; and of being expressed sometimes gaily, sometimes sadly, sometimes fiercely. He groups variations together in accordance with their affinities, and distributes the different moods so as to illustrate one another, and to make a complete composite design.

The texture of his work as a whole is far more polyphonic than that of his predecessors, and illustrates the tendency of the time to revert to the methods of Bach, in the free motion of the bass and the internal organisation of the harmony—adapting the methods at the same time to the system of harmonic form. The case is parallel to the reversion to the methods of the old ecclesiastical music after the speculative revolution of Peri and Monteverde, described in Chapter VII. But the counterpoint is by no means that of Bach; it is less ostensible, and the various inner parts and figures that move are kept in relative subordination in accordance with their relative degrees of importance. Music by this means regained an immensely enhanced power of expression of the highest kind. The harmony not only became more interesting and rich, but very much more powerful at the moments when powerful and characteristic discord was required; while at the same time it afforded much more delicate gradations of degrees of harshness.

The tendency to use the art for expression naturally led Beethoven to identify his work occasionally with some definite idea or subject. As in the Eroica Symphony, which was intended for his ideal of Napoleon (so soon shattered); the Pastoral Symphony, which embodied his feelings about the fields, and brooks, and woods, and birds he loved so well; the "Lebewohl" Sonata, which embodied his ideal musical

sense of friends parting, of absence, and of the joyous coming
together again.   But with him, for almost the first time, the
true principle of programme music is found, and he indicates
it with absolute insight into the situation in his remark on
the Pastoral Symphony.   That it was " mehr Ausdruck der
Empfindung, als Malerei "—" More the expression of inner
feeling than picturing."   The most common failing of minds
less keen than Beethoven's is to try to make people see with
their ears.   Beethoven goes to the root of the matter.   For,
as pointed out in the first chapter, it is not the business
of music to depict the external, but to convey the inner impressions which are the result of the external.   And music
is true in spiritual design only when it is consistent in the
use of the resources of expression with the possible workings
of the mind in special moods or under the influence of
special external impressions.   With Beethoven and Bach the
consistency of the harmonic, melodic, and rhythmic elements
f expression is so perfect, that with all the infinity of change,
    e variety that is necessary for design's sake, the pos-
     ing of a mind affected by some special exciting
      stently represented by the kind of treatment
      That people often can feel this for them-
      by the general adoption of such a name as
      " which was not given by Beethoven, but
       ified in every particular by the contents

         n the comprehensive develop-
         d in the fact that the princi-
          ype of design were ready to
          pon the scene.   His imagina-
          concentration were equal to his
        resources of effect were as yet not so
       him to extravagance.   Indeed he himself
      d develop and systematise much of them,
      them more than any other man except
      ata form, moreover, was new enough to
      e without forcing him either to risk common-
      esort to hyper-intellectual devices to hide its

familiarities. In his hands alone the forces of design and of expression were completely controlled. Self-dependent instrumental art on the grandest and broadest lines found its first perfect revelation in his hands, not in a formal sense alone, but in the highest phase of true and noble characteristic expression.

any subject which has impressed an artist as worthy of permanent record. The instinct for beauty and the feeling for
design may still have plenty of scope in accordance with the
disposition of the artist, but they are by no means so
prominent and necessary a part of art as they were; and
many pictures have had immense fame which have been
nothing but the baldest presentations of totally uninteresting
everyday occurrences, without a trace of anything that shows
a sense of either beauty or design.

It is much the same in literature. Nothing is more conspicuously characteristic of the present age than the immense
increase of short illustrative stories which make vividly alive
for all men the varieties of human circumstances and dispositions, from the remotest districts of India and the steppes
of Russia, to the islands of Galway Bay and the backwoods
of Australia. The few men that still have the instincts of
great art cling to the great traditions and deal as much as
they can with great subjects, but the preponderant tendency
in all arts is towards variety and closeness of characterisation.

As has before been pointed out, the premonitions of this
tendency are already discernible in Beethoven; and many
other external facts in his time and soon after show in what
direction the mind of man was moving. A characteristic
feature which illustrates this is the much more frequent
adoption by composers of names for their works; which
evidently implies taking a definite idea and endeavouring to
make the music express it. No one emphasises this fact
more than Spohr. By natural musical organisation and
habit of mind he was the last composer of whom one might
expect unclassical procedure. Mozart was his model, and
Beethoven was barely intelligible to him except in his least
characteristic moods. But Spohr set himself in a very marked
way to emphasise illustration. To many of his symphonies
he gave definite names, and made it his endeavour to carry
out his programme consistently. The well-known "Weihe
der Töne" is a case in point. He meant originally to set a
poem of that title by Pfeiffer as a cantata, but finding it un-
suitable he wrote the symphony as an illustration of the poem,

and directed that the poem was to be read whenever the symphony was performed. Moreover, he endeavoured to widen the scope and design of this symphony to carry out his scheme, with eminently unsatisfactory results, as far as all the latter part of the work is concerned. His "Historical Symphony" has a similarly definite object, though not so close an application; as it was merely a very strange attempt to imitate the styles of Bach and Handel, Mozart and Beethoven in successive movements. More decisively to the point is his symphony called "The Worldly and Heavenly Influences in the Life of Man," in which the heavenly influences are represented by a solo orchestra, and the worldly by an ordinary full orchestra. The general idea is very carefully carried out, and the heavenly influences are made particularly prominent in the early part, and apparently succumb to the power of the worldly orchestra towards the end. Another symphony of Spohr's is called "The Seasons," which is a very favourite subject, and also a very suitable one, for true musical treatment. Weber was naturally on the same side, both on account of his romantic disposition and the deficiencies of his artistic education. His one successful instrumental work, on a large scale, the Concertstuck for pianoforte and orchestra, deliberately represents a story of a knight and a lady in crusading times. The inference suggested is even stronger in the case of Mendelssohn, who was ultra-classical by nature, but gave names and indicated a purpose or a reason for the particular character of all his best symphonies—The Reformation, the Italian, and the Scotch. Even the symphony to the "Lobgesang" has a very definite and intelligible relation to the cantata which follows; while as far as musical characterisation is concerned, the overture and scherzo in the "Midsummer's Night's Dream" music are among the vivid things of modern times.

To all appearance the line which Berlioz took is even more decisive. But important as it is, the fact of his being a Frenchman reduces its significance a little. The French have never shown any talent for self-dependent instrumental music. From the first their musical utterance required to be put in

motion by some definite idea external to music. The great
Parisian lute-players wrote most of their neat little pieces to
a definite subject; Couperin developed considerable skill in
contriving little picture-tunes, and Rameau followed in the
same line later. The kernel of the Gallic view of things is,
moreover, persistently theatrical, and all the music in which
they have been successful has had either direct or secondary
connection with the stage. Berlioz was so typical a Frenchman
in this respect that he could hardly see even the events of his
own life as they actually were; but generally in the light of
a sort of fevered frenzy, which made everything—both ups
and downs—look several times larger than the reality. Some
of his most exciting experiences as related by himself are conceived in the spirit of melodrama, and could hardly have
happened as he tells them except on the stage. This was not
the type of human creature of whom self-dependent instrumental music could be expected; and it is no wonder that
when he took to experimenting in that line of art he made it
even more theatrical than ordinary theatrical music; because
he had to supply the effect of the stage and the footlights and
all the machinery, as well as the evolutions and gesticulations
of the performers, by the music alone. His enormous skill
and mastery of resource, brilliant intelligence, and fiery energy
were all concentrated in the endeavour to make people see in
their minds the histrionic presentation of such fit histrionic
subjects as dances of sylphs, processions of pilgrims, and orgies
of brigands. Even the colossal dimensions of his orchestra,
with its many square yards of drum surface, and its crowds
of shining yellow brass instruments, is mainly the product of
his insatiable theatrical thirst. It imposes upon the composer
himself as much as it imposes upon his audience, by looking
so very big and bristling to the eye of the imagination. But
though it makes a great noise, and works on the raw impressionable side of human creatures, and excites them to an
abnormal degree, the effect his music produces is not really
so imposing as that of things which make much less show—
for instance, the opening of Beethoven's B♭ Symphony, which
requires only seven different instruments to play it, and is

all pianissimo. The means are in excess of the requirements; or rather what should be means become requirements, because the effect is made by the actual sound of the instruments, and often not at all by the music which they are the means of expressing. And this aspect of Berlioz's work is even more noteworthy in relation to modern musical development than the fact that he uniformly adopted a programme for his instrumental works. He was a man of unusually excitable sensibility, and the tone of instruments appealed to him more than any other feature in music. He was also a man of literary tastes, and had no inconsiderable gifts in that line, and was more excited by the notion of what music might be brought to express than by the music itself. The result of such influences and predispositions was to impel him to endeavour to express literary or theatrical ideas in terms of colour and rhythm. He was the first composer who emphasised the element of instrumental tone quality or colour to such an extent; and so strong was his predisposition in this direction, that it can easily be seen that he often speculated in original effects of colour, and afterwards evolved or worked up musical ideas to fit into them, just as a painter might cover his canvas with the strangest tints he could devise, and work them up into a subject-picture or a landscape afterwards. But quite independent of these very marked peculiarities in his character, his genius and originality are incontestable. When the spirit of a situation like the opening scene of "Faust" or Margaret's meditation in the prison inspired him wholesomely, he was capable of rising to very high and genuinely musical conceptions.

The sum total of his work is one of the wonders of the art —unique in its weirdness and picturesqueness; and notable for the intense care with which every detail that ministers to effect is thought out. Not only are the scores very complicated in respect of the figures and rhythms of the actual music; but they are full of minute directions as to the manner of performance; extending to the putting of wind instruments in bags, and playing drums with sticks with sponge at the end, and many other original contrivances

The tendency to exaggeration is all of a piece with the high
tension of his nervous organisation; but inasmuch as the
whole object is to intensify characteristic expression in every
conceivable manner, his work is very noteworthy as an illustration of the general tendencies of modern art since Beethoven.
His methods have not found any very conspicuous imitators,
though some very successful French composers have learnt a
great deal from him in many ways. Indeed the modern
French have more natural gift for colour, and a greater love
for it, than for any other department of art. It appears to
express most exactly their peculiarly lively sensibility; and
their passion for it, and for what they call *chic*, has enabled
them to develop in recent times a style of orchestration
which is quite their own, and is generally very neat, graceful,
finished, and telling, especially for lighter kinds of music and
for opera.

Even that very serious and reserved branch of art, the
oratorio, was influenced by such tendencies of modern art,
and gained a new lease of life through the development of
richer means of effective expression. The oratorio had almost
collapsed after the time of Handel and Bach, for the universal
domination of Italian operatic style affected it more vitally
than any other branch of art. The growth of the singularly
perverted taste for having church music in the same style as
opera, with set arias for "prima donnas" at what might be
expected to be extremely solemn moments, and the emptiest
and baldest commonplace harmonisation in place of the old
polyphonic choral music, affected oratorio almost fatally. For
though oratorio was not necessarily a part of any ecclesiastical
function, its associations were of a religious order, and the
style was closely assimilated to that of the various works
written for church use. But it could not afford to be as
empty as either church music or opera, for it stands mainly
on its own footing; and if the music is not interesting in
itself, there is neither scenic effect, nor action, nor the glamour
of an ancient ceremonial to help it out. Other conditions told
in the same direction; for it is probable that people did not
use performances of oratorios quite so much as operas for

19

fashionable gatherings and gossip; and if the music was
tiresome they were bound to become aware of it. Hence the
formality of the arias which were introduced, and the graceful
futility of the Italian style in general, had full effect, and
oratorios fell completely into the background. People would
not listen to things in the lofty style of Bach's Passions, and
so composers were driven to write things that were not worth
listening to at all. Composers like Philip Emmanuel Bach,
who tried to put good work into their oratorios, wasted their
efforts; for even they had to put in some of the usual arias
as a sop to the public, and the conventional stiffness of that
form ultimately counterbalanced the parts of their works
which were of superior quality.

It was not until operatic art had had the benefit of Gluck's
reforms and Mozart's improvements, and the arts of orchestration had been substantially founded upon definitely modern
lines, that a revival became possible. Quite at the end of
the eighteenth century the appearance of Haydn's "Creation"
serves as a sort of landmark of the new departure. It is full
of obvious traces of operatic influence in the forms of the
movements and the style. But the sincere peasant-nature of
the great composer gave a special flavour even to the florid
and conventional airs, which distinguishes them from the
ordinary types, and gives them a characteristic ring which
the world was not slow to recognise. Moreover, his experience of Handel's choral work while in London inspired
him to treat his choruses in a more animated style than usual,
and his great skill and experience in orchestration enabled
him to make the most of that important element of effect;
and so, after a long period of coma, the oratorio form was felt
to have come to life again. The traces of operatic style are
strongly apparent in Beethoven's "Engedi," but the dramatic
character and picturesqueness of some of the details quite
distinguish it from earlier works, though it is by no means
among the great master's most happy productions. The
emancipation from Italian operatic influence becomes more
complete in Spohr's works of this kind. Being a Protestant,
he escaped the influence of the Italianised music of the Roman

Church, and learned to see things in the same sort of light as J. S. Bach. His treatment of the choral portions of his oratorios is much more like what such work ought to be; and there was just sufficient dramatic sense and sentiment in his disposition to enable him to deal with his subjects characteristically and consistently; while his very exceptional gifts as a master of orchestral effect placed in his hands one at least of the most prominent of the new resources which brought about the revival of this form of art. The impulse to cultivate oratorio took special hold of Protestant countries, and those which were the homes of the higher orders of instrumental music—such as the symphony and various forms of chamber music; and the first important crisis in the modern story of oratorio is undoubtedly centred in the work of Mendelssohn in that department. He was one of the earliest of modern musicians to become intimate with J. S. Bach's work, and to a certain extent to understand it. His insight was keen enough to see the wonderful interest of the Passion-music type, and the possibility of adapting it to modern conditions; while Bach's intensely earnest style served him as an inspiring example. His critical feeling was subtle enough to hit the true standard of style, just poised half-way between the strict clearness and reserve of instrumental music and the loose texture of the dramatic style; and his scheme proved so generally successful that it has served most composers as a model ever since the appearance of "Elijah" and "St. Paul." The works are so well known that it is hardly necessary to point out the degree in which they make for expression rather than for mere technical effect. To many people they have long formed the ideal of what such expression ought to be. Mendelssohn undoubtedly emphasised melody, but by no means to the exclusion of other means of expression. He was one of the few composers to whom, in his best moments, all the resources of art were equally available. His choral writing was on the whole the most practical and most fluent that had been seen since Handel and Bach, and for mastery of orchestral effect he had no real superior in his time. His harmony is full of variety and

sufficiently forcible; and his facility in melody quite unlimited. He applied his resources almost to the highest
degree of which he was capable in this line of art, and it
naturally followed that his solution of the problem of oratorio
has satisfied the constant and exacting scrutiny of most
musicians ever since.

To make this the better understood it will be as well to consider shortly what are the conditions which govern the style
and scheme of oratorio. The essence of the situation is the
intention to present a dramatic story in a musical setting without action. The absence of scenic accessories, and of all such
things as are conveyed to the mind and feelings through the
eyes, has drawn the form in the same direction as abstract
instrumental music; for people are more critical about details
when their whole attention is concentrated on the music than
when it is distracted by other elements of effect. So that
oratorio has been found to require more definite and clear
forms and more distinct articulation in minutiæ than opera.
In opera slovenly workmanship has generally been preferred
by the public to artistic finish which bores and distracts them
from the play. In oratorio slovenly workmanship or faulty
designing cannot long pass without being resented. And
moreover, the conditions are more favourable for careful and
scrupulous artistic work. The absence of action reduces the
stringency of the need to keep the music continuously going.
In opera the action is impeded and weakened by breaking up
the music into disconnected pieces, however finished and beautiful they may be in detail; but in oratorio it is a distinct
advantage to have breaks that rest the mind and even to emphasise points in the movements themselves by occasional and
discreet repetition. So that it is not only necessary to make
design clear and artistic workmanship thorough, but the situation actually gains by the use of set forms which render such
treatment possible. On the other hand, in point of style and
dramatic force oratorio is much more limited than opera.
Even positively vulgar music is sometimes defensible in connection with the stage when a character is presented in the
drama who would not be completely represented in the music

associated with him without some suggestion of his vulgar side.
And a much more undisguised use of frank appeals to the
unsophisticated animal side in man has always been tolerated,
even generally welcomed, in operatic matters. But in oratorio
such things would soon betray their artistic falseness. The
ignoble has very often to be dealt with on the stage, but in
the music of the concert-room the responsibilities of a great
and serious form like oratorio cut composers off from everything that is not in a high sense dignified and elevated. But
as a compensation the resources of oratorio are much more
elastic. In opera the attention is centred upon the individual
singers and their stage fortunes; and the chorus, who cannot
learn anything at all complicated by heart, are little better
than lay figures. But in oratorio the prominence of the soloists
is immensely toned down, and is more on a level with the
other elements of effect; and the form of art is in no respect
more strongly distinguished from all other branches of music
than by the inevitable prominence of that democratic element,
the chorus.*

In the oratorio of the eighteenth century the chorus
generally had but a very perfunctory share. They had to
sing things which were intended to be inspiring, but were
in reality quite mechanical—such things as formal theorists'
fugues, and movements consisting of mere successions of
chords, with a great deal of dull note-repetition to fit the
syllables, and no individuality in the parts at all—such as
the passage "Jam plebis devote canentis una est vox, exaudi
precantes exaudi," &c., in Mozart's "Splendente te." The
comprehensive change of the whole aspect of the chorus is
one of the most significant features of modern art; and
nothing emphasises more signally the change from the formal
to the spiritual. Composers did not always take a perfunctory view of the possibilities of chorus in the formal age, as
Mozart's splendid conception of "Rex tremendæ majestatis"

* It is perhaps worth while to remark in passing that the element of
the chorus has always thriven best in societies and branches of society
with very strong democratic energies; while music of the soloists is the
delight of the courtly, fashionable, and plutocratic branches of society.

testifies; but as a rule the choral body was a mere heavy aggregate of figures with lungs and throats whose humanity was merged in a submissive crowd. The modern chorus becomes more and more like an organised group of human beings with human passions and feelings, and with collective ways of expressing them, which are as near as the circumstances allow to what human beings might be expected to adopt in the dramatic situations suggested in the oratorios. The choruses of Baal's priests behave and sing in a way which conveys the impression that they are meant for Baal's priests and not for lay figures; and in one of the finest of recent modern oratorios the choruses of angels and of devils sing passages which express the characteristic impulses of angelic and diabolic natures to a nicety. This recognition of the personal nature of the singers in a chorus was prefigured very strongly in Bach's choral works, and also frequently in Handel's; but the development of orchestral music and of the resources of general dramatic effect have so enhanced the opportunities of composers that the chorus tends more and more to be the centre of interest in such works—and as choral singing is the department of music in which the largest number of people can take an active share, it is all of a piece with the interlacing of the endless phases of cause and effect which conduce towards important results, that the development of the methods of art which make chorus singing interesting in detail, and identify those who sing in them as human beings, should coincide with the great growth of democratic energy which marks the present age. And in such respects the forms of secular choral music, such as odes and cantatas, which are cast on the same general lines as oratorios, and are controlled by absolutely the same conditions of presentation, tend to become even more important and comprehensive than oratorio itself. There is nothing more ideally suited to the inward nature of music than the presentation, in the closest and most characteristic terms, of great reflective and dramatic poems and odes by genuine poets; and for such purposes the chorus is ideally suited. The declamatory method of treating the voices which is growing up and increasing makes every member of the chorus take a share in the recital of the poem ; and the practice of choral singing may yet become a happier means for the diffusion of real refinement of mind and character among large sections of the people than the world has hitherto ever had the fortune to contrive. A composer who has enough cultivation and refinement of mind to appreciate great poems, and commensurate mastery of the arts of choral music and instrumentation, may emphasise the beauties of a poem and bring out its meaning far more effectually than any amount of commentary and explanation. This is eminently a case which illustrates the value of the rich accumulation of resources of various kinds, and the wide facilities which they offer to modern composers ; for till comparatively lately the range of design and the power of composers to wield varieties of means so as to make the form intelligible was so limited, that unless poems were constructed purposely to fit into conventional types of musical form, they could not be effectively set. But since Beethoven has shown how various are the means of making a work of musical art coherent, systematic, and intelligible, and other composers of the modern school have discovered how to adapt various means of expression to the requirements of musical form, there need be but few poems which are in a mood adapted for music that will not admit of an effectual treatment. And the advantages composers now enjoy are so copious that there is little excuse for their adopting the feeble resource which once was so universal, of repeating words and sentences without reference to their importance ; for with increased range of means of expression and design poems can perfectly well be presented in conformity with the poet's intentions.

The same conditions which make possible the characteristic treatment of poems on a grand scale of this kind, with all the splendid resources of orchestration and choral effect, have brought about the profuse cultivation and diffusion of the typical modern song. In no branch of art is the tendency towards expressive characterisation more prominently displayed, for in the best modern "Songs" the music is brought into relation to the poems set to an extent of closeness which was altogether unknown, and indeed would be impossible in any less elaborately organised artistic system. Songs there have been at all periods in history. Solo song is the thread that runs from end to end of the story; but it is only in late years that a system has been devised which is elastic enough to follow every turn of the poet's thought, every change of his mood, every subtlety of his wit, and every beauty of his diction. Till comparatively recent times the scheme of song as a setting of poetry was tune and tune only. Tune can be admirable, and can express a good deal when properly dealt with; but it is not very comprehensive, and the same tune cannot adequately represent different moods unless the performer has great skill in putting extra expression into it which is not necessarily in the music itself. A genuine singer of folk-tunes takes unlimited liberties with them. He makes them fast or slow at will—agitated or quiet—loud or soft—alters the accents and the rhythms, and even the length of the notes. There are even in modern times many public singers who like to have their songs as empty as possible, in order that they may put in all the expression for themselves. But a composer cannot now be satisfied with such conditions, and wants to put in for himself the expression which the words convey to him; and he prefers to have singers who can fall in with his feeling and make their art serve to interpret what is in itself worth expressing, instead of making what does not deserve any interpretation at all seem to be worth it by their art.

In old days composers did not trouble themselves much about the poems which they set. They regarded them as a collection of syllables which admitted of being used for a singable tune. When the poet, for expressive, or structural, or rhythmic reasons, slightly altered the disposition of the accents, the musician rode roughshod over the difficulty it presented to him, and presuming that his tune was of more importance than the poet's intentions, set short syllables to long notes, and accented syllables to unaccented notes with equal impartiality. The composer's habits were similarly inconsiderate with regard to changes in the mood of the words. The relation of the poem to the music was almost ignored, except in a very general sense. This was especially the case in respectable artistic circles. In the music of the people the words counted for a good deal, and plebeians liked to hear them. But in respectable circles the situation was much the same in songs as in operas of the formal period. There were exceptional occasions now and then when composers paid close attention to the words, but as a rule the object was to make a nice piece of melodious music rather than to make it characteristic, or in any way to represent the intention of the poet. The Italian domination was a little in fault here also; for people who did not understand the language, but liked the music the great singers sang, got into the habit of thinking that the words were of no consequence in other things as well as Italian arias. Songs had a better chance out of the range of that kind of civilisation, and in quarters where democratic conditions or national predispositions prevailed, the means for adequately interpreting poems as solo songs improved. Composers saw how to make the harmonisation of a tune alter its character, and how to make their accompaniments characteristic of the mood of the poem or of the situation it expressed, instead of adopting purely mechanical formulas like an Alberti bass for all sentiments alike. The excessive prominence of the element of mere tune was thereby reduced; while the capacity of melody for expression was enhanced by the circumstances with which it was surrounded. Then as harmony was more richly developed and tonality better understood, modulation came in as an additional means of effect. And so, little by little, under various influences, the final blossoming of the form was approached.

The culmination was rather sudden when it came, and was favoured by singular circumstances. Schubert is conspicuous among great composers for the insufficiency of his musical education. His extraordinary gifts and his passion for composing were from the first allowed to luxuriate untrained. He had no great talent for self-criticism, and the least possible feeling for abstract design, and balance, and order; but the profusion of his ideas was only limited by lack of time for writing them down. And these ideas were instinct with genuine

individual life, not mechanical artificial products like opera
arias. They had a form and a character which meant something over and above mere adaptation to formulas of design.
In instrumental music he was liable to plunge recklessly, and to
let design take its chance. The thirst in him was for expression. And when he looked at a manuscript of Beethoven's,
and saw the infinite labour of rewriting again and again to
get all the climaxes and changes of harmony and progressions
of all sorts exactly in their right places from every point
of view, he shook his head and doubted whether such labour
was worth while. With him, perhaps, it would not have
been worth while, for he is hardly likely to have developed
enough perception in that direction to know where to stop
or where to press on. But this was the ideal nature for
modern song writing. That form of art did not require any
great scope of intellect or self-control. The poems he set had to
supply him with the design, and his receptive mind, as it were,
spontaneously reproduced in musical terms the impressions
which they made upon him. The wonder is that he could find
such varieties of characteristic expression so soon after the
formal period. "Gretchen am Spinnrade" was written in
1814, and the Erl König in 1815, within six years after the
death of Haydn, and even before Beethoven's Ninth Symphony.
But they are both instinct with the full measure of vitality in
every part; and are absolutely complete representatives of
the modern spirit of musical expression. Harmony, rhythm,
colour, tonality—all minister to the full utterance of the poems
as well as melody. In the Erl König the vivid portrayal
by the accompaniment of the rage of the storm is familiar to
every one. But the subtlety of instinct is even more remarkable in less obvious directions. For instance, if people's
sense of tonality had not become so developed by his time
the skilful device of beginning the question, "Wer reitet so
spät durch Nacht und Wind?" upon a secondary harmony
would have been merely obscure; and the modulation to a
different key from the opening in the second line of the song
would have been yet more so. Here a highly developed feeling
for keys is made use of for purposes of expression. The ques-

tion and answer which give the clue to the spirit of the song
are isolated, so as to make them stand out from the context.
Then again, instead of having a tune for the solo voice like
earlier songs, the vocal part is so exactly a reproduction of what
a good reciter might do in declaiming, that each rise and fall
seems to belong inherently to the words. Its melodic significance is much more the result of the accompaniment than of
the solo part itself. When a more definitely tuneful phrase
makes its appearance, it comes because it is so particularly suitable to the moment; as when the Erlking is made to wheedle
the child with promises of flowers and pretty games. The characters of the several speakers are perfectly identifiable throughout, notwithstanding the ceaseless rush and turmoil; and the
changes of moods are perfectly conveyed without any break of
continuity. The musical portrayal gains in intensity as the
song proceeds, and is finally concentrated into the characteristic passage in the bass just at the end, where it goes stamping
upwards till it arrives at a point that is purposely obscure in
relation to the key of the song, so as to accentuate the cadence
and isolate the dénouement. The rush and turmoil suddenly
cease, and the consummation of the tragedy is conveyed in the
mood of awe which is as near as possible to silence. And, just
as in the passage described on p. 266 from Beethoven's "Appassionata," the very tension of the situation gives the cadence all
the requisite degree of impressiveness to round off the design
into completeness. This is indeed one of the most significant
instances of the relation between expression and design in
modern art, for in such cases it is the quickness of perception
generated by the exciting qualities of the music which enables
the mind to grasp a mere suggestion of an important factor
in the musical design, which is so slightly emphasised that
a man in cold blood would probably feel it to be inadequately
presented.

The wonderful "Gretchen am Spinnrade" is dealt with in
precisely the same manner. It is unified by the suggestion
of the spinning-wheel in the accompaniment, while the perfect management of the harmonic scheme of the music gives
perfect freedom to the treatment of the words. How vivid

such a situation can be made in musical terms may be illustrated from the treatment of the words "Und ach, sein Kuss!"

The rise to the highest emotional point, with the acutely
sensitive harmonies enforcing the complicated mood of the
moment; the pause in the spinning and then the sudden
drop to the silence of reflection—the broken fragments of
the characteristic spinning accompaniment—which might from
one point of view suggest the sobs and the difficulty of getting
back to the spinning again; and the exact adjustment of the
harmony to the desperate sadness of the mood. Every resource is thus made use of to emphasise the expression. And
so it is with numbers of other songs of Schubert's which will
bear the closest analysis; especially when the poems happen
to be fine enough to inspire fine music and close and consistent treatment.

In the gigantic mass of Schubert's songs there is necessarily a large quantity that is of no great value—that is even flat and pointless. But this is all of a piece with the spirit of the new age which he prefigured so ripely. His aims were in a sense speculative. He had no preconceived idea of the form in which to put his utterances; as far as design was concerned he only felt that he had to start from a given point of tonality and get back to it. If the thought of the poet suggested modulations which were not too copious or too ill distributed to be intelligible, the result was a success; if the poet's imagery was too flat and his thought too mechanical, or on the other hand too turgid and too indefinite, the chances were in favour of a failure. Schubert had the good fortune to have some truly superb poems to inspire him; and even in lower standards, whenever any "local colour" or strong human characteristics can be associated with the words, his mind would fasten on them and make them the cue for his manner, and for the musical material he gave to his accompaniment.

It is very significant that with a divine gift of melody he rarely condescends to rely upon that alone. The greater number of his melodies gain their very expressive character through his harmonisation. He instinctively understood the relation of harmony to melody, and its power of emphasising definite expression at a moment; where melody would have to express a thing—if it could do it at all—by a long phrase. It is also characteristic of the time that his melodies are often constructed of successions of figures which are very definite and decisive in themselves. The articulation is sometimes almost as clear as in Beethoven's subjects. Mozart, and the Italians among whom he represents the highest type, usually made long meandering passages of melody with no very definite articulation. The true Teuton aiming at concentration of expression compresses his thought into figures which are specially definite and telling. They become the nuclei by which he indicates the spirit of his work. The process of figure development is specially characteristic of instrumental music, because in that branch of art the rhythm helps the concentration and definition; and the use of such character istic figures in the instrumental part of songs is a very conspicuous feature in Schubert's work and that of all other great song-writers; but it is also characteristic in a lesser degree of the finest vocal melody.

The development of song art after Schubert's time is mainly notable in respect of the application of new resources as they came into being, and the special attitude towards poetry taken by the composer. Schumann, as a man of exceptional cultivation, highly imaginative, and closely in sympathy with poetry, was of the ideal type to follow in Schubert's steps. He was gifted with more of the familiar Teutonic disposition to reflect and look inwards than Schubert, whose gaiety of the Viennese type generally kept him in touch with the outward aspect of things. There is more passion and depth and sensibility in Schumann, but less of the gift of portrayal. Schumann excelled in the things that are direct utterances of inner feeling. Many phases of the impulses of love find most vivid expression with him, which Schubert could not have touched. "Du meine Seele," "Ich grolle nicht," are moods which are eminently characteristic of a later phase of human musical sensibility than Schubert's, and help to fill up the whole circuit of song types; which is still further enriched by the remaining great German song-writer of the present day, Johannes Brahms. The three between them fill up almost the whole range of the higher type of song-writing. Numbers of other successful song-writers there are—and some honourably unsuccessful ones—who fully understand what an opportunity the association of a solo voice with an instrumental accompaniment affords for definite and close characterisation. And composers of different nations impart the flavours of Slav, English, Norwegian, and French to their songs, but make them, if they have any sense, on the same general terms as the great Germans. Each national flavour lends a special interest to the product, if the product is a sincere and genuine musical utterance; but the methods upon which the finest songs are constructed remain as they were with Schubert and Schumann.

The advantage of the song branch of art is that the expressive resources of music are applied for purposes which the words make plain. Where the words are thoroughly musical, and the composer particularly sensitive and skilful, the music fits the lyric at every instant, and makes the words glow with intensified meaning. In some ways the other principal branch of domestic music labours under the apparent disadvantage that its exact meaning is often left obscure. Even when pianoforte pieces are identified with ideal subjects by titles, composers do not very often attempt to emphasise the details of their working in the mind; and such realistic devices as were popular in former days to depict "The Battle of Prague," and similarly exciting events, are recognised by all the world as laughable. Unconsciously the development of the musical world's sense of criticism tends to arrive at the truth, that though realism is admissible as a source of suggestion, the object of the expressive power of music is not to represent the outward semblance of anything, but to express the moods which it produces, and the workings of the mind that are associated with them. When Beethoven called a movement "Am Bach," he justifiably used a suggestion of the ripple of the water as his accompaniment. But the ripple does not make the sum total of the effect, and is not the aim of the movement; it only forms the musical atmosphere or medium in which the expressive material is embodied. The little disjointed fragments of figure which float on the rustling sound of the water are, as it were, broken ejaculations of happy contentment, which gather into volume at length with the full sweep of pure delight expressed in the melody:—

In such a movement, indeed, Beethoven's power of giving utterance to human feeling seems even to be intensified by associating it with realistic device. And it may at once be granted that a little of such realism is sometimes at least a help to the composer, for it keeps his moods in tune; but it is also a dangerous weapon to handle, and every one is conscious in a moment if the subordinate relation of realistic to inward presentation is exceeded.

These conditions help to explain the peculiarities of the course of one important department of modern music. The pianoforte has become one of the most familiar objects of domestic life, and occupies the position at one time held by the lute, at another by the harpsichord and clavichord. It is eminently a practical instrument, and can be made to serve for the wildest excesses of vulgarity as well as for a very comprehensive variety of fine and noble music; which gives it a great advantage over previous instruments from a purely practical point of view. The lute was slow moving, soft and delicate; it could neither rage nor rattle. The harpsichord could rattle, and tinkle counterpoint, and present fine effects of harmony, and give a picturesque sound; but it was only moderately efficient for rhythm and *cantabile*. The pianoforte, while lacking certain beauties which both the earlier instruments possessed, is infinitely more efficient for every kind of characterisation. It combines common sense with a very fair capacity for becoming poetical. It puts a wide range of musical expression into the hands of one performer, and enables him to present music in all the phases of harmony, polyphony, colour, melody, and rhythm which have become necessities of modern music. It is the compendium of musical performance, and as such is most apt for domestic use. Its sphere of public activity, the great concert room, is secondary to this; and is the mere outcome of the need for giving a large general public the opportunity of hearing celebrated performers. It is rather its position as the chosen instrument of intimate home life which has induced composers to write so much for it; and the consciousness that its real function is to deal with things intimately has had considerable influence upon the style of music written for it, especially in the earlier stages of pianoforte music. The intimate music of home life is that which people like to have always with them. It is the music that they like to dwell upon, and to hear again and again both as the true presentation of human feeling, and as finished and refined art. The purest conceivable ideal of such intimate music is to be found in Bach's "Wohltemperirte Clavier." But that lacks the modern sensibility, the modern luxury of tone, and the phases which represent those developments of harmonic design and colour which have become part of modern musical life. Later composers have aimed at supplying all varieties of tastes with pianoforte music which is for home consumption; and inasmuch as this implies dealing with characteristics at close quarters, and addressing themselves to an infinite variety of small groups of individuals, the circumstances have produced a wider range of characteristics in pianoforte music than in any other branch of the art. What people like to have at home is the true test of their standard of refinement. The diversity is obviously immense; ranging from Bach and Beethoven to mere arrangements of popular items from the latest Italian opera, or the buffoonery of nigger minstrels. And this happily illustrates the process of constant differentiation which is characteristic of evolution; for indeed the growth of diversity of character in such things has become so extensive that in these days nearly every taste can be satisfied.

To come finally to the working of the influences which have made modern pianoforte music what it is under these circumstances. In Beethoven's work the world felt that the high water mark of well-balanced art and expression in sonata form had been reached. Certain expansions of it were, no doubt, possible; and in such branches as quartetts, trios, and other forms of pianoforte chamber music which are cast in "sonata forms," there still is vitality. But in essentially pianoforte music it was not worth while to do again what had been done as well as seems humanly possible. Moreover, composers have become conscious that the sonata form is spread rather wide, and is best suited for rather special occasions; and further, that it is not quite perfectly suited to many modern types of thought which are quite fit to be treated musically, though not at such great length. And so there has grown up a common

20

consensus of opinion to explore new possibilities of design
and expression. And here men of various types have necessarily taken various lines. There were all sorts of ways in
which new departures might be made. Some men delight in
neatness of design, some in ardent expression, some in ingenuity, and some in display. All types found their exponents.
Schubert left many beautiful little movements in very characteristic style; Field made an important mark with his nocturnes;
even studies were made to have a poetical aspect in the hands
of J. B. Cramer; while Mendelssohn came very prominently
before the world in a similarly independent line with his
"Lieder ohne Worte," which rightly took a very comprehensive hold upon the artistic public through their thoroughly
refined character and the finished qualities of their art. It is
patent to all the world that even these last are totally different
in form as well as expression from sonatas. Their title admirably expresses them, and the more so if it be remembered that
"Song" has come to mean something quite different from
the old conception; and implies a work of art in which all
the factors—melody, harmony, figure, rhythm—are combined
to the common end. Under such conditions, when the name
"Song" had become almost inappropriate, a "Song without
words" is not such an anomaly as it would have been in
less developed stages of art. Mendelssohn, however, as was
natural in his days, rather emphasised the melody which is
the counterpart of the absent voice, and thereby somewhat
restricted his resources of expression; so his work may be
said to lean in the formal direction more than many later
productions.

Of conspicuously different type were the wild theories of a
certain group of enthusiasts, whose eagerness to solve artistic
problems was in excess of their hold upon the possibilities and
resources of art. They emphasised unduly the expressive aims
of Beethoven, and thought it possible to follow him in that
respect without regard to his principles of design; and sought
to develop a new line of art by the use of clearly marked musical
figures, which were to be presented in an endless variety of
guises in accordance with some supposed programme. The

aspiring innovators recognised the expressive possibilities of music to the fullest possible extent, and their efforts might have come to a more successful issue but for two circumstances. One of these was that through taking the superficial theorists' view of sonata form to represent all the facts, they entirely overlooked the deeper principles, and rejected those deeper principles along with some of the superficial conventions of the theorists. And this rendered the failure of their scheme inevitable until they arrived at a better understanding of the situation. The second circumstance was the accident that they were closely connected with the most advanced school of technicians; indeed, one of the foremost representatives of their views was the greatest pianoforte virtuoso of modern times; and the outcome of this connection was that their reforming efforts were completely drowned and extinguished by the flood of ornamental rhetoric to which the abnormal development of pure technical facility in performance gave rise. Nearly all the energy of composers of this section of humanity was expended in finding ways to make scales and arpeggios sound more astonishing than they used to do when they were played in the old-fashioned ways; and further, of finding opportunities for showing off such futile dexterities. It so happens that their root theory of working up figures and fragments of tune into programme movements adapts itself well to the requirements of display. It is only people of inferior organisation who are taken in by such empty extravagance of barren ornament; and for people of that type tunes out of operas which they already know, or familiar popular tunes, are the most intelligible forms of musical material. So, when a composer of this school addressed himself to his task of showing off the new kinds of scales and arpeggios, he had only to collect a few familiar tunes and intersperse them with all the ornamental resources of which he was master, and the scheme was complete. Curiously enough, though works of such kind are totally worthless intrinsically, the skill which the composers developed in technique materially widened the resources of effect which thereby became available for better composers to use. In that sense the development of technique, and of the effect which comes of it, is of great historical importance; and his achievements in that direction give Liszt a noteworthy position quite apart from the actual quality of his musical effusions. He, indeed, summed up a great period of brilliant development of pianoforte technique, and put the crown on that branch of music.

However, the result of technical development has not been all gain. It has been carried to such an excessive extent that pianoforte music has been rather overburdened than benefited by it. A faulty tradition has got into the very marrow of this branch of art, and a composer has to address himself so much to technical effect that there is little energy left over for genuine expression.

But by the side of the school of virtuosi, and in touch with it, the spirit of Chopin has laid a spell upon musical people all the world over, and has coloured a singularly wide range of musical activity in all countries. His circumstances were specially suited to the necessities of the moment. The Poles are peculiarly different from the more happily regulated races of the western part of Europe; and the fact of having been unfortunate in their relations with their most powerful neighbours has intensified nationalist feeling. Such feeling, when repressed, generally bursts into song, and very often into very expressive song; and in Chopin's time everything combined to enhance the vividness and individuality of Polish music. Chopin, with Polish blood in his veins, and brought up in pure Polish surroundings, absorbed the national influences from his early years. Under such circumstances a national dance becomes a vital reality of more than ordinary calibre. A mazurka was a rhythmic expression of the national fervour. A polonaise symbolised the exaggerated glories of the Polish chivalric aristocracy. Music which was so vivid and direct, and had such a touch of savage fervour, was not of the kind to go satisfactorily into sonatas. There needed to be very little intellectuality about it, but a great deal of the rhythmic element and of poetic feeling, and these things Chopin was eminently fitted to supply. On the other hand, his sensitiveness was acute even to morbidity; and being less gifted with force and energy than with excitability, he applied himself instinctively to the more delicate possibilities of his instrument. With him ornamental profusion was a necessity ; but, more than with any other composer except Bach, it formed a part of his poetical thought. With most of the player-composers who cultivate virtuoso effects the brilliant passages are purely mechanical, and have little relation to the musical matter in hand. With Chopin the very idea is often stated in terms of most graceful and finished ornamentation, such as is most peculiarly suited to the genius of the instrument. Beethoven had grown more and more conscious of the suitableness of very rapid notes to the pianoforte as his experience and understanding of the instrument increased, and he had tried (in a different manner from Chopin) to achieve the same ends. But the reserve and grandeur of his style did not admit of the sort of ornaments that Chopin used ; for these are made peculiarly vivid by profuse use of semitones and accessory notes of all kinds, which do not form part either of the harmony or the diatonic scale in which the passages occur. It gives a peculiarly dazzling, oriental flavour to the whole, which, joined with a certain luxurious indolence, a dreaminess of sentiment, and a subtlety of tone, makes Chopin's the ideal music for the drawing-rooms of fairly refined and prosperous people. But there is enough of genuine humanity and dramatic feeling to make his works appeal to a larger public than mere frequenters of drawing-rooms. There are even passages of savagery, such as those in the polonaises in A♭ and F♯ minor, which sound like some echo from a distant country, and ring of the proud fervour of patriotic enthusiasm. The "Ballades" and so-called Sonatas and Scherzos convey a rich variety of moods and effects on a considerable scale, while the nocturnes, and some of the preludes and mazurkas, exactly hit the sensuous perceptions which are so highly developed in modern life. Fortunately, with Chopin the general departure from sonata lines was no result of theory, but the spontaneous action of his nature. His music was the spontaneous utterance of a poetic and sensitive disposition, in the terms ideally suited to the instrument whose inner

most capacities he understood more thoroughly than any one
else in the world. Design of a classical kind was comparatively unimportant to him. He did not know much about it.
But he most frequently cast his thoughts in simple forms,
such as that of the nocturne—which Field had brought successfully into vogue just before his time—or the ordinary
forms of the dance. When he struck out a form for himself, as in some of the best preludes and studies, it was like
a poem on new lines. But the methods by which they were
unified were much the same as those employed by J. S. Bach
in his Preludes. Only in respect of their much more vivid
colour, and intensity of feeling for modern expression, do they
differ from the far more austere master. Of the degree
in which expression is emphasised rather than form there
can hardly be a question. But when the form is original it
is extraordinarily well adapted to the style of the expression ;
as, for instance, in the preludes in E minor and D minor,
where the form and expression are as closely wedded as in
the most skilful and condensed poetical lyric. But such types
of thought could not be expanded into great schemes of design.
His largest works in original forms are the Ballades, and
these are as unlike sonatas as any. The whole collection of his
works is an illustration of the wide spread of possible variety
which the new departure in the direction of expression, after
the formal age, made inevitable.

Utterly different as was the nature of Schumann, his work
in general tends in the same direction ; and, as it were, fills
up the other half of the circle which Chopin left comparatively
vacant. Schumann was a typical Teuton in his introspective
disposition, his mystic imaginings, his depth of earnestness.
The rhythmic side of music did not appeal to him with anything like the elastic, nervous intensity with which it excited
a Pole, but rather with the solemnity and orderliness of a
German waltz. His natural sphere was rather the type of
music which belongs to the reflective mind; and the types of
thought, both emotional and noble, which appeal to a cultivated intellectualist. As it was not intended to make music
his life's occupation, his education in his art was not as com-

plete and thorough as that of many other composers; but it brought him into closer contact with the expression of human feeling in poetic forms and in general literature, and forced him to take an unconventional view of his art. He saw from the first that something different from sonatas was wanted; and though he did write a few sonatas, the one that is most like the old sonatas, though brilliant in effect, is rather weak in design; while the sonata in F♯ minor is a deliberate attempt to distribute the ideas in a manner totally different from the old sonata order. In forms which afforded some fresh opportunities for treatment and effect, as in the quintett and quartett in E♭, he is very much more successful in contriving something like the old sonata forms; but in the main his works for the pianoforte are attempts to open up a new path, and to increase the variety of types of form and expression in music. To a great many of his epigrammatic musical poems he affixes names—such as the familiar "Warum," "Träumeswirren," "Grillen"; the numbers of Carnival figures, the beautifully finished and neatly expressive Kinderscenen; in some cases he gives no names to individual numbers, but makes it very clearly felt that he has a decided poetic purpose, as in the Kreisleriana and the Davids-bündler. Moreover, the general names he gave to these sets supply the clues to those who know his particular lines of reading, and his special enthusiasms at particular times in his life, and indicate what he meant to express by them. In other cases he gives general names, such as Novelletten, to imply new experiments in form without so much of an acknowledged poetic purpose. In the case of the fantasia in C, he tried to develop a work on a scale fully equal to sonatas, but totally different in character and principle of design. In most of these works his idea seems to be to give the full sense of design by the juxtaposition of ideas which illustrate one another in a poetical sense, and to contrive their connection by means which are in consonance with the spirit of the ideas, or by making some characteristic musical figure into a sort of text which pervades the tissue of the whole. The experiments are so far novel that it is almost too much to expect of them to be always entirely successful. But at least in the last movement of the fantasia, the novel principle of design and the development of the whole scheme is as successful as the ideas themselves are beautiful and poetical.

Schumann, like Beethoven, revels in a mass of sound. But his sound is far more sensuous and chromatic. He loved to use all the pedal that was possible, and had but little objection to hearing all the notes of the scale sounding at once. He is said to have liked dreaming to himself, by rambling through all sorts of harmonies with the pedal down; and the glamour of crossing rhythms and the sounding of clashing and antagonistic notes was most thoroughly adapted to his nature. A certain confusion of many factors, a luxury of conflicting elements which somehow make a unity in the end, serves admirably to express the complicated nature of the feelings and sensibilities and thoughts of highly-organised beings in modern times. Chopin's style has coloured almost all pianoforte music since his time, in respect of the manner and treatment of the instrument; and many successful composers are content merely to reproduce his individualities in a diluted form. But Schumann has exerted more influence in respect of matter and treatment of design. With him the substance is of much greater significance, and he reaches to much greater depths of genuine feeling. There must necessarily be varieties of music to suit all sorts of different types of mind and organisation, and Chopin and Schumann are both better adapted to cultivated and poetic natures than to simple unsophisticated dispositions. That is one of the necessities of differentiation; and music which is concentrated in some especial direction can only meet with response from those who possess the sensitive chord that the music is intended to touch. There are natures copious enough to have full sympathy with the dreamers as well as the workers; but as a rule the world is divided between the two. People who love much imagery and luxury of sensation do not want to listen to Cherubini's best counterpoint, and those who only love energy and vital force do not want to listen to the love scenes in the Walküre. But as illustrating the profusion of sensations, the poetic sensibility, and even the luxury and intellectuality, the passion and the eagerness of modern life, Chopin and Schumann between them cover the ground more completely than all the rest of modern pianoforte composers put together.

For greatness of expression and novelty of treatment Johannes Brahms stands out absolutely alone since their time. Disdaining the ornamental aspects of pianoforte music, he has had to find out a special technique of his own; and in order to find means to express the very original and powerful thoughts that are in him, he resorts to devices which tax the resources of the most capable pianists to the utmost. Moreover, he taxes the power of the interpreter also; which is a thing a great many virtuosi pianists are not prepared for. There is something austerely noble about his methods, which makes thought and manner perfectly consistent; and though it cannot be said that his line of work is so easily identifiable with the general tendency towards independence of design, he has produced many works that are decidedly not on the line of sonatas—such as his Rhapsodies and Clavier-Stücke and Intermezzi; all instinct with the definiteness and decisiveness of individuality which mark him as an outlying representative of the great family of Teutonic musical giants.

The aspect of pianoforte music in general seems to indicate that composers are agreed that the day for writing sonatas is past, and that forms of instrumental music must be more closely identified with the thoughts or moods which are expressed in them. The resources of harmonic and polyphonic effect, combined with rhythm and melody, are much richer than the resources of simple accompanied melody; and the growth of fresh resources is by no means at an end. There is plenty of room for characteristic work. Composers have begun to import national traits into their pianoforte compositions with perfect success; and the identifying of a nation's essential character with its music can be aptly and very considerably extended in pianoforte music as in other branches of art. The field of characteristic musical expression is certainly not exhausted; and composers who have any gift for devising consistent and compact forms which are perfectly adapted to the

mood of their ideas, have still room to achieve something new
in the most interesting modern phases of art. The sonata
type was no doubt adapted to the highest and noblest kind of
musical expression; and it is not likely that anything so noble
and so perfect in design as Beethoven's work will be seen in
the world for a long while. But even if illustrations have not
so elevated a dignity as the works of a great artistic period,
they may serve excellent purposes, and be in every way admirable, and permanently interesting and enjoyable, if they are
carried out with fair understanding of the true necessities of
the situation, and with the sincerity of the true artistic spirit.

One of the most obvious features of the modern condition
of music is the extraordinary diversity of forms which have
become perfectly distinct, from symphony, symphonic poem,
and opera, down to the sentimental ballad of the drawing-
rooms. And in all of them it is not only the type of design
which has become distinctive, but the style as well. For
instance, one of the branches of music which is still most
vigorously alive is chamber music, which consists mainly of
combinations of varieties of solo stringed or wind instruments,
with pianoforte, in works written on the lines of sonatas. Its
present activity is partly owing to the fact that it has rather
changed its status from being real chamber music, and is
becoming essentially concert music. The instruments are
treated with less delicacy of detail than they were by
Beethoven, with a view to obtain the sonority suitable to
large rooms. The style has therefore necessarily changed to
a great extent; but nevertheless it is still as closely differen-
tiated from the style of all other branches of art as ever. A
touch of the operatic manner instantly betrays itself as inconsistent, and so do the devices of symphonic orchestration.
Even the national tunes, and the original subjects which belong
to that type, which are such a welcome and characteristic
feature in Dvořák's works of this order, are so transformed
and translated by the subtle genius of the composer into terms
which are apt to the style of this highly specialised branch of
art, that the remoteness and diversity of the branch of art from
which they spring is almost forgotten. In other lines the same

law holds good. The features of brilliant and vivacious fancy which adorn the orchestral works of the Bohemian master— probably the greatest living master of orchestral effect—are in like manner translated into the terms suited to the particular branch of art he is dealing with. And even the wild experiments of younger aspirants after a poetical reputation and picturesquely astonishing novelty unconsciously fall into line with the limitations of style and diction which are characteristic of their branch of musical utterance.

Thus there is an average mood and style of idea which composers have instinctively adopted for each branch of art, so that the examples of different orders are distinct not only in technical details but in spirit. And moreover, even in the highest branches of art, represented by the noble symphonies of Brahms, which illustrate the loftiest standard of style of the day, the significant change from the old ideals in respect of subject-matter is noticeable. For the aim in his works on the grandest scale is but rarely after what is equivalent to external beauty in music. What beauty is aimed at is beauty of thought, the beauty of nobleness, and high musical intelligence. Even beauty of colour is but rarely present ; but the colours are always characteristic, and confirm the reality of the powerful and expressive ideas. So the rule holds good even in the most austere lines, that the latest phase of art is characterisation

CHAPTER XIV

MODERN PHASES OF OPERA

GLUCK's theories of reform had strangely little effect upon the course of opera for a long while. The resources of art were not sufficiently developed to make them fully practicable, and even if they had been, it is quite clear that in many quarters they would not have been adopted. The problem to be solved in fitting intelligible music to intelligible drama is one of the most complicated and delicate ever undertaken by man; and the solution is made all the more difficult through the fact that the kind of public who frequent operas do not in the least care to have it solved. Operatic audiences have always had the lowest standard of taste of any section of human beings calling themselves musical. They generally have a gross appetite for anything, so long as it is not intrinsically good. If the music is good they have to be forced to accept it by various forms of persuasion; and a composer who attempts any kind of artistic thoroughness has to look forward either to failure, or to the disagreeable task of insisting on being heard. It follows that progress towards any ideal assimilation of the various factors of operatic effect has to be achieved in spite of the taste of the audiences, and by the will and determination which is the outcome of a composer's conviction. Nations vary very much in their capacity to take sensible views of things, as they do in their capacity for enjoying shams and taking base metal for gold; so a composer's opportunities of emancipating himself from convention, and of solving the problems he sees to be worth solving, are much better in one country than another. It is conspicuously true in operatic matters that the public decide what they will have, unless a man is strong enough to force them to listen to what they have at first no mind for; and even then the public have, as it were, a casting vote.

It cannot be pretended that all the causes of the different aspects of opera in different countries can be conclusively shown; but the general and familiar facts are strangely in accordance with the general traits of national character which are commonly observed. The Italians appear to have been the most spontaneously gifted with artistic capabilities of any nation in Europe. In painting they occupy almost the whole field of the greatest and most perfect art; especially of the art produced in the times when simple beauty of form and colour was the main object of artists. In music too they started every form of modern art. Opera, oratorio, cantata, symphony, organ music, violin music, all sprang into life under their auspices. But in every branch they stopped half-way, when the possibilities of art were but half explored, and left it to other nations to gather the fruit of the tree which they had planted. Numbers of causes combine to make this invariable result. One of the most prominent is curiously illustrated by the history of opera. The Italians are generally reputed to be on the average very receptive and quickly excitable. The eagerness of composers for sympathetic response is found in the same quarters as quick receptiveness of audiences to the music that suits them. The impressions which are quickly produced do not always spring from the most artistic qualities. But the Italian composer cannot take note of that; he is passionately eager for sympathy and applause, and is impelled to use all the most obvious incitements to obtain them, without consideration of their fitness. The way in which Italian opera composers resort to the most direct means to excite their audiences is a commonplace of everyday observation. The type of opera aria, which was polished and made more and more perfectly adapted to the requirements of the singer from Scarlatti's time to Mozart's, was ultimately degraded, under the influence of this eagerness for applause, into the obvious, catchy opera tunes which are the most familiar features of the works of the early part of this century. The good artistic work which used to be put into the accompaniment, and was often written in a contrapuntal form by the composers of the best time, degenerated into worthless jigging formulas, like the accompaniments to dance tunes, which have neither artistic purpose nor characteristic relevancy to the situation. The blustering and raging of brass instruments when there is no excuse for it in the dramatic situation, and such tricks as the whirling Rossinian crescendo (which is like a dance of dervishes all about nothing), produce physical excitement without any simultaneous exaltation of higher faculties. These and many more features of the same calibre are the fruits of the excessive eagerness in the composer for immediate sympathetic response from his audience. He has no power to be self-dependent, or to take his own view of what is worthy of art or what is not, or of what represents his own identity. The thirst for the passionate joy of a popular triumph must have its satisfaction. What men constantly set themselves to obtain they generally succeed in obtaining; and the objects of Italian opera composers have been abundantly achieved. The furore of Italian operatic triumphs, such as the Rossini fever after Tancredi, surpasses anything recorded or conceivable in connection with any other branch of art. The opera tunes of Bellini, Donizetti, and the early works of Verdi have appealed to the largest public ever addressed by a musician; and that was till recently the sum of their contribution towards the modern development of their art. In respect of the details of workmanship of which their public were not likely to take much notice, such as the orchestration, they were careless and coarse; and the advance made from the standard of Mozart all round until recent times was made backwards.

The Italians emphasised the musical means of appealing to their audiences from the first; the French, on the other hand, always had more feeling for the drama, and stage effect, and ballet. Though the stories of Roland, Armide, Phaeton, and the other subjects Lulli used are somewhat formal in their method of presentation, they are made quite intelligible, and

the situations are often very good, and very well treated. In
that sense, indeed, Lulli's work is more genuine than Scarlatti's.
The same aspect of things continues throughout the history of
French opera. French audiences seem to have been capable of
being impressed by the pathos, tragedy, and human interest
and beauty of the situations. Their minds seem to have been
projected more towards the subject than the music. Gluck's
dramatic purpose found a response in Paris that he failed
to find even in Vienna, where Italian traditions prevailed.
Things would seem to have bid fair in the end for French
opera. When Italians came under French influence they did
good work. French influence helped Cherubini to achieve his
great operatic successes. Perhaps the enigmatical relation
between his reputed character and his actual work may have
been somewhat owing to Parisian influence. Personally he
appeared to be endowed with all the pride, reserve, and
narrowness of a pedant, yet his Overture to Anacreon is as
genial as the ancient poet himself may be assumed to have
been, and expresses all the fragrance and sparkle of the wine
of which he sang with such enthusiasm. He was cold and
hard and devoid of sympathetic human nature, but nevertheless he devised the tragic intensity of his opera Medea
with unquestionable success.

In later days the influence exerted by French taste upon
Rossini is even more notable and pregnant with meaning.
After his wild triumphs in Italy he came into contact with the
French operatic traditions, and they at once brought out whatever there was of real dramatic sincerity in his constitution.
"William Tell," the one work which he wrote for a Parisian
audience, puts him in quite a new light; for under the influence of a more genuinely dramatic impulse even his artistic
work improved; the orchestration becomes quite interesting,
the type of musical ideas is better, and they are better expressed, and the general feeling of the whole is more sincere
and rich in feeling.

In light comic operettas and operatic comedies the acute
sympathy of the French with the stage produced the happiest
results of all. In this line the French took their cue from the

Italian opera buffa, which had been introduced a little before Gluck's time, and became very noticeable by reason of the ferment of controversy that it produced. Once rooted in the soil and cultivated by French composers, it was found to be even more at home than in Italy. The quick wit, and the sense of finish—even the element of the superficial which the French cultivate with so much interest and care—all told to make the product peculiarly happy. A special style was developed, which in the hands of many composers was singularly refined, neat, and perfectly artistic. The music is merry, and attains the true comedy vein without descending to buffoonery; carelessly gay, without being inartistic in detail. In the early days no doubt the resources of art were not very carefully used; and however excellent the spirit and wit of Grétry, it cannot be pretended that he attempted to deal with the inner and less obvious phases of his work with any artistic completeness. He professedly contemned musicianship, and in a sense he was right. The typical pedant never shows more truly the inherent stupidity of his nature than when he obtrudes conscious artistic contrivance into light subjects. But the perfect mastery of artistic resource does not obtrude its artistic contrivances. It uses them so well that they are perfectly merged in the general effect. The fact that Bach was the most perfect master of artistic contrivance did not prevent his writing perfectly gay dance tunes; and Mozart's careful education in the mysteries of his craft enabled him to write his comic scenes in a fully artistic manner, without putting up sign-posts to tell people when to look out for a piece of artistic skill. In that respect Grétry was wrong, and his successors much wiser. For men like Auber and Bizet and Gounod, and other still living representatives of this branch of art, use the resources of their orchestra with most consummate skill at the lightest moments; just hitting the balance of art and gaiety to a nicety; while the rounding and articulation of their phraseology, the variety and clearness of their ideas, and the excellence of their design, up to the point required in such work, is truly admirable. In no other branch of music is the French genius so completely at home and happy. Even in the coarser types of the same family of operetta, which have become rather popular in recent times, the composers who set the licentious and unwholesomely suggestive dialogue at least caught something of the spirit of their more refined brethren, and showed a skill of instrumental resource and a neatness of musical expression and treatment which are surprising in relation to such subjects. Whenever the play aims at real human interest, and the capacity of the composer for looking at it as human interest is equal to the demand, French effort, even in the more serious branch of opera, produces eminently sincere and artistic results. But in the more serious subjects it has been generally happiest in very reserved phases like those illustrated by Cherubini and Méhul. The dangerous susceptibility of the French nature to specious show and mere external effect seems peculiarly liable to mislead them when it comes to great or imposing occasions. The French are so devoted to "style" that they omit to notice that it is a thing which may be very successfully cultivated to disguise inherent depravity and falseness. It seems to be chiefly owing to this weakness that the result of their enthusiasm for musical drama does not come nearer to the complete solution of the problem of opera. At all events, the most imposing result obtained in the direction of French opera is strictly in accordance with those characteristics of the nation which have persisted so long that they were even noticed by the conquering Romans.

The influence is apparent even in Lulli's and Rameau's work. The spectacular side is carefully attended to, and forms a conspicuous element in the sum-total. Gluck had to submit, and to satisfy the taste to a certain extent; and its effect is even more noticeable in the works of his successor, Spontini. In many ways, however, French influence had an excellent effect upon the latter composer. His operas are singularly full of true dramatic expression; the details of orchestral effect are worked out with marvellous care, and are extremely rich and full of variety for the time when he wrote. The scores are marked almost as fully and carefully as Wagner's, and the inner and outer phrases are thoroughly articu

21

late, and well suited to the instruments used. He wielded all his resources with power and skill—chorus, soloists, and orchestra alike. He saw his dramatic points clearly, and often rose to a degree of real warmth and nobility of expression. But with all these excellences his tendency to the pomp and circumstance of display is unmistakable. The situations are often really fine, but many of them are rather weakened by being overdone. The coruscations of the long ballets, the processions, the crowds of various nationalities, and even the very tone and style of much of the music, show clearly which way things are tending. The same specious element of show peeps out now and then in the works of other composers, such as Halévy; and when ultimately the type of man arrived who knew how to play upon the weak side of French society's susceptibility to display, the true portent arose; and the crown which was put upon the long development of French grand opera, and embodied most of the results of French operatic aspiration, proved to be very imposing, but not of the most perfect metal.

Meyerbeer was of the brilliantly clever type of humanity. His gifts were various, and of a very high order. At first he was known as a brilliant pianist, and was famous for his quickness in reading from score. Then, a pianist's career not appearing imposing enough for his aspirations, he conceived the notion of becoming an opera composer. He tried several styles in succession. First he wrote German operas, without success. Then he went to Italy, and wrote operas in the Italian style, and met with a good deal of success. But as even this did not satisfy his aspirations, he inspected the situation in Paris, and seems to have made up his mind that the audience there was just suited for him. Indeed, the Oriental love of display which is so frequently found still subsisting in people of Jewish descent marked out Meyerbeer as essentially the man for the occasion. He is said to have studied things French with minute care— both history and manners—and he made his first experiment upon the Parisians in 1831 with "Robert le Diable," and achieved full measure of success. At long intervals he followed it up with further experiments—"The Huguenots" in 1836, "Le Prophète" in 1849, and so on—till he had built himself a monument so large that if size were any guarantee of durability he would be as secure of perennial honour as Horace himself.

The fact which is conspicuously emphasised by these works is the gigantic development and variety of the resources of effect in modern times.   Meyerbeer thoroughly understood the theatre, and he took infinite pains to carry out every detail which served for theatrical effect.   He tried and tested his orchestral experiments again and again with tireless patience.   He had "L'Africaine" by him for at least twenty years, and never got it up to the point of satisfying him, and finally died before it was performed.   He was so painfully anxious that his effects should tell, that his existence at the time when any new work was in preparation for performance is described as a perfect martyrdom.   Beethoven, too, took infinite pains, and wrote and rewrote constantly.   But his object was to get his ideas themselves as fine and as far from commonplace expression as possible, and to get the balance and design as perfect as his own critical instinct demanded. Meyerbeer's object was to make the mere externals tell.   He did not care in the least whether his details were commonplace or not.   His scores look elaborate and full of work, but the details are the commonest arpeggios, familiar and hackneyed types of figures of accompaniment, scales, and obvious rhythms.   Musically it is a huge pile of commonplaces, infinitely ingenious, and barren.   There is but little cohesion between the scenes, and no attempt at consistency to the situations in style and expression.   No doubt Meyerbeer had a great sense of general effect.   The music glitters and roars and warbles in well-disposed contrasts, but the inner life is wanting.   It is the same with his treatment of his characters. They metaphorically strut and pose and gesticulate, but express next to nothing ; they get into frenzies, but are for the most part incapable of human passion.   The element of wholesome musical sincerity is wanting in him, but the power of astonishing and bewildering is almost unlimited.   His cleverness is equal to any emergency. For instance, when a situation requires something impressive, and he has nothing musical to supply, he takes refuge in a cadenza for a clarinet or some other instrument, and the attention of the public is engaged by their interest in the skill of the performer, and forgets to notice that it has no possible relation to the significance of the situation. The scenes are collections of the most elaborate artifices carefully contrived and eminently effective from the baldest theatrical point of view. But for continuity, development, real feeling, nobility of expression, greatness of thought, anything that may be truly honoured in the observance, there is but the rarest trace. He studied his audience carefully, developed his machinery with infinite pains, carried out his aims, and succeeded in the way he desired. No doubt his works are worth the amusement of getting up, and of seeing and hearing also, because of the extraordinary dexterity with which the immense resources are wielded; but it cannot be said that he attempted to face the problem of musical drama at all. In that respect "Faust" and "Carmen" are much nearer the mark. In both of these the types of expression are infinitely more sincere, there is more artistic work in the details, more genuine sense of characterisation, and a much higher gift both of harmony and melody. Even the feeling for instrumental effect is really much finer; for there is more of real beauty of sound and more indication of ability to use colour to intensify situations. But in the end, neither of these approaches the complete solution of the problem. The traditional formulas of cheap accompaniment, the laxness in the treatment of inner minutiæ, the set forms of arias, and the detachable items that only hang together and are not intrinsically continuous, and many other features of convention and habit, prevent their being acceptable as completely satisfactory types of musical drama from the highest standpoint.

Germans were much slower than other nations in finding a national type of opera. They learnt very early how to succeed in writing operas for other nations, and surpassed the Italians in their own lines when it was worth doing it. But the discovery of the style and method suited to their more critical aspirations took many centuries. Mozart had done something for the cause in Seraglio and the Zauberflöte. Then there was a pause of many years, till Beethoven at last found a subject which he thought worthy of musical treatment, and gave the world Fidelio. In the interval musical art had advanced a good deal, chiefly through Beethoven's own efforts. He had written his first three symphonies, and got to the end of his "first period"; which implies a considerable develop-ment of the resources of real expression. As is natural, it is in the scenes where human circumstances become deeply interesting, and deep emotions are brought into play, that Beethoven is at his best. In the lighter scenes between Marcellina and Jacquino, in Rocco's song, he is less like himself; and even Pizarro's fierce song rings a little hollow. Beethoven could hardly bring such things within the range of his particular methods of thought and utterance. But for the more truly emotional situations, especially in the prison scene, he wrote the finest and truest music that exists in the whole range of opera. In fact, the whole work is too reserved and lofty to be fit for any but extremely musical audiences, and it has never been a genuine success with the public. Moreover, though the language of the play was German, and the serious spirit in which the music was written is worthy of the great German's attitude towards music, it was not essentially a German subject, and traces of old Italian influence through Mozart are still appa-rent. It was reserved for a man of far less personality to satisfy the aspirations of the race after true Teutonic music drama.

The chief advantages of Weber's early years were the opportunities he obtained for getting into touch with the theatre, through his father's eagerness to possess an opera-producing prodigy after the Mozart pattern. He was not especially identified with national sentiments till after Napo-leon's failure in the expedition to Moscow. Then, in common with many patriotic enthusiasts, the hope for independence inspired him, and he became the mouthpiece of national feeling in his superb settings of patriotic songs by Körner. These gave him a position which was emphasised by his being appointed successively at Prague and Dresden to organise a genuine German operatic establishment. Dresden had long been under the domination of the Italians, headed by the conductor Morlacchi, and the constant plotting and opposition which went on even after Weber's appointment only served to intensify his patriotic feeling. This at last found its full expression in "Der Freischütz," which was brought out at Berlin in 1821, and was immediately taken by the Germans to their hearts. It was indeed the first successful fruit of their aspirations, and its out-and-out German character in every respect gives it a great prominence in the history of the art. The style is consistently German almost throughout; the tunes are the quintessence of German national tunes and folk songs; the story is full of the mystery and romance which the Germans love, and is about real German people with thoroughly German habits and German characters. Apart from that, the musical material and the actual workmanship are Teutonically admirable. Weber's sense of instrumental effect was always very great, but in this work he rose to a higher point than usual. The tones and characteristics of the various instruments are used with unerring certainty to strengthen the emotional impression. The score is alive in all its parts, not full of dummy formulas and fragments of scales and arpeggios that have no relation to the situation. The various characters are also perfectly identified with the music that they have to sing. Kaspar, the reckless meddler in dangerous magic, was easily drawn; but the heroine Agathe, and the lighter-spirited Aennchen, both also keep their musical identity quite well, even when they are singing together. The scenes are separate, but the final transition to the continuous music of later times is happily illustrated in such a case as Agathe's famous scena, in which a great variety of moods and changes of rhythm and speed and melody are all closely welded into a perfectly complete and well-designed unity.

In Freischütz the German tradition of spoken dialogue is still maintained; the music being reserved for the intenser moments. In Euryanthe, Weber set the whole of the dialogue, and thereby approached nearer to the ideal which the first originators of the form had conceived. The work in other respects keeps the same consistently German style, and possibly contains finer individual passages than its forerunner; but the desperate foolishness of the libretto makes the whole almost unendurable, except to people who have the capacity to attend to the music alone and to ignore what is going on on the stage. Weber had a curious inclination for stories of a romantic and chivalric cast, as well as delight in the supernatural, which is probably to be explained by the instinct of a composer for finding things out of the hackneyed range of common everyday experience. For light and comic music the familiar dress of everyday life answers perfectly well. It may even accentuate the funniness of things. But when there are highly emotional, serious, heartfelt things to be dealt with, the association of the familiarities of everyday life with dialogue passionately sung, becomes too conspicuously anomalous. Thoughts that have any genuine greatness about them do not fit easily into commonplace terms. At any rate, Weber tried to escape from such familiarities in his librettos, and had the ill luck to fall into extremes of childish unreality which prevent his two later works being acceptable in more matter-of-fact times. But the excellence of the musical material, the freedom and breadth with which the scenes are developed without the requirements of musical design interfering in the least with the action, the complete achievement of a genuinely Teutonic theatrical style, quite different from the style of classical quartetts and symphonies and such self-dependent music, give Weber a position among the great representatives of musical art. Wagner fitly characterised him as most German of the Germans; and he himself was not a little indebted to him for mastering one of the last points of vantage necessary for the full attainment of the ideal of pure dramatic music.

Weber's style powerfully influenced his successors, even in

domains outside opera; his supernatural line was followed in something of the same style by Marschner and others, while Spohr plodded on by the side of them writing operas with very little dramatic style about them, but with good feeling for artistic finish and refined effect. But Germans are slow-moving as well as tenacious, and act as if they meant to do great things, and knew that great things took time to mature. It was many years before another great stroke for essentially German opera was achieved. German energy was not entirely relaxed, but it was concentrated in the person of Meyerbeer, who was busy writing French grand operas, and was best fitted for that occupation. Wagner, though born in Weber's lifetime, did not begin to put his singular powers to any definite use till nearly twenty years after Weber had passed out of the world. Born of a family of actors, brought up in constant contact with the stage, inspired with dramatic fervour from early years, and passionately devoted to Beethoven and Weber, he had sufficient to impel him to the career of an opera composer. But at first he struck out at random. The impulse in him was mainly dramatic, and only experience could reveal to him what line and style of composition would serve best for his purposes. His musical education was extremely defective, and his first experiments in opera contained things that were at once feeble and feebly expressed. Many were his changes of position. First he was chorus-master at a theatre at Wurzburg, then conductor at various places; he wrote several works which were inevitable failures; and finally, with the ardent conviction of his mission, characteristic of his curious personality, he made up his mind to take by storm the central home of the art in the Grand Opera in Paris. Meyerbeer was then in the full plenitude of his glory, and the need of propitiating Meyerbeer's own particular audience probably prompted him to write his grand opera "Rienzi" in Meyerbeer's style, with all the glitter, blaze of brass, and scenic splendour he could think of. But as far as Paris was concerned, his journey was a failure. His importunities were in vain, and after many weary months he returned to Germany. But meanwhile he had been busy with a new work,

"Der fliegende Holländer," which, when completed, marked
the definite commencement of his real career. The essence of
the situation is that Wagner is throughout as much dramatist
and master of theatrical requirements as musician. In fact,
at first the spontaneous musical gift was comparatively small;
but the intensity of his dramatic and poetic feeling produced
musical figures and musical moods in his mind which he found
out by degrees how to express in more and more powerful and
artistic musical terms. The vitality of the Flying Dutchman
lies more in the superbly dramatic story than in the music.
But at the same time there are scenes and passages in which
the music rises to an extraordinary pitch of vivid picturesqueness and expressiveness. The whole of the overture is as
masterly a musical expression of omens and the wild hurly-
burly of the elements as possible, and carries out Gluck's
conception of an overture completely; Senta's ballad is one
of the most characteristic things of its kind in existence,
and hits the mood of the situation in a way that only a
man born with high dramatic faculty could achieve; and
the duet between Senta and the Holländer is as full of
life and as fine in respect of the exact expression of the
moods of the situation, and as broad in melody, as could
well be desired. "Rienzi" looks back to the past of Meyerbeer, and is comparatively worthless; "Der fliegende Holländer" looks forward along the way in which Wagner is
beginning to travel, and already embodies traits of melody
and characteristic devices of modulation and colour which
become conspicuous, with more experienced treatment, in his
maturer works.

His progress from this point was steady and steadfast in
direction. Having struck on the vein of old-world myths,
and found their suitableness for musical treatment, he soon
saw the further advantage of using stories which were essentially Teutonic in their source and interest. He wisely chose
such as symbolised a great deal more than the mere stories
convey, and so have a deeper root in human nature and a
wider scope than mere typical stage dramas. The story of
Tannhäuser and the hill of Venus, and of Lohengrin the

knight of the Holy Grail, each in their way show the growth
of his powers of musical resource. Lohengrin is not so
vigorous as its predecessor, but there are fewer crudities and
formalities in it, and fewer traces of an unwholesome influence which made some parts of Tannhäuser run very near to
vulgarity—splendid as the whole work is. A long time inter-
vened between the production of Lohengrin and Rheingold, the
preface to the great mythic cycle—and the step in point of style
and artistic management is as wide as the interval of time.
He seems to have thought out his scheme more thoroughly.
Indeed, it may well be doubted if he had any scheme or method
at all in the earlier works. In the Flying Dutchman the
traces of the old operatic traditions are extremely common.
The complete set movements merely holding together by their
ends, the musical isolation of scene from scene, the discon-
nection of the overture from the opening of the drama, and
many other points, show that he had as yet by no means
made up his mind to break away from the conventional traditions. In Tannhäuser and Lohengrin he made the musical
texture of the scenes much more continuous, but the long
operatic tunes still make their appearance together with many
other familiar signs of the old genealogy. The use of the
same characteristic musical figures in various parts of the
works wherever some special personality or characteristic
thought or situation recurs, is frequently met with ; but the
figures are not used with the systematic persistence that is so
conspicuous in the later works. It seems extremely probable
that it was reflection upon the earlier works, and writing
about his artistic theories at the time of his exile, that led
him to the uncompromising attitude of the later ones. The
impulse which led to the new features in his earlier works
was simply his dramatic feeling. He had no theoretic idea
of replacing the principles of the old operatic formulas of
design by "Leit motive." They were the result of the
accident that he was trying to illustrate a dramatic subject
in musical terms ; and when any one so essential to the
story as the Holländer or Lohengrin or Elsa came prominently forward, it was natural to repeat a figure which best

expressed their character. It conduced to unity as well as to characterisation. But it was done unsystematically in the earlier works; and "Leit motive" only began to pervade the whole texture of his musical material at last in the cycle of "Der Ring des Nibelungen."

The change from the earlier works even to Rheingold, the first drama of "The Ring," is as great as the change from Beethoven's earliest symphonies to his C minor; and apart from style and materials, the changes are the same in principle. In the Symphony in D No. 2, the manner of expressing the ideas is often very much like that of the earlier generation. Even in the presentation of the first idea there is a certain stiffness and formality, which is not quite like the full-grown Beethoven. It seems to express the same kind of complacent attitude as is implied in the work of John Christian Bach or Galuppi. But in the C minor the first four notes are quite enough to give the mind the impression that music has passed into a different region  from that of the formal politeness of the previous century.

Analogously in Tannhäuser there are many passages which have the flavour of Italian opera about them—many that even suggest the influence of Meyerbeer and the Grand Opera; —long passages of melody of the formal type, and frequent traces of things like the relics of rudimentary organs, that have not perfectly merged into the rest of the organism. But the first dozen bars of Rheingold give indication of quite a different spirit. His object clearly is to express the situation at the beginning of the first act. The depths of the Rhine are there, the swaying waters, darkness. The music is the exact equivalent of the central idea of the situation; and at the same time it supplies a principle of design without having to fall back on familiar formulas to make that design appreciable. The dramatic conception is formed first, and is then expressed in terms of art which follow every phase and change of mood without having to stop to make the music intelligible apart from the drama. The principle of treatment is the same as in Schubert's great songs, the "Junge Nonne," or "Doppel-gänger," or the "Erl König"; only the scale is larger and the style different. Wagner wrote his own dramas, always with a clear feeling of what was fit to be expressed musically; and as he grew more experienced, he was able to hold all the forces he had to use for dramatic ends more surely in hand, and to control their relations to one another with more certainty. While writing the poems he probably had a general feeling of what the actual music was going to be, just as a dramatist keeps in his mind a fairly clear idea of the scene and the action of the play he is writing; and as certain general principles of design are quite indispensable in musical works of this kind, he evidently controlled the development of his stories so as to admit of due spreading of groundwork and of variety of mood; and devised situations that admitted of plain and more or less diatonic treatment, and crises which would demand the use of energetic modulation, and so forth. But in reality this requires less restriction than might be imagined; for the working and changing of moods in a good poem is almost identical with the working and developing and changing of moods adapted for good music. They both spring from the same emotional source, only they are different ways of expressing the ideas. As poetry and music approach nearer to one another, it becomes more apparent that the sequence of moods which makes a good design in poetry will also make a good design in music.

One thing which strikes the attention at once from the very commencement of "The Ring" is the difference in the treatment of the musical material from the earlier works. As has been pointed out before, there is a constant tendency in music to make the details more distinct and definite. The instinctive aim of the most highly gifted composers is to arrive at that articulation of minutiæ which makes every part of the organism alive. The type of vague meandering melodies which formed the arias of Hasse and Porpora became far more definite in organisation in Mozart's hands; the contrast is even greater between their treatment of orchestral material and Mozart's. The very look of the score of Idomeneo is busier than any earlier score; and moreover, Mozart made his own details more finished and more definite as his view of instrumental music matured. In the next generation the process of defining details progressed very fast in Beethoven's hands. Even in his first sonata the tendency to concentrate his thoughts into concise and emphatic figures is noticeable, and the habit grew more decisive with him as his mastery of his resources improved. The same tendency is shown in almost every department of art. Schubert's accompaniments to songs are often made up of little *nuclei* which express in the closest terms the spirit of the situation, and the way in which he knits them together is a perfect counterpart, in little, of Wagner's ultimate method. The advantages of the plan are obvious. It not only lays hold of the mind more decisively, but it enables the musical movement to be knit into closer unity by the reiteration of the figures. Wagner, in his earlier works, appears to have realised the advantage of condensing the thought into an emphatic figure, as every one knows who has heard the overture to the "Fliegende Holländer," though he did not make much use of such figures in the actual texture of the earlier music. But from the beginning of the Rheingold he seems to have clearly made up his mind not only to condense his representative musical ideas into the forms which serve to fix them in the mind, but to weave them throughout into the texture of the music itself, to dispense with the old formulas of accompaniment, and to use next to nothing except what was consistent and definite. The result is that in the main the texture of the music is something of the same nature as a fugue of Bach. Wagner often uses harmony as a special means of effect, but in a great measure the harmony is the result of polyphony, often of several distinct subjects going on at once, as they used to do in the ancient fugues. This immensely enlarges the range of direct expression, as it is possible by making such familiar devices as accented passing notes and grace notes occur simultaneously in different parts, to produce transient artificial chords of the most extraordinary description; such as are heard in the following passage from the first act of Parsifal :—

Wagner notoriously rejected the conventional rules of the theorists about resolving chords and keeping strictly within the lines of keys, and many other familiar phases of orthodox doctrine. He tried to get to the root of things, instead of abiding by the rules that are given to help people to spell and to frame sentences intelligibly. But he by no means adopts purely licentious methods in treatment of chords, nor does he forego the use of tonality—the sense of key which is the basis of modern music—as a source of effect. He did not attempt to define his design by the means required in sonatas and symphonies, because the situation did not warrant it ; neither would he submit to the conventions which forbade his using certain progressions which he thought the situation required because they happen to mix up tonalities. Many of the progressions which Beethoven used outraged the tender feelings of theorists of his day who did not understand them, and thought he was violating the orthodox principles of tonality. Yet Beethoven's whole system was founded on his very acute feeling for it He expanded the range of the key as much as he could, and Wagner went further in the same direction. But he is so far from abandoning tonality as an element of design and effect, that he uses it with quite remarkable skill and perception of its functions. When he wants to give the sense of solid foundation to a scene, he often keeps to the same key, even to the same harmony, for a very long time.

The introductions to Rheingold and Siegfried are parallels
in this respect, the first almost all on one chord, the second
almost all in one key; and the principle of design is the same
in both cases; consisting in laying a solid foundation to the
whole work by rising from the lowest pitch, and gradually
bringing the full range of sounds into operation. In the
accompaniment of the ordinary dialogue he is often very
obscure in tonality, just as J. S. Bach is in recitative; some
instinct prompting them both to avoid the conditions which
make the music that approaches nearest to ordinary speech
seem too definite in regular design. When he wants to express
something very straightforward and direct, like the character
of Siegfried, he uses the most simple diatonic figures; but
when he wants to express something specially mysterious,
he literally takes advantage of the fact that human creatures
understand modern music through their feeling for tonality,
to obtain a weird and supernatural effect by making it
almost unrecognisable. For in that case he almost invariably
makes his musical idea combine chords which belong to two or
more unassimilable tonalities, on purpose to create the sense
of bewilderment, and a kind of dizziness and helplessness,
which exactly meets the requirements of the case. If people's
sense of tonality were not by this time so highly developed,
such passages would be merely hideous gibberish; and they
often seem so at first. It is just on a parallel with language.
A man may often say a thing that is most copiously true
which his audience does not see at once, and everybody has
experienced the puzzled, displeased look that the audience
gives—till, as the meaning dawns upon them, a cloud seems
to pass away, and the look of pleasure is all the brighter
for the transition from bewilderment to understanding.
Wagner's device stands in the same relation to the musical
organisation of the present day as Beethoven's employment
of enharmonic transition did to that of his time. Men judge
such things instinctively in relation to the context. The
transition from the first key to the second in Beethoven's
great Leonora Overture produces the same sort of feeling of
momentary dizziness, in relation to the simpler diatonic style

of the rest of the music, that Wagner's subtle obscurities do in
relation to his far more chromatic and highly-coloured style.
It need not be supposed that he deliberately adopted such
a device. True composers very rarely work up to a theory
consciously, in the act of production ; but they may afterwards try to justify anything very much out of the common on
some broad principles in which they believe. It is much more
likely to have been the impulse of highly developed instinct
that caused Wagner to adopt the same procedure so invariably. A familiar example is the musical expression of that
really marvellous poetic conception, the magic kiss of the god
which expels the godhead from the Valkyrie and makes her
mortal.

Even more conspicuous is the figure associated with the
"Tarnhelm," the helm of invisibility. But in that case
the effect often depends a good deal upon the way in which
the figure is taken in relation to a context in an obscurely
related key. The motive of the magic ring* is condensed
very closely, and is much to the point.

The death-figure in Tristan is constructed on similar principles, but curiously enough the figure used for the magic love-potion, which pervades the whole musical material of that drama, is not of mixed tonality, but only made to seem so by the use of chromatic accessory notes. The opening passage of Tristan is, indeed, peculiarly interesting in respect of clearness of tonality, for Wagner uses the same device of sequence (which is the repetition of an identical phrase at different levels) which is familiar in ancient folk-song (pp. 55 and 69), in the opening movements of several of Corelli's Sonatas (in just the same position in the scheme of design), at the beginning of Beethoven's E minor Sonata (Opus 91), and in Brahms' Rhapsody, No. 2, where the device is carried to even greater lengths in the matter of distantly related tonalities than by Wagner. The subject of the love-potion is necessarily puzzling to the mind; but the use of the sequence gives a sense of orderliness and stability which is clearly essential at the beginning of a great work. The sequence is perfectly familiar in its order, and turns on nearly related keys—first, A minor, then its relative major C; then, taking the same step of a third as the cue, E major, which is the dominant of A, and therefore completes the circuit. And the process keeps things in the right place too, for despite the very close involutions of subordinate secondary tonalities, the system of design in that wonderful Vorspiel is mainly centralised on the relationships of A minor and C, and its general scheme is the same as that of the introductions to Rheingold, Siegfried, and Parsifal; and in Parsifal, moreover, he uses precisely the same device of sequence at the beginning, only developing it on a very much wider scale, as suits the solemnity of the subject. It may be concluded, therefore, that Wagner is very far from ignoring tonality. His use of it is different from that of composers of sonatas and symphonies, but he shows a very clear understanding of the various opportunities that it affords for the purposes of effect and design.

In the use of the effects of tone producible by various instruments (which people for want of a better word seem to have agreed to call colour) he is clearly the most comprehensive

22

of masters. Instinctively he adopted the true view for his
particular work. In old days colours were disposed in relation to one another principally in order to look beautiful.
Some of the greatest early Italian painters and Mozart seem
much alike in that respect. Gluck used the moderate variety
of colours at his disposal to add to the vividness of his situations. Beethoven used colour to the extreme of conceivable
perfection; and all to the ends of expression, as far as the
conditions of abstract self-dependent instrumental music admitted.

Wagner took the uncompromising position of using every
colour, whether pure or composite, to emphasise and intensify
each dramatic moment, and to complete the measure of expression which is only half conveyed by the outline and rhythmic
movement of the musical ideas themselves. The great development of instrumental resources gave him enormous advantages
over earlier composers. The improvement of instruments, the
general improvement in the skill and intelligence of players,
both served his turn. From the first his excitable nature was
particularly susceptible to colour; but the more his powers
matured, the better he used his colours with absolute apt-
ness to the end in view. The composite vividness of the 'cellos,
hautboys, corno inglese, horns, and bassoons at the beginning
of the Vorspiel of Tristan, is not more absolutely to the point
than the wonderful quietude and depth of solemnity of the
tone of the strings alone at the opening of the third act.
The magic sound of the horns in the music of the Tarnhelm
is not more nor less suggestive than the merry cackle of the
wood-wind in the music of the apprentices in " Die Meister-
singer," or the vivid combination of various arpeggios for
strings, with the solemn brass below, and the tinkling of the
Glockenspiel at the top, which represent the rising of Loge's
flames that shut out Brunnhilde from the world. Even with
regard to the honourable old-world devices which have not much
place in opera, the requirements of the situations brought out
the requisite skill. The art of combining many subjects together, of which theoretic composers make so much, is carried
by Wagner to a truly marvellous extent. The texture of the

music is often made of nothing but a network of the various melodies and figures which are called "Leit motive," each associated with some definite idea in the drama. The extent to which this subtle elaboration is carried on escapes the hearer, because it is done so skilfully that it passes unperceived. But it is one of those respects in which the work of art bears constant close scrutiny, as a work of art should, without ceasing to be wonderful. It makes most of the difference between the earlier types of such departments of art, when the figures of accompaniment had been only so many tiresome formulas, and the later work in which everything means something, and yet is not obtrusive. The elaboration of all the detail is still subordinate to the general design and the general effect. When a work is faulty in such respects it is because the composer tries to produce all his effect by the multiplicity and ingenuity of his details alone. The importunity of minutiæ soon makes works on a large scale insupportable. But Wagner's minutiæ are not importunate, because the effect in general is proportionately great. The wide sweeps of his sequences, the long and intricate growth towards some supreme climax, the width and clearness of the main contrasts, the immense sweep of his basses, the true grandeur of many of his poetic conceptions, keep the mind occupied enough with the larger aspects of the matter. And though, as in human life, all the little moments are realities, their prominence is merged in the greater events which form the sum of them.

Wagner's use of the voice part illustrates musical tendencies in the same way as every other part of his work. The traditions of solo singing which still persist in some quarters imply that the human voice is to be used for effects of beauty only. The old Italian masters subordinated everything to pure vocal effect; they made the utmost of pure singing, and singing only. Occasional reactions against so limited a view, and in favour of using the human voice for human expression, came up at various points in history. Purcell is often a pure embodiment of ill-regulated instinct for expression. John Sebastian Bach's recitatives and ariosos are still stronger in that respect. The Italian reaction that followed him was all in favour of beautiful vocal sound and simple intrinsic beauty of melody; but in Schubert the claims of expression again found an extremely powerful advocate. He appealed to human creatures a good deal by means of melody, but much more by his power of general expression. He often produces much more effect by a kind of recitative than by tune. He uses tune when it is suitable, otherwise musical declamation. He appeals to intelligent human beings who want music to mean something worthy of human intelligence; and Schumann does eminently the same, though he too knows full well how to express a noble sentiment in a noble melodic phrase. Wagner again takes an attitude of " no compromise." The voice has an infinity of functions in music. It may be necessarily reduced to the standard of mere narrative, it may have to utter dialogue which in detail is near the level of everyday talk; it must rise in drama to the higher levels of dramatic intensity, and it may rise at times to the highest pitch of human ecstasy. For each its appropriate use. The art is not limited to obvious tune on one side, and chaotic recitative on the other, but is capable of endless shades of difference. Wagner makes Mime sing melody because he is a sneaking impostor, who pretends to have any amount of beautiful feelings, and has none; that no doubt is a subtlety of satire; but otherwise he generally reserves vocal melody for characteristic moments of special exaltation. That is to say, the actor becomes specially prominent when the development of the drama brings his personality specially forward. The human personality is an element in the great network of circumstances and causes and consequences which make a drama interesting, and no doubt it is by far the most interesting element; but there is no need that the actor should always be insisting upon his own importance, and the importance of his ability to produce beautiful sounds. The human voice is for use, and not only for ornament. People must no doubt learn to sing in a special way in order to do justice to the beautiful old-world artistic creations; and art would be very much the poorer if the power to give them due effect was lost. But the expression of things that are worth uttering because they express something humanly interesting is much more difficult, and implies a much higher aim. Both objects require a great deal of education, but the old-fashioned singer's education was limited chiefly to the development of mechanical powers; the singer of the genuine music of Bach, Schubert, Schumann, Brahms, amd Wagner requires the old-fashioned singer's education and education of the mind as well.

Of Wagner's general reforms in connection with music-drama this is not the place to speak in detail. His hiding away the unsightly fussy notions of the orchestra under the stage, and his alteration of the arrangements of the theatre, are accessories which do not immediately bear on the musical question here under discussion. His aim in all is to control the multitudinous factors and elements, from small minutiæ up to the largest massing of combined powers to the ends of perfect expression of his dramatic and poetic conceptions. His personality, and the particular subjects that he chooses, and the manner in which he looks at them, affect people in different ways; that is a matter apart from the development of resources or the method of applying them. Of the method itself it may be said that it is the logical outcome of the efforts of the long line of previous composers, and the most elaborately organised system for the purposes of dramatic musical expression that the world has ever yet seen.

Of what has been done in the line of opera since Wagner's death, it is not yet time to speak in detail. Some of the most successful opera composers have been considerably influenced by his personality, and a few have endeavoured to apply his methods; but it can hardly be said as yet whether the results make any fresh advance of artistic importance. A disposition to compromise is obvious, and it may well be that a step backwards is necessary, as a preliminary to another larger stride forwards. But so far the number of new operas which have any genuine pervading vitality may be counted on the fingers of one hand, and from a few individual instances no one can gather substantial grounds for generalisation. The happiness of the idea of adopting subjects which are raised above the common-place, even in modern clothes, by embodying some deeply set patriotic enthusiasm, may fairly be acknowledged; and so may the genuine success of the special class of comic and satiric light operas which have been so much in vogue in England in recent years. But the artistic methods adopted in such works do not yet suggest new extension of principles, or attainment of new points of vantage; and their consideration may well be deferred till the field of vision becomes wider, and the world has not to judge of the phenomena at close quarters.

SUMMARY AND CONCLUSION

THE long story of the development of music is a continuous and unbroken record of human effort to extend and enhance the possibilities of effects of sound upon human sensibilities, as representing in a formal or a direct manner the expression of man's inner being. The efforts resolve themselves mainly into impulses to find means to produce the effect of design, and to contrive types of expression which are capable of being adapted to such designs. And as the difficulty of coping with two things at once is considerable, men have generally concentrated their efforts on design at one time, and on expression at another. So that some periods are characterised by special cultivation of principles of form, and others by special efforts in the direction of expression ; and owing to the interlacing of various causes in human affairs, these conditions have generally coincided with conditions of society which are adapted to them. The formal character of the music of Mozart's and Haydn's time agrees very well with the character of society in their time; and when a more vehement type of expression became possible the style agreed well with the character of the time, which was specially marked by that impulse to shake off the old conventions which found its most violent expression in the French Revolution.

The first steps in the direction of the essentially modern type of music were made when men attempted to improve upon pure melodic music by singing melodies simultaneously at different pitches. It took an immense time to produce a satisfactory result in part singing ; but by degrees men found out how to vary their bald successions of fifths and fourths by ornamental notes, and to make their various simultaneous tunes move without too hideous a cacophony. They found out how to systematise their experiments at least so far as to make the closing points bear some relation to the beginnings, and to contrive something which had the effect of a cadence. And in the course of some centuries, without making the inner organisation of their movements at all definite in design, they succeeded in stringing harmonies together by means of independent voice parts in such a way as to produce the most purely beautiful sound possible. Things arrived at the first crisis under the influence of the Roman Church, and almost all music was then written in the contrapuntal style used in the Church services.

Then, having apparently exhausted the possibilities in this direction, a new impulse seized upon composers, to apply music more decisively to secular uses, and to find a method of treatment better adapted to secular ideas. They began to employ some of the devices which had been mastered in the way of chord effects in a new way, and gave a solo voice something like musical talking to do. It was like going back to chaos at first; but they had something to build upon, and as the solo voice-part grew more definite, so did the order of the chord successions. They found out that a chord made up of one definite set of notes afforded an excellent contrast to another chord made up of a different set of notes, and that certain chords were more nearly allied to one another than others. They also found that the old scales that they had used in ecclesiastical music were not accommodating enough for the successions of chords they wanted ; and under the influence of their growing feeling for systematisation of these chords, they modified these old modes till they had got the tones and semitones in better order for harmonic purposes, and had added a fair quantity of extra chromatic notes to give variety to their progressions. Music began to expand into a variety of types. Instrumental music began to take a different character from choral music, and secular from sacred vocal music. And by degrees, as the various resources made available by the new arrangement of the scales became better understood, and the devices of the old counterpoint were adapted to the new system, the second great crisis was achieved, which is mainly illustrated in the great works of Bach and Handel, who gave utterance to the new vigour of the Protestant impulses.

Here again men seemed to have arrived at the highest point possible without another change of method; and they applied themselves to developing new types of design, in which melody and harmony were combined in new ways. Their feeling for the relationships of harmony enabled them to spread their bases of structure over wider areas, and to obtain effects of contrast by making one long passage represent one key, and another represent a contrasting one; and by combining various types of contrast into one complete design. The ease with which such a type of design could be handled, enabled them to make use of other elements of effect. The element of colour began to come in very noticeably, and a new climax was reached when all the resources so far attained were combined in symphonies and operas. Art had by this time branched out into a very considerable number of forms, but their actual style was not very distinct. The respective styles of opera and of symphony, of sonata and of Church music, were all very much alike. The principles on which the various forms were constructed were the same; and their internal organisation, as far as minutiæ were concerned, was rather indefinite and conventional.

But in the next age things began to move at a very much increased speed. It was the age of revolutionary ideas; and men were bent on getting rid of conventions, and on seeing things as they are. The art began branching out right and left; the style of orchestral works such as symphonies began to differ more intrinsically from opera style; song style from sonata style; oratorio style from the style of Church services, and all from one another. Men found that different objects entailed different treatment; and the subtleties of style had their full measure of attention from men gifted at last with a fine critical sense of relevancy and appropriateness. Again, the internal organisation of works began to be much more definite and articulate. Ideas were put into compact and vivid forms, and the various inner and secondary parts gained more distinct vitality.

Then came the time when men, having many resources at their disposal, sought to use them more decisively for the purposes of expression. The differentiation of forms went on faster than ever. Each large group was subdivided into subordinate groups, and each different item received different treatment. Pianoforte music came to comprise dances of various kinds and calibres, nocturnes, lyrics of all sorts, sonatas, scherzos, capriccios, fugues, and endless other varieties. Operas came to comprise the grand, the comic, the buffa, the seria, and various other national and distinctive types. And each form that had vitality showed a still further advance in effects of colour, articulation of detail, and close approximation to dramatic or expressive consistency. The principle of tonality was expanded to the utmost limits of intelligibility both for design and effect; and with all the resources of harmony and polyphony for form and direct expression; with melody—both inward and outward—for general tone and all that corresponds to vocal utterance, and with rhythm to convey the impression of gesticulatory expression and colour to intensify meaning, mankind seems finally to have full measure of almost unlimited materials available to illustrate anything he will.

But the resources are so immense, that none but composers gifted with special vital energy, and power to grasp many factors at once, seem likely to use them to the full. There are plenty of indications that men are tired of the long journey, and find the rich variety of resource rather overwhelming, and long for things a little less copious in detail and artistic fulness. Those who aim highest must have command of all resources; but there must be music for all types of mind and all varieties of nature; and there is no necessity that because a thing employs only the minutest fraction of the available resources of art, that it need be bad. The song from the music hall may be excellent and characteristic, and often is; the music of people who have every opportunity to be refined and cultivated may be detestably bad, and often is. There is an infinite variety of moods which admit of being expressed, from the noble, aspiring, human sincerity of a great nature like Brahms', to the rank, impudent, false sentimentality of impostors who shall be nameless. The unfortunate art may be made to grovel and wallow as well as to soar. A man may use slender resources to very good ends, and great resources to very bad ones. It rests with a very wide public now to decide what the future of the art shall be; and if its members can understand a little of what music means and how it came to be what it is, perhaps it may tend to encourage sincerity in the composer, and to enable themselves to arrive at an attitude which is not too open to be imposed upon by those who have other ends in view than honouring and enriching their art.

If the art is worthy of the dignity of human devotion, it is worth considering a little seriously, without depreciating in the least the lighter pleasures to which it may minister. If it is to be a mere toy and trifle, it would be better to have no more to do with it. But what the spirit of man has laboured at for so many centuries cannot only be a mere plaything. The marvellous concentration of faculties towards the achievement of such ends as actually exist, must of itself be enough to give the product human interest. Moreover, though a man's life may not be prolonged, it may be widened and deepened by what he puts into it; and any possibility of getting into touch with those highest moments in art in which great ideals were realised, in which noble aspirations and noble sentiments have been successfully embodied, is a chance of enriching human experience in the noblest manner: and through such sympathies and interests the humanising influences which mankind will hereafter have at its disposal may be infinitely enlarged.

Note to pp. 49 and 51.

The brilliant idea of phonographing the tunes of savage and semi-civilised races seems to offer such opportunities of getting at the real facts of primitive and barbarous music as have never before been available for the investigation of such subjects. It has been put into practice by a Mr. J. W. Fewkes to record the tunes of the Zuni Indians of the southern states of North America, and the results have been published in the "Journal of American Ethnology and Archæology," vol. i.

Several tunes are given, and some of them afford happy illustrations of the uncertainty of savage intonation referred to on p. 49, and also of the singularly unsystematic manner in which the savages reiterate the characteristic intervals or musical figures which have taken their fancy.

The following is an approximate record of one of their curious tunes, which is stated to have been considerably irregular in the details of pitch and intonation :—

INDEX

ACCIDENTALS, 45, 112.

Accompaniment, 89, 127, 137, 140, 168, 196, 220, 222, 224, 287, 289, 290, 292, 323.

Ainu music, 50.

Alberti bass, 211, 287.

Alceste, 217, 219.

Allemande, 185, 200.

Arcadelt, 109, 110.

Aria, 144, 146, 214, 219, 231.

Arpeggio subjects and figures, 190, 238.

Arpeggio tunes, 70, 73, 74.

Artistic disposition, 2.

Auber, 310.

Australian native music, 49, 54.

BACH, John Christian, 205, 208, 242, 244.

Bach, John Sebastian, 45, 54, 119, 162, 176, *et seq.*, 189, 197, 273, 276, 279, 281, 300, 335.

Bach, Philip Emmanuel, 192, 193, 209.

Bagpipe scale, 39.

Ballet, 139, 184, 219, 312.

Balletti, 113.

Bas Quercy, tune from, 65.

Beethoven, 252, *et seq.*, 273, 293, 321, 325.

Berlioz, 276.

Boccherini, 245.

Brahms, 303, 305.

Buffa opera, 215, 227.

Byrd, 121, 155.

CACCINI, 127, 132.

Cadences, 99. 120.

Cadences, Church, 43.

—— of the voice, 18, 19.

Canons, 97, 122, 184.

Cantatas, 284.

Canto fermo, 89, 92, 98.

Canzonas, 113, 177.

Caribs, music of, 48.

Carissimi, 136.

Cavaliere, 133.

Cavalli, 135, 139.

Cesti, 137.

Chamber music, 304.

Characterisation, 135, 149, 162, 165, 219, 221, 275, 296, 303.

Cherubini, 309, 311.

Chinese scale, 21, 33, 34.

Chinese tune, 57.

Chopin, 241, 298.

Choral music, 80, 102, 106, 119, 163, 283.

Church modes, 41.

Classification of notes of the scale, 44.

Clavichord, 183.

Clementi, 256.

Concerto, 151, 152, 186.

Contrasts, 10, 11, 13, 129, 153, 200, 236, 240, 260.

Corelli, 151.

Counterpoint, 89, 90, 101, 106, 177, 183, 195.

Couperin, 155, 184.

DANCE movements, 115, 116, 184, 199, 247, 260.

Dance music, early, 116.

Dancing, and dance gestures, 6, 7, 9.

Declamation, **127**, 130, 139, 141, 284, 289, 330.
Design, 2, 3, 4, 12, 13, 48, 62, 70, 109, 113, 129, 131, 140, 146, 157, 175, 234, 249, 259, 262, 273, 289, 297, 324, 327, 330, 335.
Discord, 99, 119, 120, 134, 323.
Domestic life, music of, 116, 294.
Doric mode, 24, 41.
Dunstable, **105.**
Dvořák, **304.**

Ellis, 21.
English folk-music, **55, 74.**
English music of Elizabethan period, 114, 121.
Equal temperament, **45, 187.**
Erl König, 288.
European scale system, modern, 16, 18, 45, 187, 188.
Expression, 3, 7, 8, 9, 14, 48, 62, 72, 77, 83, 123, 129, 134, 136, 148, 149, 150, 160, 162, 165, 172, 173, 183, 185, 189, 219, 220, 252, 258, 260, 276, 284, 289, 293, 296, 303, 319, 328, 330, 336, &c.

Fantasia, 191, 301.
Feejee music, 53.
Field, 296.
Flying Dutchman, The, **319.**
Folk-music, 47, 96.
—— Types of, 61.
Forty-eight, the, 186, 300.
Freischütz, Der, 316.
French characteristics in music, 138, 155, 218, 277, 308.
Frescobaldi, 119, 154, 179.
Fugue, 122, 153, 180, 189.

Gabrieli, Giovanni, **121.**
Galician tune, 64.
Gaultier, Denis, 155.
German folk-music, 70, 72, **74.**
—— Opera, 227, 230, 314.
Gibbons, Orlando, 121, **155.**

Gipsy music, 59.
Gluck, 216, 250, 306.
Gossec, 209.
Gounod, 314.
Greek scales, 22.
Gretchen am Spinnrade, **288, 289.**
Grétry, 310.
Ground bass, 54, 140.

Hale, Adam de la, 95.
Halevy, 312.
Handel, 162, 165, 168, 170, **185, 195.**
Harmonic form, 199, 235.
Harmony, 43, 88, 108, 110, 134.
—— incipient, 82.
Harpsichord music, **117,** 183, 202, 256.
Haydn, 241, 288.
Heptatonic scales, 21.
Histrionic music, 133, 139, 277, 311
Hobrecht, 121.
Hungarian music, 48, 59, 63, 77.
Hypolydian mode, **25.**

Idomeneo, 224.
Indian scales, 30.
—— tune, 57.
In dulci jubilo, 66.
Instrumental music, 114, 137, 150, 175, 273, 293.
Instrumentation, 135, 139, 141, 143, 167, 206, 209, 220, 221, 224, 246, 257, 278, 281, 308, 314, 316, 327.
Intermezzi, 214.
Iphigénie en Aulide, **219.**
—— en Tauride, 220.
Irish folk-music, 79.
Israel in Egypt, 170.
Italian choral music, 113, 114, 121. 160.
—— Opera, 127, 143, 223, 307.

Japanese scales, 37.
Javese scales, 38.
—— music, 92.
Josquin, 121.

Keiser, 227.

Lasso, Orlando, 121.
Leit-motive, 320, 323, 329.
Liszt, 298.
Lohengrin, 320.
Lulli, 138, 311.
Lus, 34.
Lute, 116, 294.

Maousi native music, 50.
Madrigals, 109.
Mannheim, 209.
Marenzio, 121.
Marschner, 318.
Mascarades, 138.
Masques, 138.
Material of music, 13.
Méhul, 311.
Melodic element, 7, 9.
—— music, 18, 56, 93.
—— systems, 18.
Melodies, several sung simultane-
ously, 92.
Mendelssohn, 281, 284, 296.
Mexican tune, 69.
Meyerbeer, 312, 318.
Minuet, 247, 260.
Modes, 110; Greek, 24; Indian, 32.
Modulation, 111, 133, 324.
Monteverde, 133, 250.
Motets, 93.
Mozambique, native music of, 51.
Mozart, 223, 240, 244, 251, 263.
Murcian tune, 78.

Netherlands, music of, 120.
Notation, 83, 91.
Nozze di Figaro, 228
Nuove musiche, 133.

Odes, choral, 284.
Opera, 129, 145, 213, 306.
—— and oratorio, beginnings of,
127.
Oratorio, 133, 136, 157, 283.

Orchestral music, 183, 206, 257, 277.
Orchestration, 135, 141, 156, 206,
220, 224, 241, 257, 278, 327.
Organ, 117, 152, 179.
Organum, 91.
Oriental music, 57.
Ornament, 59, 67, 70, 78, 90, 117,
132, 141, 192, 299, 314.
Overtures, 139, 147, 206, 217, 325,
327.

Palestrina, 121, 273.
Paradisi, 204.
Partitas, 184.
Passion music, 173.
Pattern tunes, 62.
Pentatonic scales, 21, 28.
Peri, 129.
Persian scales, 28,
Phrygian mode, 25, 28.
Pianoforte, 256, 294.
Piccini, 219, 220.
Poitevin tune, 64.
Polynesian cannibals, 48.
Preludes, 189, 300, 327.
Programme music, 276, 292, 296.
Purcell, 142, 149, 274.

Quality of tone, 105, 124, 168, 220,
257, 328.
Quartetts, 245.

Racial characteristics, 61, 306.
Radical reforms, 125.
Ragas, 32.
Rameau, 155, 311.
Realism, 149, 165, 290, 293.
Recitative, 128, 130, 136, 146, 166,
220, 226, 325.
Reduplication of melodies, 85.
Religion and music, 82.
Rheingold, 321.
Rhythmic element, 7, 9, 109, 115,
181, 201, 203, 260, 261.
Rienzi, 319.
Ring of the Nibelung, the, 321.

Rondo, 52, 241.
Rossini, 308.
Roumanian folk-music, 60.
Rules of early music, 89, 98.
Russian folk-music, 53, 55, 62, 66.

SARABANDE, 185.
Savages, music of, 6, 8, 48.
Scales, 15 ; Heptatonic and Penta-
 tonic, 21 ; Greek, 22 ; Persian,
 28 ; Indian, 30 ; Chinese, 34 ;
 Japanese, 37 ; Javese, 38 ;
 Siamese, 38 ; European, 16, 19,
 49, 203.
Scandinavian folk-music, 74.
Scarlatti, Alessandro, 144, 206, 214.
Scarlatti, Domenico, 10, 202.
Scherzo, 260.
Schubert, 287, 296.
Schumann, 10, 302, 331.
Schütz, 136, 145, 231.
Scotch bagpipe, scale of, 39.
Scotch tunes, 67, 77.
Secular music, rise of, 125.
Sequence tunes, 55.
Sequences, 55, 182, 266, 269, 327.
Servian tune, 65.
Solo song, 285.
Sonata form, development of, 196,
 232, 241, 253.
Sonatas, 151, 196, 198, 233, 241,
 253, 262, 270, 303, 304.
—— for harpsichord, 202.
—— for violin, 197.
Song, 285, 296.
Spanish tune, 68, 69.
Spohr, 275, 280, 318.
Spontini, 311.

Stamitz, 208.
Stradella, 137.
Subjects, 101, 124, 178, 180, 238,
 240, 270, 322.
—— based on tonic chord, 238.
Suites, 184.
Symphony, 147, 206, 217, 244, 246,
 257, 276.

TANNHÄUSER, 320.
Temperament, equal, 45, 188.
Toccatas, 118, 192.
Tonality, 56, 156, 198, 234, 324,
 325.
Tongataboo, music of natives of, 49.
Troubadours, 102.
Trouvère music, 95.
Tyrolese music, 74.

VAGUENESS of early music, 123.
Variations, 54, 184, 270.
Violin music, 150, 196.
Violins, 150, 196.
Viols, 115.
Vittoria, 121.
Vivaldi, 152.
Vocal music, 7, 19, 23, 48, 51, 70,
 72, 74, 86, 89, 90, 94, 103, 129,
 149, 162, 165, 171, 219, 226, 284,
 285, 329.

WAGNER, 318.
Weber, 315.
Welsh tune, 64.
Wohltemperirte clavier, 186, 300.
Writing, methods of, 89.

ZAUBERFLÖTE, Die, 230.

(14)

THE END